Getting straight "A"s doesn't have to be a mystery...

these practical, concise, and affordable study guides will tell you how!

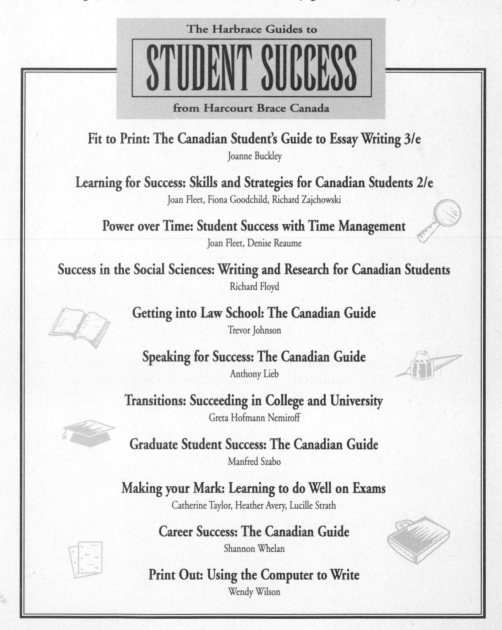

The Harbrace Guides to

STUDENT SUCCESS

from Harcourt Brace Canada

Fit to Print: The Canadian Student's Guide to Essay Writing 3/e
Joanne Buckley

Learning for Success: Skills and Strategies for Canadian Students 2/e
Joan Fleet, Fiona Goodchild, Richard Zajchowski

Power over Time: Student Success with Time Management
Joan Fleet, Denise Reaume

Success in the Social Sciences: Writing and Research for Canadian Students
Richard Floyd

Getting into Law School: The Canadian Guide
Trevor Johnson

Speaking for Success: The Canadian Guide
Anthony Lieb

Transitions: Succeeding in College and University
Greta Hofmann Nemiroff

Graduate Student Success: The Canadian Guide
Manfred Szabo

Making your Mark: Learning to do Well on Exams
Catherine Taylor, Heather Avery, Lucille Strath

Career Success: The Canadian Guide
Shannon Whelan

Print Out: Using the Computer to Write
Wendy Wilson

Look for copies of these best-selling books in your college or university bookstore.

The Bare ESSENTIALS

FORM A

FOURTH EDITION

Sarah Norton

Brian Green

HARCOURT
BRACE
CANADA

Harcourt Brace & Company, Canada

Toronto Montreal Fort Worth New York Orlando
Philadelphia San Diego London Sydney Tokyo

Canadian Cataloguing in Publication Data

Norton, Sarah,
    The bare essentials, form A
4th ed.
Includes bibliographical references.

ISBN 0-7747-3361-6

1. English language—Rhetoric. 2. English language—Grammar. I. Green, Brian. II. Title.

PE1408.N674 1996   808'.042   C95-931728-7

Publisher: Heather McWhinney
Acquisitions Editor: Kelly V. Cochrane
Projects Manager: Liz Radojkovic
Developmental Editor: May Su Mei Ku
Director of Publishing Services: Jean Davies
Editorial Manager: Marcel Chiera
Production Editor: Louisa Schulz
Production Manager: Sue-Ann Becker
Production Co-ordinator: Sheila Barry
Copy Editor: Maryan Malone
Cover Design: Opus House
Typesetting and Assembly: Publications Development Company of Texas
Technical Art: Publications Development Company of Texas
Printing and Binding: Webcom Limited

This book was printed in Canada.
1 2 3 4 5   00 99 98 97 96

Preface

Most of the changes to this fourth revision of *The Bare Essentials, Form A*, have been made in response to suggestions from our teaching colleagues across Canada whose recommendations and endorsement have made this new edition possible.

In addition to revising and updating most of the exercises, we have added instruction and practice in using the dictionary; expanded the chapter on revision and included exercises; consolidated the information on verbs and pronouns in the unit on grammar; moved apostrophes and capital letters from the punctuation unit to the spelling unit; reorganized the remaining chapters within the unit on punctuation; and added two new readings on the topic of multiculturalism. Teachers familiar with the earlier editions of the text should note that, as a consequence of these changes, the chapters have been renumbered. The Quick Revision Guide has been revised and moved to the inside front cover.

Like its predecessors, *The Bare Essentials, Form A*, Fourth Edition is intended for Canadian college students taking a first-semester or first-year writing course. Although we have not designed *The Bare Essentials* specifically as a remedial text, we have tried to accommodate the varying levels of ability represented in a typical first-year composition class by limiting our use of technical vocabulary, writing the expository material in an accessible style, and designing the exercises within each chapter to progress from simple to challenging. The concise explanations, numerous exercises, and easy-to-use answer key make *The Bare Essentials* appropriate for individualized, self-paced learning programs as well as for traditional composition classes.

As the title suggests, *The Bare Essentials* covers only those writing practices that are indispensable to effective communication: organization of ideas, sentence structure, grammar, spelling, diction, and punctuation. This book presents the basic skills, leaving teachers free to supplement the text according to the needs of their classes or the requirements of their particular courses.

Each "essential" is presented in a discrete unit. A glance at the table of contents will show that we have arranged the units in what might be called the "order of visibility" of composition errors, starting with spelling and ending with diction, but the instructor may introduce the units in any order. The chapters within each unit, however, should be covered in the order in which they appear. The exercises within a unit are often cumulative: those in later chapters include questions that assume mastery of knowledge or skills covered in earlier chapters.

The Bare Essentials is based on our experience that students can learn to write clear, error-free prose if they understand the principles involved, master the principles through practice with appropriate exercises, and apply the principles in their own writing. We acknowledge that students will not learn unless they *want* to learn. We've tried to help motivate them by beginning most chapters with a few words about the practical significance of the material. A short, nontechnical explanation of the writing principle appears next, followed by illustrative examples. Where the material is complex, we've broken it down into easy-to-follow steps. Most of each chapter is devoted to practice exercises of gradually increasing difficulty, and the student is directed to do as many as necessary to master the rule. Working through grammar exercises can be a mind-numbingly dull experience; we've tried to forestall boredom, if not spark enthusiasm, by appealing to the interests of Canadian college students and by incorporating a little humour. In an effort to engage and motivate students, we've used a casual, informal tone throughout the book.

Several features of this edition make it easier to use than its predecessors. Students can do some of the exercises right in the book, and the answers in the back of the book are easy to find. The first exercise in each chapter refers the student to the page on which the answers for that chapter begin, and all exercises are numbered by chapter as well as by exercise, both in the text and in the answer key. For example, the heading "Exercise 21.2" indicates the second exercise in Chapter 21. Students are instructed to check their answers right after they have completed an exercise. If they follow this instruction, they get immediate feedback on their grasp of the principle and can review the explanation, if necessary, before proceeding. We encourage instructors to emphasize the importance of this procedure. If students ignore this instruction and complete an entire set of exercises before checking their answers, they run the risk of reinforcing rather than eliminating the error the exercises have been designed to correct.

The Quick Revision Guide now appears on the inside front cover. Students can use the Guide as a checklist to help them revise and edit their work. Instructors can duplicate the Guide, attach a copy to each student's paper, and use it to explain the grading of assignments.

We hope you and your students will find *The Bare Essentials, Form A,* Fourth Edition profitable and painless, perhaps even fun, to use. We look forward to your comments and criticisms.

Sarah Norton

Brian Green

Introduction

Why You Need This Book

Who needs to write anyway? If I get a general labour job, I won't ever need to write, and if I'm in management, a secretary will fix all my mistakes.

(college student)

We can train a person on the job to do the specific tasks we require in about two weeks . . . maximum. What we need you people at the colleges to do is teach them to communicate—with other workers, with their supervisors— orally and in memos, reports, and letters.

(president of a steel-fabricating firm
speaking to college faculty)

You look at the people who move up in this industry. They're the ones who can write intelligently and who can read and understand other peoples' writing. Hard work helps, and so does being the owner's nephew . . . but you've got to be able to read and write reasonably well to get a job and keep it these days— and those who can't *know it better than anyone. Ask them.*

(former employee in the Canadian mining industry)

To an employer, any employee is more valuable if he or she is able to write correctly and clearly. No one can advance very far in a career without the ability to construct understandable sentences. It's that simple. Fairly or unfairly, employers and others will judge your intelligence and ability on the basis of your use of English. If you want to communicate effectively and earn respect, both on and off the job, you need to be able to write well.

That's the bad news. The good news is that *anyone who wants to* can achieve the standards of written English that are acceptable anywhere. All that is needed from you, really, is caring. If you care enough about what others think of you and about career advancement, then you'll put out the effort necessary, whether that means looking up spelling, revising what you've written, or doing all the exercises in this book twice!

How to Use This Book

In each chapter, we do three things: explain a point, illustrate it with examples, and give exercises to help you master it. The exercises are arranged in sets that get more difficult as you go along. By the end of the last set in a chapter, you should have a good grasp of the skill.

Here's how to proceed.

1. Read the explanation. Do this even if you think you understand the point being discussed.
2. Study the examples carefully.
3. Now turn to the exercises. If you've found an explanation easy and feel you have no problems with the skill, try a set near the end of the group of exercises following the explanation. If you get all the sentences right, do one more set. If you get that one all right too, skip the rest and go on to the next point. Skip ahead only if you're really confident, though.

    If you don't feel confident, don't skip anything. Start with the first set and work through all the exercises until you're sure you understand the point.
4. ALWAYS CHECK YOUR ANSWERS TO ONE SET OF EXERCISES BEFORE GOING ON TO THE NEXT. If you ignore this instruction, this book can't help you. Only if you check your accuracy after every set can you avoid repeating your mistakes and possibly reinforcing your error.
5. When you discover a mistake, go back to the explanation and examples and study them again. Make up some examples of your own to illustrate the rule. When you're sure you understand, continue with the exercises.

On the inside of the front cover you'll find the Quick Revision Guide. Use it to check over your papers before handing them in. This book is meant to be a practical tool, not a theoretical reference. Apply the lessons in all the writing you do. Explanations can identify writing problems and show you how to solve them; exercises can give you practice in eliminating errors; but only writing and revising can bring real and lasting improvement.

A Note from the Publisher

Thank you for selecting *The Bare Essentials, Form A*, Fourth Edition, by Sarah Norton and Brian Green. The authors and publisher have devoted considerable time and care to the development of this book. We appreciate your recognition of this effort and accomplishment.

We want to hear what you think about *The Bare Essentials, Form A*. Please take a few minutes to fill in the stamped reply card at the back of the book. Your comments and suggestions will be valuable to us as we prepare new editions and other books.

Contents

UNIT THREE
Grammar

UNIT FOUR
Punctuation

UNIT FIVE
Organizing Your Writing

UNIT SIX
Beyond the Bare Essentials

Appendixes

Index   375

Meat me hear in have an our—you end up with a tangle of misspellings no computer can unravel.

Careful pronunciation sometimes helps to correct this problem. For example, if you pronounce the words *accept* and *except* differently, you'll be less likely to confuse them in your writing. It's also useful to make up memory aids to help yourself remember the difference between words that sound alike but have different meanings.

accept **except**	*Accept* means "take." It is always a verb. *Except* means "excluding." Everyone *except* Mia *accepted* my explanation.
advice **advise**	The difference in pronunciation makes the difference in meaning clear. *Advise* (rhymes with *wise*) is a verb. *Advice* (rhymes with *nice*) is a noun. I *advise* you not to listen to free *advice*.
affect **effect**	*Affect* as a verb means "influence." As a noun, it means "a strong feeling." *Effect* is a noun meaning "result." If you can substitute *result*, then *effect* is the word you need. Occasionally, *effect* is used as a verb meaning "to bring about." Learning about the *effects* of caffeine *affected* my coffee-drinking habits. Depressed people often display inappropriate *affect*. Antidepressant medications can *effect* profound changes in mood.
a lot **allot**	*A lot* (often misspelled *alot*) should be avoided in writing. Use *many* or *much* instead. *Allot* means "distribute" or "assign." He still has ~~a lot of~~ (many) problems, but he's coping ~~a lot~~ (much) better. The teacher will *allot* the marks according to the difficulty of the questions.
are **our**	*Are* is a verb. *Our* shows ownership. Farley Mowat and Alice Munro *are* two of Canada's best-known writers. Canada is *our* home and native land.

choose
chose

Pronunciation gives the clue here. *Choose* rhymes with *booze* and means "select." *Chose* rhymes with *rose* and means "selected."

> Please *choose* a topic.
> I *chose* film making.

coarse
course

Coarse means "rough, unrefined." (Remember: the word **arse** is co**arse**.) For all other meanings, use *course*.

> That sandpaper is too *coarse* to use on a lacquer finish.
> You'll enjoy the photography *course*.
> Of *course* you'll come with us.

complement
compliment

A *complement* completes something. A *compliment* is a gift of praise.

> A glass of wine would be the perfect *complement* to the meal.
> Some people are embarrassed by *compliments*.

conscience
conscious

Your *conscience* is your sense of right and wrong. *Conscious* means "aware" or "awake"—able to feel and think.

> After Ann cheated on the test, her *conscience* bothered her.
> Ann was *conscious* of having done wrong.
> The injured man was *unconscious*.

consul
council
counsel

A *consul* is a government official stationed in another country. A *council* is an assembly or official group. Members of a *council* are *councillors*. *Counsel* can be used to mean both "advice" and "to advise."

> The Canadian *consul* in Venice was very helpful.
> The Women's Advisory *Council* meets next month.
> Maria gave me good *counsel*.
> She *counselled* me to hire a lawyer.

desert
dessert

A *désert* is a dry, barren place. As a verb, *desért* means "leave behind." *Dessért* is the part of a meal you'd probably like two helpings of, so give it two *s*'s.

> The tundra is Canada's only *desert* region.
> As soon as our backs were turned, our lookout *deserted* his post.
> Jell-O is the children's favourite *dessert*.

_____ **UNIT ONE**

Spelling

CHAPTER 1

Three Suggestions for Quick Improvement

Of all the errors you might make in writing, spelling is the one that is noticed by everyone, not just English teachers. No piece of writing that is full of misspellings can be classified as good. Misspellings can cause misunderstanding, as when an English teacher promised his students a course with "a strong *vacational* emphasis." (Those students who weren't misled wondered what he was doing teaching English.)

Misspellings sometimes cause confusion. Take this sentence, for example:

Mouse is a desert with a base of wiped cream.

It takes a few seconds to "translate" the sentence into a definition of *mousse*, a *dessert* made with *whipped* cream.

Most often, though, misspellings are misleading; they spoil the image you want to present. You want, naturally, to be seen as intelligent, careful, and conscientious. But if your writing is riddled with spelling errors, your reader will think you are careless, uneducated, or even stupid. It is not true, by the way, that intelligence and the ability to spell go hand in hand.

It is true, though, that people generally think they do. So, to prevent both confusion and embarrassment, it is essential that you spell correctly.

There are three things you can do to improve your spelling almost instantly:

---

1. Buy and use a good dictionary.

A dictionary is a writer's best friend. You will need it every time you write, so if you don't already own a good dictionary, you need to buy one. A good dictionary is one that is reliable, current, and reasonably comprehensive. A convenient Canadian reference is the *Gage Canadian Dictionary,* which was last revised in 1983. It is the dictionary on which the examples and exercises in this chapter are based. Also recommended for Canadian writers are the *Funk & Wagnalls Canadian College Dictionary* (1986) and, for those whose native language is not English, the *Cobuild English Dictionary* (HarperCollins, 1995).

A good dictionary packs an astonishing amount of information into a small space. Thus, for each entry, you will find some or all of the following:

1. Spelling (if there are two or more acceptable spellings, the most common one is normally given first);
2. Syllables (to show you where hyphens can go, if you need to break a word at the end of a line);
3. Pronunciation (if there is more than one acceptable pronunciation, the most common one is listed first);
4. Grammatical form(s): e.g., noun *(n.),* verb *(v.),* adjective *(adj.);*
5. Any irregular forms of the word, such as the plural form of a noun, or the past tense and past participle of a verb;
6. Usage restrictions: e.g., slang, informal, archaic, offensive;
7. Definition(s) of the word (the most common meanings are given first, followed by the technical or specialized meanings), together with phrases or sentences illustrating how the word is used;
8. Idioms using the word;
9. Origins of the word (etymology);
10. Other helpful information: e.g., homonyms (words that sound the same as the entry word); synonyms (words that are similar in meaning to the entry word); antonyms (words opposite in meaning); and special variations in grammar, spelling, pronunciation, and usage.

Most of your doubts about spelling can be answered if you take the time to check your dictionary. The time you spend looking up words will not be wasted; your rewards will be the increased accuracy of your writing and the increased respect of your reader.

If you wonder how it's possible to look up a word you can't spell, look at the "Guide to the Dictionary," which you'll find in the front of your dictionary. In the Guide is a pronunciation key and a chart showing the common spellings for all the sounds in the English language. If you know how to pronounce a word, the chart will help you find its spelling. Another way to find a word you can't spell is to look up a synonym—a word with a meaning similar to that of the word you want. In the dictionary entry for the synonym, you'll probably find the word you're looking for.

The "Guide to the Dictionary" may not be the most entertaining reading you've ever done, but it will be among the most worthwhile. You will find a diagram of the kinds of information given for each word and an explanation of the abbreviations and symbols used. You will discover, for example, that you don't need to memorize long lists of irregular plurals: your dictionary gives the irregular plural for any word you look up. It also gives the irregular forms of verbs, adjectives, and adverbs. If you've forgotten how regular plurals, verbs, adjectives, and adverbs are formed, the Guide gives you that information, too. And it shows you how to read a dictionary entry so that you can see at a glance how to add various endings to a root word. Take half an hour to read the Guide in your dictionary; then do the following exercises. Be sure to check your answers to each set before you go on to the next. Answers begin on p. 314.

EXERCISE 1.1

1. What is a second way to spell the word *blond?* Are the two spellings interchangeable?
2. What is another spelling of the word *humour?* Which spelling must you use when you add an ending such as *-ous* or *-ist* to the root word?
3. Is *tatoo* spelled correctly? Is the word a noun or a verb?
4. How many correct spellings are there for the word *ketchup?* Which is the preferred spelling in Canada?
5. Find alternate spellings for the words *programme, theatre, centre, mediaeval,* and *judgement.* In each case, indicate the spelling most commonly used in Canada.

EXERCISE 1.2
Write the plural form of each word.

1. echo
2. ratio
3. criterion
4. ghetto
5. personnel
6. crisis
7. data
8. phenomenon
9. nucleus
10. appendix

EXERCISE 1.3

Combine each root word with the ending given.

1. lonely + ness
2. copy + ed
3. crazy + ness
4. easy + ly
5. happy + er

6. reply + s
7. reply + ed
8. twenty + eth
9. necessary + ly
10. traffic + ing

EXERCISE 1.4

Using hyphens, show where each word could be divided at the end of a line. (Some words can be divided in two or more places: *ice-break-er*, for example.)

1. process
2. management
3. accommodate
4. distribution
5. through

6. chaos
7. sociopath
8. algorithm
9. hierarchy
10. Algonquian

EXERCISE 1.5

The following words are tricky to spell because they are not pronounced the way you might expect if you've had no previous experience with them. Look them up in your dictionary and, in the space beside each word, write out its pronunciation (the information given immediately after it in parentheses). Using your dictionary's pronunciation key to help you, practise sounding out each word, one syllable at a time. (No answers are given for this question.)

1. solder
2. epitome
3. impotent
4. phlegm
5. libido

6. eulogy
7. indict
8. colonel
9. maniacal
10. posthumous

In addition to your dictionary, a spell-check program is a useful tool, if you have access to a word processor. Spell-checkers aren't foolproof, though—as we'll see in the next chapter—so don't count on your computer to solve *all* your spelling problems.

> 2. Ask a good speller.

Some people seem to have been born with the ability to spell. Such people are more reliable than a computer program. Often, they are secretly proud of their talent and pleased to demonstrate it, so don't be afraid to ask. They probably aren't as good at something else as you are; you may have a talent they could use in exchange.

> 3. Learn three basic spelling rules.

English spelling is frustratingly irregular, and no rule holds true in all cases. But there are three simple rules that do hold for most words, and mastering these rules will help you avoid many common errors.

Before learning the three rules, you need to know the difference between **vowels** and **consonants.** The vowels are **a, e, i, o,** and **u** (and sometimes **y**). All the other letters are consonants.

Rule 1: Dropping the Final *e*

The first rule tells you when to drop the final, silent e when adding an ending to a word.

> Drop the final, silent *e* when adding an ending that begins with a vowel.
> Keep the final, silent *e* when adding an ending that begins with a consonant.

Keeping the rule in mind, look at these examples:

ENDINGS BEGINNING
WITH A VOWEL

-ing: amuse + ing = amusing
-ed: live + ed = lived
-able: like + able = likable
-ible: force + ible = forcible
-er: use + er = user

ENDINGS BEGINNING
WITH A CONSONANT

-ment: amuse + ment = amusement
-ly: live + ly = lively
-ness: like + ness = likeness
-ful: force + ful = forceful
-less: use + less = useless

In the exercises that follow, combine each word with the ending to form a new word. When you have finished each set, check your answers.

EXERCISE 1.6

1. safe + ly =
2. argue + ing =
3. size + able =
4. accelerate + ing =
5. extreme + ly =

6. improve + ment =
7. reduce + ing =
8. use + able =
9. immediate + ly =
10. require + ing =

EXERCISE 1.7

1. sincere + ly =
2. cohere + ence =
3. value + able =
4. guide + ance =
5. discourage + ing =

6. ice + y =
7. complete + ly =
8. purchase + ing =
9. collapse + ible =
10. encourage + ment =

In the following exercises, add *e* in the blank space wherever it's needed to complete the spelling. If no *e* is needed, leave the space blank.

EXERCISE 1.8

1. bor____ing
2. mov____ment
3. scarc____ly
4. unus____able
5. car____ful

6. advertis____ment
7. excus____able
8. provid____ing
9. sens____ible
10. improv____ment

EXERCISE 1.9

1. saf____ty
2. rang____ing
3. reduc____ible
4. balanc____ing
5. entir____ly

6. insur____ance
7. definit____ly
8. car____less
9. respons____ible
10. distanc____ing

EXERCISE 1.10
Make up sentences using the words you got wrong in exercises 1.1 through 1.5.

Exceptions to Rule 1

Three common words do not follow the rule.

> argue + ment = argument
> nine + th = ninth
> true + ly = truly

There is one more exception to rule 1: after soft *c* (as in *notice*) and soft *g* (as in *change*), keep the final, silent *e* when adding an ending beginning with *a* or *o*. Here are two examples:

> notice + able = noticeable
> outrage + ous = outrageous

Rule 2: Doubling the Final Consonant

The second rule tells you when you need to double the final consonant before adding an ending to a word.

> When adding an ending that begins with a vowel (such as *-able, -ing, -ed,* or *-er*), double the final consonant of the root word if the word
> 1. ends with a single consonant preceded by a single vowel AND
> 2. is stressed on the last syllable.

Notice that a word must have *both* characteristics for the rule to apply. Let's look at a few examples:

begin + er ends with a single consonant *(n)* preceded by a single vowel *(i)* and is stressed on the last syllable *(begín),* so the rule applies, and we double the final consonant: **beginner**

control + ed ends with a single consonant *(l)* preceded by a single vowel *(o)* and is stressed on the last syllable *(contról),* so the rule applies: **controlled**

drop + ing   ends with a single consonant *(p)* preceded by a single vowel *(o)* and is stressed on the last syllable (there is only one: *dróp*), so the rule applies: **dropping**

appear + ing   ends with a single consonant *(r)* preceded by two vowels *(ea)*, so the rule does not apply, and we do not double the final consonant: **appearing**

turn + ed   ends with two consonants *(rn)*, so the rule does not apply: **turned**

open + er   ends with a single consonant *(n)* preceded by a single vowel *(e)* but is not stressed on the last syllable *(ópen)*, so the rule does not does not apply: **opener**

In words such as *equip, quit,* and *quiz,* the *u* should be considered part of the *q* and not a vowel. These words then follow the rule: *equipping, quitter,* and *quizzed.*

Note: There is a group of words ending in *l, t,* or *s,* which, according to our rules, do not need a double consonant before the ending. Some examples are *label, counsel, focus,* and *format.* You will sometimes see this consonant doubled: *labelled, counselled, focussed,* and *formatting.* For these words, it doesn't matter which spelling you choose, but be consistent!

The following exercises require you to combine each word with the ending to form a new word. Check your answers to each set before going on. If you make no mistakes in the first two sets, skip ahead to exercise 1.14.

EXERCISE 1.11

1. plan + ing =
2. stop + ing =
3. admit + ed =
4. nail + ing =
5. stir + ed =
6. commission + er =
7. put + ing =
8. write + ing =
9. map + ing =
10. interrupt + ed =

EXERCISE 1.12

1. suffer + ing =
2. quiz + ed =
3. permit + ing =
4. strip + ed =
5. meet + ing =
6. compel + ing =
7. crop + ed =
8. tip + ing =
9. allot + ing =
10. quarter + ed =

EXERCISE 1.13

1. prefer + ing =
2. omit + ed =
3. transfer + ing =
4. develop + ing =
5. control + er =

6. occur + ed =
7. equip + ing =
8. forgot + en =
9. write + ing =
10. prefer + ed =

EXERCISE 1.14

1. overlap + ed =
2. expel + ing =
3. quiz + ed =
4. acquit + ed =
5. focus + ing =

6. excel + ing =
7. develop + ed =
8. transfer + ed =
9. parallel + ed=
10. rebel + ing =

EXERCISE 1.15

1. occur + ence =
2. exist + ence =
3. cohere + ence =
4. concur + ing =
5. interfere + ing =

6. subsist + ence =
7. differ + ence =
8. depend + ence =
9. recur + ence =
10. insist + ence =

When it comes to adding *-ence*, three words are especially troublesome. Prefer, refer, and confer all appear to require a doubled final consonant. But they don't, because, when you add *-ence*, the stress shifts to the first syllable of the word. So you write:

prefér	preférring	*but*	préference
refér	reférring	*but*	réference
confér	conférring	*but*	cónference

EXERCISE 1.16

Make up sentences in which you use the words you got wrong in exercises 1.11 through 1.15.

Rule 3: Words Containing *ie* or *ei*

There are almost a thousand common English words containing *ie* or *ei*, so remembering the rule that governs them is worthwhile. It helps to keep in mind that *ie* occurs approximately twice as often as *ei*.

The old rhyme tells you most of what you need to know to spell these words:

> Write *i* before *e*, except after *c*,
> Or when sounded like *a*, as in *neighbour* and *weigh*.

If you remember this rhyme, you'll have no difficulty in spelling words like *belief, piece, ceiling, receive,* and *freight*.

Unfortunately, the rhyme covers only two of the cases in which we write *e* before *i*: after *c*, and when the syllable is pronounced with a long *ā* sound. So we need an addition to the rule.

> If short *ĕ* or long *ī* is the sound that is right,
> Write *e* before *i*, as in *their* or in *height*.

This rule covers words such as *Fahrenheit, seismic, heir,* and *leisure* (pronounce it to rhyme with *pleasure*). *Either* and *neither* can be pronounced "eye-ther" and "nye-ther," so they too require *ei*.

There are, of course, exceptions. This silly sentence contains the most common ones:

A *weird species* of *sheik seized caffeine, codeine,* and *protein*.

These exercises will help you master *ie* versus *ei*. Fill in the blanks with *ie* or *ei*. After you finish each set, check your answers.

EXERCISE 1.17

1. br____f
2. cash____r
3. rec____ve
4. p____rce
5. rel____f
6. retr____ve
7. c____ling
8. bel——ve
9. dec____tful
10. hyg____ne

EXERCISE 1.18

1. I gr____ved when Dracula struck a v____n.

2. The fr____ght yard was under police surv____llance.

3. She gave me a rec____pt for ____ght dollars.

4. There is no rel____f from his conc____t.

5. I would have ach____ved a good mark, but th____ves broke into my apartment and stole my essay.

EXERCISE 1.19

1. I ordered chow m____n and a st____n of beer.

2. N____ther of us knows how to use a G____ger counter.

3. Our n____ghbour has offered to hire our n____ce.

4. Harry wore a b____ge l____sure suit to the graduation party for the Fashion Design students.

5. It is conc____vable that ____ther one could do the job.

EXERCISE 1.20

No answers are given for this exercise.

1. Each w____ner w____ghed 85 g.

2. It is the duty of a pr____st to comfort those who are gr____ving the loss of a fr____nd or relative.

3. That spec____s of ape grows to a h____ght of 2 m.

4. The front____r police s____zed my camera in the bel____f that I had entered a restricted zone.

5. Orin is so conc____ted he thinks he alone should rec____ve credit for conc____ving the idea for our hit song.

There are three or four more spelling rules we could explain here, but we won't—for two reasons. First, there are many exceptions to the remaining rules for English spelling. And second, you don't need to memorize more rules if you use your dictionary.

CHAPTER 2

Sound-Alikes, Look-Alikes, and Spoilers

Using a dictionary, asking a good speller for help, and applying the three spelling rules will make an immediate improvement in your spelling. By following two additional suggestions, you will further increase your spelling accuracy, but the skills involved will take longer to master. First, learn to tell apart words that are often confused because they sound or look alike. Second, learn to spell the words that most people find difficult—words we have called spelling spoilers. Don't try to master all of these words at once. Instead, memorize a few each week, and review them frequently. In two or three months, you could be one of the people poor spellers turn to for help!

Sound-Alikes and Look-Alikes

Some of your spelling troubles are probably caused by your using words that either sound or look like the words you really want. A spell-check cannot help you with these words because, if you're like most people, you don't misspell them. What makes the spelling "wrong" is the sense of the sentence in which you've used them. *Hear, our, meat,* and *have* are correctly spelled, as isolated words. But if you combine them into a "sentence"—

dining
dinning

You'll spell *dining* correctly if you remember the phrase "wining and dining." You'll probably never use *dinning*. It means "making a loud noise."

> The dog is not supposed to be in the *dining* room.
> We are *dining* out tonight.
> The sounds from the karaoke bar were *dinning* in my ears.

does
dose

Pronunciation provides the clue. *Does* rhymes with *buzz* and is a verb. *Dose* rhymes with *gross* and refers to a quantity of medicine.

> Josef *does* drive fast, *doesn't* he?
> My grandmother used to give me a *dose* of cod liver oil every spring.

forth
fourth

Forth means "**for**ward." *Fourth* contains the number **four,** which gives it its meaning.

> Please stop pacing back and *forth*.
> The Raptors lost their *fourth* game in a row.

hear
here

Hear is what you do with your **ear**s. *Here* is used for all other meanings.

> Now *hear* this!
> Ranjan isn't *here*.
> *Here* is your assignment.

it's
its

It's is a shortened form of *it is*. The apostrophe takes the place of the *i* in *is*. If you can substitute *it is,* then *it's* is the form you need. If you can't substitute *it is,* then *its* is the correct word.

> *It's* really not difficult. (*It is* really not difficult.)
> The book has lost *its* cover. ("The book has lost *it is* cover" makes no sense, so you need *its*.)

It's is also commonly used as the shortened form of *it has*. In this case, the apostrophe takes the place of the *h* and the *a*.

> *It's* been a bad month for software sales.

later
latter

Later refers to time and has the word **late** in it. *Latter* means "the second of two" and has two t's. It is the opposite of *former*.

> It is *later* than you think.
> You take the former, and I'll take the *latter*.

led
lead

The word **lead** is pronounced "led" only when it refers to the heavy, soft, grey metal used in items such as lead bullets or leaded windows. Otherwise, *lead* is pronounced to rhyme with "speed" and is used as the present tense of the verb *to lead*. (*Led* is the past tense of the same verb.)

When I asked her to *lead* me to the person in charge, she *led* me to the secretary.
Your suitcase is so heavy it must be filled with either gold or *lead*.

loose
lose

Pronunciation is the key to these words. *Loose* rhymes with *goose* and means "not tight." *Lose* rhymes with *ooze* and means "misplace" or "be defeated."

A *loose* electrical connection is dangerous.
Some are born to win, some to *lose*.

miner
minor

A *miner* works in a **mine.** *Minor* means "lesser" or "not important." For example, a *minor* is a person of less than legal age.

Liquor can be served to *miners*, but not if they are *minors*.
For some people, spelling is a *minor* problem.

moral
morale

Again, pronunciation provides the clue you need. *Mo'ral* refers to the understanding of what is right and wrong. *Mora'le* refers to the spirit or mental condition of a person or group.

Parents are responsible for teaching their children *moral* behaviour.
The low *morale* of our employees is the reason for their high absenteeism.

peace
piece

Peace is what we want on **ea**rth. *Piece* means a part or portion of something, as in "a **pie**ce of **pie**."

Everyone hopes for *peace* in the Middle East.
A *piece* of the puzzle is missing.

personal
personnel

Personal means "private." *Personnel* refers to the group of people working for a particular employer or to the office responsible for maintaining employees' records.

The letter was marked "*Personal* and Confidential."
We are fortunate in having highly qualified *personnel*.
Yasmin works in the *Personnel* Office.

principal
principle

Principal means "m**ai**n." A princi**ple** is a ru**le**.

> A *principal* is the main administrator of a school.
> The federal government is Summerside's *principal* employer.
> The *principal* and the interest totalled more than I could pay. (In this case, the principal is the main amount of money.)
> One of our instructor's *principles* is to refuse to accept late assignments.

quiet
quite

If you pronounce these words carefully, you won't confuse them. *Quiet* has two syllables; *quite* has only one.

> The chairperson asked us to be *quiet*.
> We had not *quite* finished our assignment.

stationary
stationery

*Station**a**ry* means "fixed in pl**a**ce." *Station**e**ry* is writing pap**e**r.

> Did you want a laptop or *stationary* computer?
> Please order a new supply of *stationery*.

than
then

Than is used in comp**a**risons. Pronounce it to rhyme with *can*. *Then* refers to time and rhymes with *when*.

> Karim is a better speller *than* I.
> He made his decision *then*.
> Tanya withdrew from the competition; *then* she realized the consequences.

their
there
they're

Their indicates ownership. **There** points out something or indicates place. It includes the word **here,** which also indicates place. *They're* is a shortened form of *they are.* (The apostrophe replaces the *a* in *are*.)

> It was *their* fault.
> *There* are two weeks left in the term.
> Let's walk over *there*.
> *They're* late, as usual.

too
two
to

The *too* with an extra *o* in it means "more than enough" or "also." *Two* is the number after one. For all other meanings, use *to*.

> She thinks she's been working *too* hard. He thinks so, *too*.
> There are *two* sides *to* every argument.
> The *two* women knew *too* much about each other *to* be friends.

were
where
we're

If you pronounce these three carefully, you won't confuse them. *Were* rhymes with *fur* and is a verb. *Where* is pronounced "hwear," includes the word **here**, and indicates place. *We're* is a shortened form of *we are* and is pronounced "weer."

> You *were* joking, *weren't* you?
> *Where* did you want to meet?
> *We're* on our way.

who's
whose

Who's is a shortened form of *who is* or *who has*. If you can substitute *who is* or *who has* for the *who's* in your sentence, then you are using the right spelling. Otherwise, use *whose*.

> *Who's* coming to dinner? (*Who is* coming to dinner?)
> *Who's* been sleeping in my bed? (*Who has* been sleeping in my bed?)
> *Whose* paper is this? ("*Who is* paper" makes no sense, so you need *whose*.)

woman
women

Confusing these two is guaranteed to irritate your women readers. *Woman* is the singular form; compare **man**. *Women* is the plural form; compare **men**.

> One *woman* responded to our ad.
> The affirmative action policy promotes equality between *women* and men.

you're
your

You're is a shortened form of *you are*. If you can substitute *you are* for the *you're* in your sentence, then you're using the correct form. If you can't substitute *you are*, use *your*.

> *You're* welcome. (*You are* welcome.)
> Unfortunately, *your* hamburger got burned. ("*You are* hamburger" makes no sense, so *your* is the word you want.)

In the exercises that follow, choose the correct word in each pair. If you don't know an answer, go back and reread the explanation. Check your answers after each set. Answers begin on p. 316.

EXERCISE 2.1

1. Unemployment is having an (affect effect) on the kinds of (coarses courses) college students choose.
2. (Are Our) offer was not (accepted excepted).
3. Fresh fruit is a healthier (desert dessert) (than then) cake.

4. When (your you're) travelling abroad, (losing loosing) your ticket is a nightmare.
5. It was so (quite quiet) that you could (hear here) a pin drop.
6. (Your You're) being (conscience conscious) during class is a prerequisite to learning.
7. Alex, the (forth fourth) child, was nine years younger (then than) his sister.
8. Don't buy expensive luggage; (its it's) bound to get scratched during (its it's) travels.
9. The SPCA will (advice advise) you on what kind of dog to (chose choose).
10. (Accept Except) for (miner minor) bruises, passengers wearing seat belts sustain fewer injuries in accidents than those who do not buckle up.

EXERCISE 2.2

1. (Your You're) acting as if you had a guilty (conscience conscious).
2. Finally, on the (forth fourth) try, I (choose chose) the right answer.
3. If you don't keep (quite quiet), I won't be able to (hear here) the news.
4. If a (principal principle) is always a rule, is a (principal principle) always a pal?
5. Let your (conscience conscious) be (your you're) guide.
6. A (stationary stationery) engine is one that is fixed in (its it's) place.
7. If we (loose, lose) this game (to too two), the (moral morale) of the team will suffer.
8. (Dose Does) the average (woman women) really worry about having the cleanest bathroom on the block?
9. It's not whether you win or (loose lose), (its it's) how you play the game.
10. It's not always easy to (choose chose) the (moral morale) (coarse course) of action.

EXERCISE 2.3

1. All I want for Christmas is (peace piece) and (quiet quite).
2. Drawings of what look like extraterrestrial beings can be found in (a lot allot many) of the world's great (deserts desserts).
3. If you insist on carrying out our former plan, (than then) I'll have no choice but to (choose chose) to carry out the (later latter).
4. (A lot of, allot of, Many) people take up jogging to try to (loose lose) weight.
5. (Your You're) supposed to swallow one tablespoonful as (your you're) daily (does dose).

6. Being unemployed for a long time cannot help but (affect effect) your (moral morale).

7. A (complement compliment) is often more welcome (than then) a kiss.

8. I thought I had mastered the "*i* before *e* " (principal principle), but (than then) I read about the exceptions.

9. (Its It's) (later latter) than you think.

10. We were fortunate to be assigned a legal (councillor counsellor) who was a (woman women) of (principal principle).

EXERCISE 2.4

1. (Its It's) no longer unusual for (woman women) to be elected to public office.

2. The thieves came back (later latter) and took everything (accept except) my roller blades.

3. Let (their there they're) be (peace piece) in (are our) time.

4. Edmund Burke believed that manners are more important (than then) (morales morals).

5. (Were We're Where) do you think (were we're where) going to get the money for a vacation in Cabo San Lucas?

6. I (hear here) (your you're) sorry you (choose chose) this (coarse course).

7. Aline Chrétien is one person (whose who's) (advice advise) Jean takes seriously.

8. Following your (advice advise), I applied to the bank for a (personal personnel) loan, and (its it's) costing me a bundle.

9. I suggest that (their there they're) behaviour can hardly be described as (moral morale).

10. The deficit and unemployment are Canada's (principal principle) concerns; world (peace piece) is considered almost a (miner minor) problem in comparison.

EXERCISE 2.5

1. Do you think most Canadians (are our) (conscience conscious) of their national identity?

2. One's ability to learn is (affected effected) by one's (personal personnel) well-being.

3. I made the turn, (than then) saw the sign: "No left turn; buses (accepted excepted)."

4. If you let your dog run (loose lose), you must (accept except) the consequences.

5. Surely (its it's) a question of (principal principle).

6. Some (miners minors) have little difficulty convincing a bartender that (their there they're) of age, especially if (their there they're) using someone else's ID.
7. Last summer, Alla (choose chose) to work in the (dining dinning) room of the Banff Springs Hotel.
8. I'd rather write an essay (than then) do an oral report in front of (are our) class.
9. Sea salt is (to too two) (coarse course) (to too two) pass through the holes of a saltshaker.
10. Judging by the noise I (hear here), I'd say (your you're) car needs a tune-up.

EXERCISE 2.6

(Lead Led) by my desire to watch more television (than then) the six or seven hours a day I normally viewed, I decided to subscribe to satellite TV. The (affect effect) of this move was (later latter) to prove detrimental to my health and my wealth. First, I did not know that (their there they're) is a monthly subscription fee in addition to the initial purchase price of almost $1000 for the "unobtrusive pizza-sized (stationary stationery) dish antenna." Second, I was (quiet quite) surprised to find that I was able to get many "pay-per-view" programs in addition to the basic 40 available stations. I was even more surprised to discover how fast I was running up a bill by (choosing chosing) to view these optional programs. To restore my (peace piece) of mind, not to mention my bank balance, I telephoned the satellite service (personal personnel) to request that they limit my monthly spending for pay-per-view programs. Seven hockey games, four basketball games, (to too two) movies, six music specials, and an award ceremony (later latter), my TV screen informed me that I had reached my spending limit. I'm afraid I responded with a few (coarse course) expressions, since I was all set to see a new fine (dining dinning) show on exotic (deserts desserts) featuring papaya as the (principal principle) ingredient. Then my TV screen informed me I could override my limit simply by pressing "star." I did, and went on watching with a clear (conscience conscious) since, after all, I had limited my spending. In addition to (its it's) (affect effect) on my budget, satellite service caused me to (loose lose) what little muscle tone I had left, since the only times I leave the couch are to go (forth fourth) to the kitchen for more food. The (moral morale) of my sad story is that (your you're) probably better off with less choice and poorer quality on (your you're) TV than in (your you're) life.

In the exercises that follow, cross out any incorrect spellings and replace them with the correct words.

EXERCISE 2.7

1. Moments after it's takeoff, the plane banked to sharply to the left.
2. I certainly won't chose the one who's application was late.
3. Please check with the Personal Department before you hire legal council.
4. If he dose that again, it will effect his chances for promotion.
5. The Canada Counsel will announce its awards latter this month.
6. When I receive a complement, I feel self-conscience.
7. Who's turn is it to find the compliment of the angle?
8. If you could remember these three simple rules, than you're spelling troubles would be over.
9. Their are many children who believe the tooth fairy will come if they loose a tooth.
10. The miner skirmish before the game had the affect of making us absolutely determined to win.

EXERCISE 2.8

Correct all the spelling errors you find in the following paragraphs. No answers are given for this exercise.

There once was a sailor who, loosing his job to a steam engine, set out to become a successful businessman. His first venture was as encyclopedia salesman, but he found that he didn't have the necessary personnel touch to win exceptance from his customers. Indeed, he was fortunate to escape one encounter with his life, after calling his prospective customer "Matey" throughout they're negotiations.

He next sought the relative piece and quite of the skilled trades, turning his hand to carpentry. The affect of that decision was even more unhappy, for he no sooner set fourth on the venture then he lost too fingers while attempting to cut a board with a dull saw. Latter, after he regained conscienceness, he swore (rather coursely) that he would never again try a job that required him to handle sharp implements.

The sailor then became a minor, but concluded that his fellow minors were to unfriendly, and so he desserted. He tried his hand (or what remained of it) at selling stationary, working in a tire repair shop, and bartending. It was on this last job that he recieved the advise that would lead to his success. A women who relieved him at 8:00 every night recommended that he forget his principals and turn to politics. Her advice was sound.

From local counsel to provincial politics, and on to Parliament, our sailor leapt from success to success. He found that his previous jobs had prepared him well for his new career. His moral soared. In campaign speeches, he was able to say, "As you're MP, I shall guide the ship of state while nailing down new reforms and toiling beneath the surface to draft legislation. I shall go door to door to ask for you're support and, when I get it, I shall serve you tirelessly!" He was irresistible. Election after election, his constituency choose him as their representative.

EXERCISE 2.9

Below is a list of word pairs that are often confused. Use each word in a sentence that clearly differentiates the word from its sound-alike or look-alike. Be sure to use your dictionary to help you. No answers are provided for this exercise.

1. altar, alter
2. breath, breathe
3. capital, capitol
4. stake, steak
5. waist, waste
6. cite, site
7. cloths, clothes
8. emigrate, immigrate
9. hoard, horde
10. precede, proceed

EXERCISE 2.10

Your own writing is the best test of your spelling accuracy. Write ten or more sentences using the sound-alikes and look-alikes that cause you the most difficulty.

Spelling Spoilers

Here is a list of words that are frequently misspelled. Have someone dictate the list to you. Circle the ones you misspell and memorize them, a few at a time. Try to learn ten each week. Review your list often, until you have mastered every word. Making up memory aids for especially troublesome words will help you conquer them. Here are some examples to get you started:

accommodate: It means "make room for," and the word itself makes room for two *c*'s and two *m*'s.

business: Bu*sin*ess is no *sin*.

environment: The word *environment*, like the earth, has **iron** in it.

friend: He is a fri**end** to the **end**.

grammar: Poor gram**mar** will **mar** your writing.

absence	criticism	forty
accommodate	definitely	friend
achievement	dependent	gauge
acknowledge	desperate	government
acquire	development	grammar
across	disappear	guarantee
address	disappoint	guidance
adolescence	discipline	height
among	dissatisfied	hoping
answer	doesn't	hypocrisy
apparent	eighth	immediately
argument	embarrassed	independent
beginning	environment	indispensable
business	exercise	laboratory
careful	existence	library
category	explanation	license (or licence)
clothes	extremely	likely
committee	familiar	loneliness
conscious	February	lonely
convenience	finally	maintenance

marriage
mentally
necessary
ninety
ninth

occasion
occasionally
omission
opinion
opportunity

paid
parallel
perform
planned
possess

prejudice
privilege
procedure

proceed
professor

psychology
recommend
relevant
repetition
restaurant

rhythm
ridiculous
safety
schedule
secretary

separate
shining
similar
somewhat
speech

studying
succeed
surprise
technique
thorough

tragedy
truly
unnecessary
until
unusual

usually
vacuum
Wednesday
writing
written

EXERCISE 2.11

Make up sentences containing the words you misspelled when the list of spelling spoilers was dictated. Underline the spelling spoiler in each sentence. (If you do this exercise once a week, you will master the list very quickly.)

One final suggestion. Despite all your efforts, you may find that there are a few words you just cannot spell correctly. The solution? Either write them out on the inside cover of your dictionary or, even simpler, don't use them. Look in your dictionary or in a thesaurus to find synonyms (different words with the same or similar meanings), and use those instead. Two thesauruses that are available in inexpensive paperback editions are *Roget's Thesaurus* and Soule's *Dictionary of English Synonyms*.

Choose synonyms with caution. Inexperienced writers sometimes assume that long, obscure words are sure to impress the reader. In fact, the opposite is usually true. Most readers are irritated, if not confused, by unnecessarily "fancy" language. Why write "The children were enthralled by the antics of the prestidigitator" when what you mean is "The children loved the magician's act"? For more on this subject, see Unit 6.

CHAPTER 3

Capital Letters

Capital letters should be used in a few specific places and nowhere else. Some people seem to have "capitalitis": they put capital letters on words randomly, regardless of whether the words are nouns, verbs, or adjectives. Like "exclamatosis," "capitalitis" is a disease communicated by comic books, which capitalize every word.

Not many people have this problem. If you are in the majority who generally use capitals properly, skip this chapter and go on to something else. If you are puzzled about capital letters, though, or have readers who are puzzled by your use of them, read on.

Capitalize the first letters of words that fit these descriptions:

1. The first word in a sentence or in a direct quotation:
   > Please do not play games on this computer.
   > Our instructor inquired sweetly, "Now, who would like to go first?"

2. The names of specific persons:

Jean Chrétien	Neil Bissoondath

   The names of specific places:

Baffin Island	Robson Street
Saturn	South Africa
Marineland	Climax, Saskatchewan

   The names of specific things:

Pacific Ocean	North American Free Trade Act
Empress Hotel	Red Deer College
Mighty Morphin Power Rangers	Lake Superior

3. The days of the week, the months of the year, and specific holidays (but not the seasons or geographic directions):

Wednesday	June
Thanksgiving	Canada Day
winter	south

4. The titles of specific people (but not the names of their positions), books, films, television shows, newspapers, etc., and school courses (but not subject names, unless they are languages):

> Governor General Romeo LeBlanc (*but* the governor general)
> Bishop Terence Finley (*but* the bishop)
> Mr. Conrad Black, Ms. Barbara Amiel
> *The Bare Essentials; Schindler's List; Roseanne; The Winnipeg Free Press*
> Biology 101 (*but* the biology course)
> French 200; conversational Spanish; the English language; the study of Chinese history

5. The names of specific companies, products, businesses, organizations, and departments:

> Calona Winery   Kleenex, Tide, Kraft Dinner
> Reform Party   Human Resources Department
> Royal Trust   Kiwanis Club

Correct the capitalization in these sentences. Check your answers to each set before continuing. Answers begin on p. 318.

EXERCISE 3.1

1. diana always wanted to be a Princess when she grew up.
2. It amazes me that anyone could think *beavis and butthead* is funny.
3. Beatrix, queen of the netherlands, visited Canada last Winter.
4. The rotary club of Halifax sponsors a scholarship to dalhousie university.
5. Gina tries hard, but she'll never be as good at Data Processing as Ravi.
6. *Black robe* was a Canadian-made film that featured international stars as well as young canadian actors.
7. I should be looking for a sensible Sedan, but I'm tempted by the Sports Models every time I visit the GM, ford, or honda dealer.
8. I wonder how the College gets away with requiring us students to take english and mathematics in addition to our Major subjects.
9. We were late for professor Chan's lecture on Time Management.
10. Stock is running low, so if you need xerox paper or toner, you'd better see Carla in office supplies right away.

EXERCISE 3.2

1. My Mother and Father drive South each Fall to look at the leaves.
2. Ali went with his english class to the Calgary stampede and then to the West edmonton mall.
3. Alain took a greyhound bus to the Coast and then a ferry to Prince Edward island.

4. Her parents thought they were seeing Gina off to University, but in fact she spent the Winter in Mexico.

5. I've always wanted to be a Pope, but, unfortunately, I am not italian, catholic, or male.

6. Luc went to Paris last Summer to study french, art history, and gourmet cooking.

7. Although I am generally fairly Conservative, I consider myself a Liberal on matters such as abortion and gun control.

8. Clement works for bell canada, which has an office on Bayview avenue.

9. After the Baseball and Hockey seasons were cancelled, Sabina became a Basketball fan and now is devoted to the raptors.

10. A letter to the Editor in today's *Globe and mail* says Jean Chrétien's claim to fame is that "he is the only Canadian Prime Minister to have mastered neither of the country's two Official Languages."

EXERCISE 3.3

1. Since you have yet to pass a single Physics or Math course, I suggest you reconsider your decision to be an Engineer.

2. As the official representative of queen Elizabeth, Canada's Governor General opens each new session of Parliament.

3. During the Spring break, Saieed drove down to florida, where he toured walt disney world, the epcot center, and Busch gardens.

4. The Quebec Premier influences not only the policies of his own Province, but also those of the rest of Canada.

5. After Clive missed the meeting, the President told him angrily, "that, Young Man, was what is called a CLM: a career-limiting move."

6. Visitors to Canada are sometimes surprised to find they cannot see the rockies, Niagara falls, Newfoundland, and the arctic Tundra all in one week.

7. We stopped at safeway for the basics: spaghetti, milk, a box of kellogg's cornflakes, and a tube of crest.

8. Canada's immigration act sets out the policies that govern the conditions for entry into the Country by immigrants from all over the World.

9. We went to see Atom Egoyan's film *exotica*, which was playing at the capitol theatre.

10. Among Canada's great waterways, the St. Lawrence river, the Mackenzie river, the Fraser river, and the red river are the most interesting to me because of the role each played in developing our Nation.

EXERCISE 3.4

Correct the capitalization in this paragraph. No answers are provided for this exercise.

Rico went to france last Summer in the hope of tracing his Noble Ancestry. In a small Village just outside Lyons, he discovered an old family Bible containing a record of his family's births and deaths back to the Seventeenth Century. From this bible, he was able to conclude that his Father's ancestors came from Switzerland. Accordingly, he moved on to Geneva, where his fluent french and english were both put to the test in getting access to the information he needed. Finally, he appealed to the Mayor, and a clerk from the Municipal Office came to help him with his quest. It was with the help of this Clerk that Rico finally discovered the Truth: the founder of his family had been hanged in 1177 for stealing sheep. Far from being descended from the Nobility, as he had always assumed, rico was the descendant of a thief!

CHAPTER 4

The Apostrophe

We have chosen to deal with apostrophes as a spelling problem because, unlike other punctuation marks, apostrophes are not used to indicate the relationship between the parts of a sentence. An apostrophe indicates either a relationship between two elements of a single word, in a contraction, or a relationship between one word and the word immediately following it, in a possessive construction.

Apostrophes are often misused, causing readers to be confused or amused. Sometimes you need an apostrophe so that your reader can understand what you mean. For example, there's a world of difference between these two sentences:

> The instructor began the class by calling the students' names.
> The instructor began the class by calling the students names.

In most cases, however, a misused apostrophe just irritates an alert reader:

> Seasons Greetings from the Norton's.
> Give the baby it's soother.
> Fresh-picked apple's for sale.

It isn't difficult to avoid such embarrassing mistakes. Correctly used, the apostrophe indicates either **contraction** or **possession.** Learn the simple rules that govern these two uses, and you'll have no further trouble with apostrophes.

Contraction

You'll need to use contractions less often than possessives. Contractions lend a conversational tone to written English, and in most of the writing you do in college or on the job, you will avoid them. However, when you are writing informally, or when you are quoting someone's spoken words, you'll need to know how contractions are formed.

The rule about where to put an apostrophe in a contraction is one of the rare rules to which there are no exceptions. It *always* holds.

> When two words are shortened into one, and a letter (or letters) is left out, the apostrophe goes in the place of the missing letter(s).

she is →	she's	they have →	they've
we are →	we're	there is →	there's
he had →	he'd	he will →	he'll
you would →	you'd	do not →	don't
it is, it has →	it's	will not →	won't (Note the slight
who is, who has →	who's		spelling variation here.)

EXERCISE 4.1

Make these sets of words into contractions. Answers for this chapter begin on p. 319.

1. you are
2. we would
3. they will
4. can not
5. I will

6. did not
7. should not
8. could have
9. who had
10. everybody is

EXERCISE 4.2

Place apostrophes correctly in these words, which are intended to be contractions. Notice that when an apostrophe is missing, the word often means something completely different.

1. cant
2. shed
3. didnt
4. lets
5. shell

6. wouldnt
7. wed
8. theyre
9. wont
10. hell

EXERCISE 4.3

Correct these sentences by placing apostrophes where needed.

1. Well have to postpone the meeting because theyre still not here.
2. If Krystal finds out whats been going on, shell be furious.
3. Its been a long time since weve had a break, hasnt it?
4. Were still about 10 km away from where theyd planned to meet us.
5. Its a tough decision, but somebodys got to make it, or well never get out of here.
6. Hockey is Canada's most popular game, so Im surprised to learn its not our official national sport.
7. Everyones welcome, but if youre all coming, wed better buy another keg.
8. Hes offered to drive all those whore going to the game.
9. Lets first find out whos coming; then well know if weve bought enough to go around.
10. Youll have to wait until hes sure you havent brought along someone whos under age.

Possession

The apostrophe is also used to show ownership or possession. Here's the rule that applies in most cases:

> 1. Add *'s* to the word that indicates the *owner*.
> 2. If the resulting word ends in a double or triple *s*, erase the last one, leaving the apostrophe in place.

person + s = person's   man + s = man's
people + s = people's   men + s = men's
sisters + s = sisters'ȿ   mother-in-law + s = mother-in-law's
Socrates + s = Socrates'ȿ   goodness + s = goodness'ȿ

When you're forming possessives, you must first figure out whether the owner is singular or plural. For example:

the employee's duties (the duties belonging to one *employee*)
the employees' duties (the duties belonging to two or more *employees*)

If you remember that possession indicates *what belongs to whom,* you can figure out where to put the apostrophe by "translating" your sentence, like this:

> *Incorrect:* The bartender asked Rudolf for his drivers license.
>   1. Translation: the license belongs to one *driver*
>   2. Add *'s:*
> *Correct:* The bartender asked Rudolf for his driver's license.

> *Incorrect:* The college finally met the students demands.
>   1. Translation: the demands belonged to—the *student?* or the *students?*
>   Here's where you have to decide whether *one* or *more than one* is involved.
>   2. Add *s:*
> *Correct:* The college finally met the student's demands.
>   (Only one student was involved.)
> *Also correct:* The college finally met the students' demands.
>   (More than one student was involved.)

Possession does not have to be literal. The owner does not have to be a person or thing. Ideas or concepts can be "owners," too:

> a life's work = the work of, or belonging to, a life
> at arm's length = at length of, or belonging to, an arm
> two cents' worth = the worth of, or belonging to, two cents

There is an alternative to part 2 of the possession rule given in the box at the start of this section. Many writers prefer to keep the final *s* when it represents a sound that is pronounced, as it does in the possessive form of one-syllable words (e.g. boss, class) and of some names (e.g. Harris, Brutus). The following examples illustrate this alternative usage:

> boss's temper   Ms. Harris's promotion
> class's decision   Brutus's betrayal

You should note that a few words, called **possessive pronouns,** are already possessive in form and so do not take an apostrophe:

> your/yours   our/ours
> her/hers   their/theirs
> his, its   whose

Your decision is *yours* to make, not *his* or *hers.*

Whose turn is it next: *ours* or *theirs?*

Four of these possessive pronouns are often confused with the contractions that sound like them. When you need to decide which spelling to use, separate the contraction into its two root words and try them out in the sentence. If the sentence makes sense, then the contraction is the spelling you need. If not, use the possessive.

POSSESSIVE	CONTRACTION
its	it's = it is *or* it has
their	they're = they are
whose	who's = who is *or* who has
your	you're = you are

You'll understand the difference between these sound-alikes if you study the following examples carefully:

They're going to try their luck at cards. (They are going to try ~~they are~~ their luck.)

You're losing your hair. (You are losing ~~you are~~ your hair.)

It's obvious your car has a hole in its muffler. (It is obvious ~~you are~~ your car has a hole.)

Who's been sleeping in whose bed? (Who has been sleeping in ~~who is~~ whose bed?)

EXERCISE 4.4

Make the following words possessive.

1. woman
2. technicians
3. the Simpsons
4. management
5. workers
6. someone
7. Iguassu Falls
8. memo
9. babies
10. Dennis

In the following exercises, make the words in parentheses possessive.

EXERCISE 4.5

1. (Biff) favourite pastime is spending his (girlfriend) money.
2. (Who) fault is it that the (car) tank is empty?
3. After about one (second) hesitation, I accepted a (week) pay instead of time off.
4. (Bikers) equipment is on special at (Leather Larry).

5. Virtue may be (it) own reward, but I won't refuse (you) offer of cash.
6. Our college aims to meet its (students) social needs as well as (they) academic goals.
7. To (no one) surprise, the (children) scores were higher than ours on every game we tried.
8. The traditional male dominance in medicine and law is disappearing as (women) acceptance into these programs now exceeds (men).
9. The (college) climate survey revealed that most (students) opinion of their program is positive.
10. (The United States) vast wealth makes some Canadians wonder whether it is worth maintaining our (country) independence.

EXERCISE 4.6

1. (Mei-ling) paper got a better grade than (Louis).
2. (Gordie Howe) record may eventually fall, but his (career) achievements will never be surpassed.
3. Alicia gave one (month) notice before leaving her position as (children) wear buyer for (Eaton).
4. After the (union) strike threat, the (owners) solution was to lock out the players for the rest of the season.
5. One of (Toronto) landmarks is (Honest Ed) store at the corner of Bloor and Bathurst.
6. Canadian (authors) works are increasingly recommended by the (Ministry of Education) curriculum planners.
7. (Cassandra) fate was probably more miserable than (anyone), including (Achilles).
8. Our (group) presentation was on (Davies) *Fifth Business,* while (they) was on (Yeats) early poetry.
9. The (survey) results were not surprising: more than half the voters surveyed were unhappy with (they) (MP) performance.
10. (Dorothy Parker) solution to boredom was to hang a sign on her office door reading ("Men) Room."

EXERCISE 4.7

Correct these sentences by placing apostrophes where they are needed in contractions and possessives.

1. Todays popular music is returning to the sounds and themes of its roots in the sixties.
2. Our government is not serious about solving its financial problems; in fact, its getting deeper and deeper into debt.
3. Charles feelings about Dianas book are well-known, but who knows what Camillas thoughts are?
4. A patients fears can be eased by a sensitive nurses attention.

5. The girls won the cheaters money in Luisas fathers poker game.
6. The speakers topic was well beyond our classes ability to understand.
7. We were told to read Northrop Fryes essay, "Dont You Think Its Time to Start Thinking?" for tomorrows class.
8. In the paper today, theres a short article entitled, "Its Clear the Apostrophes Days are Numbered, Isnt It?"
9. At her wits end, the angry mother turned to her daughter and shouted, "Whore you to tell me what youll do and wont do?"
10. The Crash Test Dummies first major hit was the off-beat "Supermans Song"; in contrast, their award-winning *God Shuffled His Feet* features Brad Roberts songs, which are rich in symbolism and insight.

EXERCISE 4.8

Correct the misused and missing apostrophes in these sentences.

1. The mens' changing room is easy to find; its across the hall and around the corner from the womens gym.
2. A good grasp of grammar and spelling does'nt guarantee success in you're chosen career, but it helps.
3. Tennises appeal is probably due to the fact that its a game that can be played by people of all ages'.
4. An actors' talent can ensure a plays success, even when the critic's reviews are negative.
5. Our instructor recommended we buy either *Rogets Thesaurus* or *Soules Dictionary of Synonyms'*, did'nt she?
6. Professor Greens' patience quickly evaporated when he discovered the class had not done they're assignment on the use and abuse of apostrophes'.
7. T-shirt ads are a bonus for a products manufacturer, who doesnt have to pay for the wearers time or effort in promoting the product.
8. Its clear their idea of a good time is not the same as our's, since theyve invited us to an operas opening performance and a formal reception afterward.
9. Dwight struggled to get into his brothers tuxedo, but it's sleeves were about 8 cm too short for his arms.
10. Childrens wear and womens shoes are on the first floor, next to the odds'-and-ends' department.

EXERCISE 4.9

Correct the following sentences where necessary.

Jess decided that she should buy a dog for it's ability to protect her and

her apartment. Several of her neighbours houses had been broken into recently, and Jess felt that the dogs bark might discourage intruders. So Jess went to the library and began to research various breeds characteristics and breeders' reputations. A days work in the stacks convinced her that she couldn't possibly learn everything there was to know about every breed of dog, so she focussed her research on three who's temperament seemed suitable for her purposes: the Doberman, the Bouvier, and the German Shepherd. The Dobermans reputation for fierceness was impressive, but the Bouviers loyalty and the Shepherds intelligence were also appealing. Finally, Jess concluded that its a gamble no matter how you choose a dog, and one animals individual characteristics might well outweigh the breeds general traits. In the end, Jess decision was to go to the Humane Society and choose a mutt who's big, brown eyes and cheerful disposition she found irresistible. As she paid her money and collected her dog, together with the veterinarians certificate of the animals fitness, Jess consoled herself with the thought that even if she couldn't train it to protect it's owner, at least shed have a cuddly companion.

EXERCISE 4.10

This exercise will test your ability to use apostrophes correctly, both in contractions and in possessive constructions. Correct the errors in the following sentences. No answers are provided for this exercise.

1. Jodies roommates gerbil got loose last night and, after getting into Jodies stash of candy, it made a disgusting mess on her roommates essay.
2. The gerbils health was not permanently damaged by its chocolate feast, but it's appetite for healthy foods has been replaced by a passion for Reese's Pieces.
3. Ruths three-week visit with the Seths was great fun both for her and for the Seths daughter, Indira, who's social life was almost

nonexistent before Ruth took her out to meet people who's interests they shared.

4. The casseroles pungent aroma comes from its forty cloves of garlic, but the taste of the dish is quite mild because the garlics strong flavour is moderated by it's long, slow cooking in bouillon and wine.

5. Italys tourist appeal results partly from the countrys wonderful people, and partly from the local regions unforgettable foods and wines.

6. Im delighted to be able to tell you that the rumours about the Italians hair-raising driving habits are just that: rumours'. In fact, nowhere in Europe did I encounter drivers who's courtesy and kindness exceeded the Italians.

7. Leonard Cohens latest CD is, in the critics opinion, his best in years because its a combination of his greatest early songs, in updated versions, and some of his latest music.

8. Some members of the teachers union are concerned about our colleges interest in distance education and self-directed learning because they fear these methods of course delivery will reduce the number of faculty needed by the schools programs.

9. Krystals brother is thinking of touring with a friends band as soon as the school years over. The money wont be very good, but theres a chance that the tours outcome might be a recording session at a major labels studio.

10. Our departments computer graphics students combined Kevins chin with Keanus lips, Brads eyes, Robs nose, Toms ears, Arnolds forehead, and Seans hair to make a portrait of the ideal mans face. Id be happy with the bits they threw away.

_____ **UNIT TWO**

Sentence Structure

CHAPTER 5

Cracking the Sentence Code

There is nothing really mysterious or difficult about sentences. You've been speaking them successfully since you were two. The difficulty arises when you go to write—not sentences, oddly enough, but paragraphs. Almost all college students, if asked to write ten sentences on ten different topics, could do so without an error. But if those same students were to write paragraphs, then fragments, run-ons, and other sentence faults would creep in. These errors confuse and annoy readers.

The solution to fragment and run-on problems has two parts:

> Be sure every sentence you write
> 1. sounds right
>   AND
> 2. has a subject and a verb.

Your ear is the best instrument with which to test your sentences. If you read your sentences aloud, you'll probably be able to tell by the sound whether they are complete, clear, and satisfactory. A complete sentence is one that makes sense by itself.

Read these sentences aloud:

Ultimate is one of the world's newest sports.

Although Ultimate is still a young sport.

The second "sentence" doesn't sound right, does it? It does not make sense on its own and is in fact a sentence fragment.

Testing your sentences by reading them aloud won't work if you read your paragraphs straight through from beginning to end. The trick is to read from end to beginning. That is, read your last sentence aloud, and *listen* to it. If it sounds all right, then read aloud the next-to-last sentence, and so on, until you have worked your way back to the first sentence you wrote.

Now, what do you do with the ones that "sound funny"? Before you can fix them, you need to be able to decode each sentence, to discover whether it has a subject and a verb. The subject and verb are the bare essentials of a sentence. Every sentence you write must have both. (The only exception is a **command,** in which the subject is understood rather than expressed. Consider this command: "Do the following exercises." The subject *you* is understood.)

Finding Subjects and Verbs

A sentence is about *someone* or *something*. That someone or something is the **subject.** The word (or words) that tells what the subject *is* or *does* is the **verb.** The verb expresses some sort of action, or condition, or occurrence.

Find the verb first. One way is by finding the word whose form can be changed to indicate a change in time. In the sentence

> The prime minister called an election.

called (in the past) can be changed to *calls* (present) or *will call* (future); so *called* is the verb.

Once you have found the verb, find the subject by asking *who* or *what* the verb is referring to.

Look at these examples. We have underlined the subjects once and the verbs twice.

> Jean helps me.
> (Helps expresses an action and is the verb.
> Who or what helps? Jean helps, so Jean is the subject.)

> Finding verbs is relatively easy.
> (Is expresses a condition and is the verb.
> Who or what is [easy]? Finding, which is the subject.)

Jacques Cartier <u>described</u> Canada as "the land God gave to Cain."
(<u>Described</u> expresses an occurrence and is the verb.
Who or what <u>described</u>? <u>Jacques Cartier</u>.)

This new accounting <u>program</u> <u>will save</u> me hours of time.
(<u>Will save</u> expresses an action and is the verb.
Who or what <u>will save</u>? The <u>program</u>.)

Hint: You can test whether you've identified the subject and verb correctly by saying them together to see whether or not they make sense. For example, "<u>Finding</u> <u>is</u>" makes sense; *"<u>verbs</u> <u>is</u>" does not. "<u>This program</u> <u>will save</u>" makes sense; *"<u>me</u> <u>will save</u>" does not.

EXERCISE 5.1

Find the subject and the verb in the following sentences. Underline the subject with one line and the verb with two. Check your answers (beginning on p. 321), and if you made even one mistake, carefully reread "Finding Subjects and Verbs." Be sure you understand this material thoroughly before you go on.

1. Algy met a bear.
2. A bear met Algy.
3. The bear was bulgy.
4. Sad to say, the bulge was Algy.
5. Grizzlies are famous for their unpredictability.
6. Meeting bears unexpectedly is clearly risky.
7. According to an old myth, bears never run downhill.
8. Take it from me. They do.
9. Females with cubs are known to be especially dangerous.
10. Defending oneself presents a real problem.

EXERCISE 5.2

1. Change is the only constant in life.
2. Information doubles every 18 months.
3. Our survival depends on our ability to adapt to change.
4. Today, effective planning means training for change.
5. Otherwise, we risk becoming roadkill on the highway of life.
6. Learning to adapt to change is, therefore, everyone's challenge.
7. Silicon, a form of sand, is a computer chip's main component.
8. To get ahead in the 90s, people need knowledge from many fields.
9. Soon, a single crystal will hold the entire Library of Congress.
10. Ironically, high technology is now our forests' best friend.

   The subject usually comes before the verb in a sentence, but not always. Occasionally, we find it after the verb:

> Back to the refreshment stand for the fourth time <u>stumbled</u> the weary <u>father</u>.
> (Who or what <u>stumbled</u>? The <u>father</u>.)
>
> At the bottom of the page, in red ink, <u>was</u> my <u>grade</u>.
> (Who or what <u>was</u>? My <u>grade</u>.)

In sentences beginning with *There* + some form of the verb *to be*, or with *Here* + some form of the verb *to be*, the subject comes after the verb.

> There <u>are</u> three good <u>reasons</u> for learning to write well.
> (Who or what <u>are</u>? <u>Reasons</u>.)
>
> There <u>will be</u> a <u>test</u> next week.
> (Who or what <u>will be</u>? A <u>test</u>.)
>
> Here <u>are</u> the <u>solutions</u> to last week's problem set.
> (Who or what <u>are</u>? <u>Solutions</u>.)

In questions, the subject often follows the verb:

> <u>Are</u> <u>you</u> sure about this?   <u>Is</u> <u>he</u> late again?
> (Who or what <u>are</u>? <u>You</u>.)   (Who or what <u>is</u>? <u>He</u>.)

But notice that, in questions beginning with *who, whose, what*, or *which*, the subject and verb are in "normal" order:

> <u>Who</u> <u>met</u> the bear?   <u>What</u> <u>happened</u> to Algy?
> <u>Whose</u> <u>belly</u> <u>was</u> bulgy?   <u>Which</u> <u>grizzly</u> <u>ate</u> Algy?

   In the following exercises, underline the subject in each sentence with one line and the verb with two. Check your answers to each set before you go on.

EXERCISE 5.3

   1. Canada is a country with two official languages and no official culture.
   2. The word "Ai!" means "hello" in Inuktitut.
   3. Newfoundland is a piece of rock entirely surrounded by fog.
   4. Are you from B.C.?
   5. There is the CN Tower, the world's tallest freestanding structure.
   6. Money, like manure, does good only when spread around.
   7. Here are the steps to follow.

8. Flin Flon is named after the hero of a ten-cent novel published in 1905.
9. Whose idea was this, anyway?
10. Drive carefully.

EXERCISE 5.4

1. Doing grammar exercises is boring.
2. Were they happy with their choice?
3. In the playground were thirty-four screaming children.
4. Are you still angry with me?
5. In July each year, in Calgary, Alberta, the famous Stampede is held.
6. Please stop at the next corner.
7. Santa Claus's address is c/o The North Pole, Canada, HOH OHO.
8. Have you finished the lab yet?
9. Under our back porch lives a family of skunks.
10. Deep in the hills, over the winding river and beyond the shining desert, lived a tribe of gnomes.

More about Verbs

The verb in a sentence may be a single word, as in most of the exercises you've just done, or it may be a group of words. **Helping verbs** are often added to main verbs so that an idea can be expressed precisely. The words *shall, should, may, might, can, could, must, ought, will, would, have, do,* and *be* are helping verbs.

> The complete verb in a sentence consists of the main verb + any helping verbs.

Here are a few of the forms of the verb *write*. Notice that in questions the subject may come between the helping verb and the main verb.

You <u>may write</u> now.
He certainly <u>can write</u>!
We <u>should write</u> home more often.
I <u>shall write</u> tomorrow.
He <u>could have written</u> yesterday.
She <u>is writing</u> her memoirs.
<u>Did</u> he <u>write</u> to you?
He <u>had written</u> his apology.

You <u>ought to write</u> to him.
We <u>will have written</u> by then.
I <u>will write</u> to the editor.
The proposal <u>has been written</u>.
Orders <u>should have been written</u>.
<u>Could</u> you <u>have written</u> it in French?

One verb form *always* takes a helping verb. Here is the rule:

> A verb ending in *-ing* MUST have a helping verb (or verbs) before it.

Here are a few of the forms an *-ing* verb can take:

I <u>am writing</u> the report.
You <u>will be writing</u> a report.
He <u>should have been writing</u> it.
<u>Is</u> she <u>writing</u> the paper for him?
She <u>must have been writing</u> all night.
You <u>are writing</u> illegibly.
I <u>was writing</u> neatly.
<u>Have</u> you <u>been writing</u> on the wall?

Beware of certain words that are often confused with helping verbs:

> Words such as *not, only, always, sometimes, never, ever,* and *just* are NOT part of the verb.

These words sometimes appear in the middle of a complete verb, but they are modifiers, not verbs. Do not underline them:

I <u>have</u> just <u>won</u> a one-way ticket to Aklavik.
She <u>is</u> always <u>chosen</u> first.
Most people <u>do</u> not <u>welcome</u> unasked-for advice.

In the following exercise, underline the subject once and the complete verb twice. Correct each set of ten sentences before you go on to the next.

EXERCISE 5.5

1. Dwight is sleeping again, unfortunately.
2. You should have been paying attention.
3. Should we conclude the meeting now?
4. In Canada, fall arrives one month before winter.
5. What mark did you get?
6. We do not want to hear your band's demo tape.

7. Where and when are we meeting?
8. The old will always think young people foolish.
9. Their coach has just begun to suffer.
10. Back and forth, lazily but without stopping, swam the shark.

EXERCISE 5.6

1. The whole country is covered with hip-deep snow for several months.
2. Why would anyone want to go over the falls in a barrel?
3. Canadians should be more concerned about the national debt.
4. Never again will I agree to ride with you!
5. A person may forgive an injury, but not an insult.
6. There have been better players.
7. You can become addicted to coffee.
8. How long did you stay in Climax, Saskatchewan?
9. Have you ever been to the Gaspé?
10. Only recently has our track coach become interested in chemistry.

EXERCISE 5.7

1. By the year 2000, gasoline made from coal will be commercially available.
2. At the end of this decade, a fibre-optic network will have been completed, linking all campuses into a single system.
3. Why are the official records of Canada's Parliament called Hansard?
4. Canada's provinces were literally railroaded into Confederation.
5. I am always studying for some test or another, only to forget everything the next day.
6. Could any government have managed the economy worse than this one?
7. Have you ever been caught cheating on a test?
8. Very little is known about the Canadian victory over the Americans in the War of 1812.
9. Why don't we simply agree to disagree about the attractiveness of nose rings?
10. Aren't you glad to be finished?

More about Subjects

Very often, groups of words called **prepositional phrases** come before the subject in a sentence, or between the subject and the verb. When you're looking for the subject in a sentence, prepositional phrases can trip you up unless you know this rule:

The subject of a sentence is never in a prepositional phrase.

You must be able to identify prepositional phrases so that you will know where *not* to look for the subject. A prepositional phrase is a group of words that begins with a preposition and ends with the name of something or someone (a noun or a pronoun). Often, a prepositional phrase will indicate the direction or location of something. In the phrases below, the italicized words are prepositions:

about the book	*between* the desks	*near* the wall
above the book	*by* the book	*of* the program
according to the book	*concerning* the memo	*on* the desk
after the meeting	*despite* the order	*onto* the floor
against the wall	*down* the hall	*over* a door
along the hall	*except* the staff	*through* the window
among the books	*for* the manager	*to* the staff
among them	*from* the office	*under* the desk
around the office	*in* front *of* the desk	*until* the meeting
before lunch	*inside* the office	*up* the hall
behind the desk	*in* the book	*with* a book
below the window	*into* the elevator	*without* them
beside the computer	*like* the book	*without* the software

Before you look for the subject in a sentence, cross out all prepositional phrases. For example:

The keyboard ~~of your computer~~ should be cleaned occasionally.
What <u>should be cleaned</u>? The <u>keyboard</u> (not the computer).

~~In case of an emergency~~, a member ~~of the class~~ should go ~~to the nearest security office~~ for help.

Who <u>should go</u>? A <u>member</u> (not the class).

In the following exercises, first cross out the prepositional phrase(s) in each sentence. Then underline the subject once and the verb twice. Check your answers to each set of ten sentences before going on. If you get three sets entirely correct, skip ahead to exercise 5.13.

EXERCISE 5.8

1. A bird in the hand is worth two in the bush.
2. Only a few of us have done our homework.
3. Most of your answers are entertaining but wrong.
4. More than a dozen brands of video recorders are now on the market.
5. Meet me at six at the corner of Robson and Granville.
6. A couple of hamburgers should be enough for each of us.
7. Do you know anything about the latest rumours in the government?
8. There is a show about laser technology on television tonight.
9. After eight hours of classes, the thought of collapsing in front of the TV set is very appealing.
10. One episode of *Geraldo* was more than enough for me.

EXERCISE 5.9

1. The verb in this sentence is "is."
2. For many students, lack of money is probably the most serious problem.
3. In the middle of May, after the end of term, the Intercollegiate Arm-Wrestling Championships will be held.
4. One strand of fibre optics can carry both telephone and television signals.
5. During the second week of term, the class will be taken on a tour of the resource centre.
6. Contrary to your expectations and despite the rumours, your instructor does not bite.
7. On Callisto, one of Jupiter's thirteen moons, snow "falls" up, not down.
8. On the eastern shore of Vancouver Island, you can find both oysters and clams.
9. One of the most entertaining comedies of the 1990s was *Wayne's World*.
10. In similar circumstances, most of us would probably have taken the money.

EXERCISE 5.10

1. By this time, you must be tired of the pointless game shows on TV.
2. The happiness of every country depends on the character of its people.
3. Above my desk hangs someone else's diploma.
4. During the course of the discussion, several of us lost our tempers.
5. In law, a sentence is a decision by a judge on the punishment of a criminal.

6. The "short side" of a goalie is the side closer to the post.
7. New steps should be taken to encourage the flow of capital into small businesses.
8. After waiting for more than an hour, we finally left without you.
9. So far only two of your answers to the questions have been incorrect.
10. One of the country's most distinguished reporters will speak on the responsibilities of the press.

EXERCISE 5.11

1. The average height of Canadian women, excluding those in Quebec, is 165 cm.
2. By waiting on tables, babysitting, and doing other jobs, I manage to make ends meet.
3. The pile of books and papers on your desk is about as neat as a tossed salad.
4. Only a few of the news reporters on television are responsible for researching and writing in addition to reading the news.
5. Except for Biff, everyone understands prepositions.
6. No book of Canadian humour would be complete without a couple of "Newfie" jokes.
7. Our teacher's uncertainty about the date of the War of 1812 made us less than confident about his knowledge of Canadian history.
8. A daily intake of more than 600 mg of caffeine can result in headaches, insomnia, and heart palpitations.
9. Six to ten cups of coffee will contain 600 mg of caffeine.
10. Despite its strong taste, espresso contains no more caffeine than regular coffee.

EXERCISE 5.12

1. The current trend in electronics is to put telephones in our pockets and televisions in our telephones.
2. Like many other Canadian expressions, the term *bluenose*, meaning a Nova Scotian, is of uncertain origin.
3. Within a week, please give me your report on the pyrazine anion project.
4. In the spring, parked in front of his TV set, Barry trains for the Stanley Cup playoffs.
5. Government programs to encourage training in basic skills have been cut back steadily over the past few years.
6. In the Arctic wastes of Ungava, there is a mysterious stone structure in the shape of a giant hammer standing on end.

7. There is no obvious explanation for its presence in this isolated place.
8. According to archeologist Thomas E. Lee, it may be a monument left by Vikings in their travels west from Greenland.
9. Here, on an island called Pamiok, are the ruins of what may have been a Viking longhouse.
10. If so, then centuries before Columbus's "discovery" of America, the Vikings were in what is now northern Quebec.

EXERCISE 5.13

Write ten fairly long sentences of your own. In at least three of them, place the subject after the verb. Cross out all the prepositional phrases, and underline the subject once and the complete verb twice.

Multiple Subjects and Verbs

So far, you have been working with sentences containing only one complete subject and one complete verb. Sentences can, however, have more than one subject and verb. Here is a sentence with a multiple subject:

Southlands and West Point Grey are suburbs of Vancouver.

This sentence has a multiple verb:

He elbowed and wriggled his way along the aisle of the bus.

And this sentence has a multiple subject and a multiple verb:

The sergeant and the detective leaped from their car and seized the suspect.

The elements of a multiple subject or verb are usually joined by *and*. Multiple subjects and verbs may contain more than two elements, as in the following sentences:

Clarity, brevity, and simplicity are the basic qualities of good writing.

I finished my paper, put the cat outside, took the phone off the hook, and crawled into bed.

In the following exercises, underline the subjects once and the verbs twice. Be sure to underline all the elements in a multiple subject or verb. Check your answers to each set of ten sentences before continuing.

EXERCISE 5.14

1. Maple sugar and wild rice are native Canadian products.
2. Kim or Avi will go next.
3. Professor Singh handed out the tests and wished us luck.
4. I tried and tried but didn't succeed.
5. The two canoeists and their dog were missing for four days.
6. Point and Click, my nerdy brother's two cats, are sleeping peacefully on the sofa.
7. Point and Click killed two pigeons and slaughtered a squirrel before breakfast.
8. Timothy Findley farms, writes, and lectures—in that order.
9. Wait ten minutes and then call again.
10. Shooting often and scoring occasionally are not marketable talents.

EXERCISE 5.15

1. Misspellings can create misunderstandings and cause embarrassment.
2. Several years ago, the *Durham County Review* printed an article about a British military leader.
3. In the article, the old soldier was highly praised but unfortunately was described as "battle-scared."
4. Furious, the soldier called the paper and demanded an apology.
5. The writer and the editor soothed the old man and promised to publish a retraction.
6. In the retraction, the paper apologized for the error and explained, "What we really meant, of course, was 'bottle-scarred.'"
7. Drive slowly and see our city; drive fast and see our jail.
8. Good drivers obey all traffic regulations and never lose their heads.
9. Drink if you want, but don't drive if you do.
10. Come-by-Chance, Blow-Me-Down, Run-by-Guess, and Jerry's Nose are places in Newfoundland.

EXERCISE 5.16

I have news for all you short people out there. Being tall is not an enviable condition. First of all, tall people are the butt of constant jokes: "How's the weather up there?" "What great kneecaps you have!" The humour is pretty lame. Next, there is the risk of serious head injury. I have been bashed by cupboard doors, concussed by sign boards, and even, on one memorable occasion, knocked senseless by a chandelier. Clothes present another problem. Finding anything to fit is a challenge. Finding anything remotely fashionable is next to impossible. Clerks in men's clothing departments are apparently hired for their ability to humiliate outsized men. They seem genuinely surprised at one's reluctance to appear in public wearing pants that end at the mid-calf. And finally, there is basketball. Like many tall people, I detest the game. Contrary to popular belief, not all persons more than 2 m tall have been blessed with the natural ability to dribble, jump-shoot, and slam-dunk. Many of us would rather join a chain gang than a basketball team. To be honest, though, for the most part, I do like being tall. But I wouldn't mind fewer jokes, more sympathy, and less basketball.

EXERCISE 5.17

This exercise will test your subject- and verb-finding ability. Underline the subjects with one line and the verbs with two lines. Be sure to underline all elements in a multiple subject or verb. No answers are given for this exercise.

1. Take only pictures. Leave only footprints. (Sign posted in Banff National Park)
2. Dwight and Rudolf studied for more than a week but failed the exam anyway.
3. In the tidal pool were two starfish, several sand dollars, and dozens of tiny crabs.
4. He worked and saved all his life and died miserable and alone.
5. Everybody but me went to camp or spent a few weeks at a cottage.
6. Among the many kinds of cheese made in Canada are Camembert, Fontina, and Quark.
7. Shoe companies, video companies, and exercise equipment manufacturers are all profiting from the fitness craze.

8. We took a train from Clarenville to Bonavista and then went by bus to St. John's.
9. The politicians of our time try in vain to change the world but seldom try to change themselves.
10. According to its campaign literature, the incoming government will provide jobs for all Canadians, eliminate the national debt, find a cure for cancer, land a Canadian on Pluto, and lower taxes, all in its first year of office.

CHAPTER 6

Solving Sentence-Fragment Problems

Any group of words that is punctuated as a sentence but does not have a subject or a complete verb is a **sentence fragment.** Fragments are appropriate in conversation and in some kinds of writing, but normally they are not acceptable in college, technical, and business writing. You've already learned how to spot a sentence fragment: read the words aloud, and check to see whether the subject or the verb (or both) is missing. Let's look at a few examples:

Now, as always, is greatly influenced by her willful neighbour.
(Who or what <u>is influenced</u>? The sentence doesn't tell you. The subject is missing.)

The argument being over sharing responsibility for housework and child care.
(The verb is missing.)

The committee attempting to analyze Canada's participation in U.N. peacekeeping missions.
(Part of the verb is missing. Remember that a verb ending in *-ing* must have a helping verb in front of it.)

To help students in every lab but this one.
(Subject and verb are both missing.)

Regarding the matter we discussed last week.
(Subject and verb are both missing.)

Now, what do you do with the fragments you've found?

> To change a sentence fragment into a complete sentence,
> add whatever is missing: a subject, a verb, or both.

You may need to add a subject:

Now, as always, <u>Canada</u> is greatly influenced by her willful neighbor.

You may need to add a verb:

The argument <u>was</u> over sharing responsibility for housework and
child care.

You may need to add part of a verb:

The committee <u>is attempting</u> to analyze Canada's participation in
U.N. peacekeeping missions.

You may need to add both a subject and a verb:

A <u>technician</u> <u>is</u> available to help students in every lab but this one.

And sometimes you need to add more than just a subject and a verb:

I <u>have written</u> to <u>the dean</u> regarding the matter we discussed last
week.

Don't let the length of a fragment fool you. Students sometimes think
that if a string of words is long, it must be a sentence. Not so. No matter
how long the string of words is, if it doesn't contain both a subject and a
verb, it is not a sentence. Consider this example, taken from "The Men of
Moosomin," by Sara Jeannette Duncan:

Here and there a ruddy little pond, like a pocket looking glass dropped on the prairie, with a score or so of wild ducks swimming in it, or a slight round hollow where a pond used to be, with the wild ducks flying high.

Do you know what's missing? Can you change the fragment into a sentence?

In the following exercises, read each "sentence" aloud. Put S before each complete sentence and F before each sentence fragment. Make each fragment into a complete sentence by adding whatever is missing: a subject, a verb, or both. After you complete each set of ten sentences, check your answers. If you get three sets entirely correct, you may skip the rest. Answers begin on p. 325.

EXERCISE 6.1

1. _____ About sentence fragments.

2. _____ To go to the wall.

3. _____ Glad to do it for you.

4. _____ Falling asleep in class, after working all night.

5. _____ The Doom players meeting in the upper lounge.

6. _____ Look at the helicopter.

7. _____ Watching television a cheap form of entertainment.

8. _____ Hoping to hear from you soon.

9. _____ Saved by the bell.

10. _____ Thinking the class was over, I left.

EXERCISE 6.2

1. _____ To whom it may concern.

2. _____ Turtles being both cheap and easy to train.

3. _____ Never cared for them, frankly.

4. ____ Learning how to write a computer program.

5. ____ The reason being they love hockey.

6. ____ Jackie Burroughs, famous for her role in *Road to Avonlea*.

7. ____ Are you sure about that?

8. ____ Many of whom have seen the film dozens of times.

9. ____ Suddenly screeched to a stop.

10. ____ Never put off until tomorrow what you can put off until next week.

EXERCISE 6.3

____ Professional athletes making millions of dollars a year. ____ At the same time, owners of sports franchises growing fantastically rich from the efforts of their employees, the players. ____ The fans, the forgotten people in the struggle for control over major league sports. ____ The people paying the money that makes both owners and players rich. ____ I have an idea that would protect everyone's interests. ____ Cap the owners' profits. Cap the players' salaries. ____ And most important, the ticket prices. ____ A fair deal for everyone. ____ Fans should be able to see their teams play for the price of a movie ticket, not the price of a television set.

EXERCISE 6.4

____ Procrastination is my most serious fault. ____ Worse even than my addiction to Saturday morning cartoons. ____ I will do almost anything to avoid doing what I'm supposed to be doing at any given time. ____ Sometimes the things I do in order to avoid my real task are more difficult or more distasteful than the task itself. ____ Which makes no sense. ____ For example, phoning old friends, or new acquaintances, or co-workers, or, when I'm really desperate, even relatives. ____ Other <u>examples</u> of my time-

<u>subject</u>

wasting activities <u>include</u> cooking, cleaning the apartment, doing laundry,

<u>verb</u>.

rearranging my books or my CD collection, or walking the neighbours' dog. ____ Finally, confronted with the inescapable: deadline day. ____ Only then, kicking into overdrive, working day and night until the job is fin- ished, and collapsing from exhaustion. ____ It's an exciting, if not very sen- sible, way to live.

EXERCISE 6.5

_F_ ____ The fact being that I have to hold down at least one part-time job to go to school. _F_ ____ The cost of tuition, books, rent, food, and other living expenses, not to mention clothing and a little money for entertain- ment. ____ I can't survive without working. _F_ ____ Getting the minimum wage for work that is heavy, dirty, and boring. _F_ ____ Jobs such as dish- washer, stock clerk, warehouser, cleaner, and short-order cook throughout my college years. _F_ ____ What I do find upsetting, though. _F_ ____ Some teach- ers not understanding that I work out of necessity, not out of choice. ____ I wish I did have the luxury of concentrating on nothing but school work. _F_ ____ Instead of dealing with problems such as class schedules that conflict with my work schedule. _F_ ____ Or assignments that are due with less than a week's notice. _F_ ____ The inescapable fact, however, being that I can't attend all my classes and hand in all my assignments on time because

I'm too busy working to pay for the education I'm not getting!

Independent and Dependent Clauses

A group of words containing a subject and a verb is a clause. There are two kinds of clauses. An **independent clause** is one that makes complete sense on its own. It can stand alone, as a sentence. A **dependent clause,** as its name suggests, cannot stand alone as a sentence; it depends on another clause to make complete sense.

Dependent clauses are easy to recognize, because they begin with words such as these:

DEPENDENT-CLAUSE CUES

after	so that
although	that
as, as if	though
as long as	unless
as soon as	until
because	what, whatever
before	when, whenever
even if, even though	where, wherever
if	whether
in order that	which, whichever
provided that	while
since	who, whom, whose

Whenever a clause begins with one of these words or phrases, it is dependent.

A dependent clause must be attached to an independent clause.
If it stands alone, it is a sentence fragment.

Here is an independent clause:

I am a poor speller.

If we put one of the dependent clause cues in front of it, it can no longer stand alone:

> Because I am a poor speller

We can correct this kind of fragment by attaching it to an independent clause:

> Because I am a poor speller, I have chained my dictionary to my wrist.

In the following exercises, put an S before each clause that is independent and therefore a sentence. Put an F before each clause that is dependent and therefore a sentence fragment. Circle the dependent clause cue in each sentence fragment.

EXERCISE 6.6

1. F (After) the game was over.

2. F (Whatever) Kiki told you.

3. F (Even if) I did agree to go with you.

4. F (As long as) we understand each other.

5. F (When) the term is over.

6. F (Unless) you can pass a simple vocabulary test.

7. F All those (who) finish before the time is up.

8. S I went since no one else was interested.

9. F (When) you move to a new apartment.

10. F Repulsive, (although) she seems to be fond of it.

EXERCISE 6.7

1. F (So that) you can learn the system.

2. F (Though) the decision was not easy.

3. F (Since) I believe she's doing the best she can.

4. _F_ If you miss the next class, too.

5. _F_ Provided that the company is pleased with your work.

6. _F_ Even if that toad turns into a prince.

7. _S_ Before the college accepted me, I worked as a dog walker.

8. _F_ Whenever we meet like this.

9. _S_ Luckily, the horse that we bet on won.

10. _F_ Occasionally, so that you don't get homesick.

EXERCISE 6.8

1. _F_ All those who are late coming back from lunch.

2. _F_ The party that was in power being full of crooks and scoundrels.

3. _S_ Although we're poor, we're happy.

4. _S_ What we think doesn't seem to matter.

5. _F_ Where you left them yesterday, I guess.

6. _F_ Frequently, when she's away on business.

7. _F_ Whether she believes him or not.

8. _F_ In a situation like this, whichever decision you make.

9. _F_ Despite our efforts to help you, until you decide you want to learn.

10. _F_ In view of the fact that you lied about your age, education, and work experience.

EXERCISE 6.9

1. _S_ She frowns because it gives people the impression she's thinking.

2. _F_ Though most of us don't even know who the candidates are.

3. _F_ A job that demands intelligence, physical fitness, and a genuine liking for people.

4. ___S___ Wherever you go, I'll follow.

5. ___S___ Whether or not you want me is irrelevant.

6. ___S___ Unless you conceal yourself, I'll be there.

7. ___F___ If I wrote his letters for him and typed his résumé.

8. ___F___ Because jargon is full of long words, uses more words than necessary, and contains long, awkward sentences.

9. ___F___ Until death do us part, or as long as we love each other, whichever comes first.

10. ___F___ When Kim approached the table where the five of us sat indulging in quantities of food that had been prepared by the students themselves.

Most sentence fragments are dependent clauses punctuated as sentences. Fortunately, this is the easiest kind of fragment to recognize and fix. All you need to do is join the dependent clause either to the sentence that comes before it or to the one that comes after it—whichever linkage makes better sense.

One final point. If you join your clause fragment to the independent clause that follows it, put a comma between the two clauses (see Chapter 17, p. 186).

Read the following example to yourself; then read it aloud, beginning with the last sentence and working back to the first.

> Montreal is a sequence of ghettos. Although I was born and brought up there. My experience of French was a pathetically limited and distorted one.

The second "sentence" sounds incomplete, and the dependent-clause cue at the beginning of it is the clue you need to identify it as a sentence fragment. You could join the fragment to the sentence before it, but then you would get "Montreal is a sequence of ghettos, although I was born and brought up there," which doesn't make sense. The fragment should be linked to the sentence that follows it, like this:

> Montreal is a sequence of ghettos. Although I was born and brought up there, my experience of French was a pathetically limited and distorted one. (Mordecai Richler, "Quebec Oui, Ottawa Non!")

EXERCISE 6.10

Correct the sentence fragments in exercises 6.6 through 6.9. Make each fragment into a complete sentence by adding an independent clause either before or after the dependent clause. Remember to punctuate correctly: if a dependent clause comes at the beginning of your sentence, put a comma after it. When you have completed this exercise, exchange with another student and check each other's work.

Identify the sentence fragments in the paragraphs below. Circle the dependent clause cue in each fragment you find. Then correct each fragment by joining it to a complete sentence before or after it—whichever makes better sense. Check your answers on p. 327.

EXERCISE 6.11

Although spring is my favourite season and I look forward eagerly to its arrival after the long winter. There are some things about the season. That I could do without. When the warm weather begins. I am always tempted to buy new, fashionable shoes. Which are ruined in the wet muck. That is everywhere. Unless I act quickly. My dog also becomes a problem in the spring. She delights in tracking mud from the backyard into the house. After she creates a mess that Mr. Clean would need steroids to tackle. She will go back outside and find something sticky and smelly to roll in. Until the warm weather dries up the mud, and my dog loses the annual urge to coat herself with disgusting substances. My joy at the arrival of spring is always a little restrained.

EXERCISE 6.12

Since my marks at the end of high school were anything but impressive. I thought the chances of my acceptance at college or university were not very good. Secretly, however, I wasn't at all sure that college or university was where I wanted to go. I had also applied to the Armed Forces program that pays for your education. If you agree to serve for four years after graduation. Provided that you meet certain conditions. On the same day that the official transcript of my dismal marks appeared in the mail. Two schools I had applied to sent their rejections. As did the Armed Forces, calling me "an academic risk." Until the next day. When a fourth letter arrived. I hid the marks and the rejection letters from my parents and suffered. As I have never suffered before or since. Fortunately, since the fourth letter was an acceptance from an unusually enlightened (or desperate) school. I was able to enjoy the summer. Eventually, I graduated with a respectable average. And became a writer. Last year I got my revenge on the Armed Forces for their lack of faith in my academic potential. When they bought three thousand copies of my text book to teach their recruits how to write.

Correct the fragments in the two paragraphs below in any way you choose. Try to use a variety of the techniques for fixing fragments that you have learned in this chapter. When you are finished, compare your answers with our suggestions on p. 327.

EXERCISE 6.13

My parents own a diesel car. A car that they claim was a wonderful buy because it gets good mileage and seldom needs a tune-up. Apparently not being concerned about the smell. Or the noise. If I borrow it to go anywhere with my friends, laughing at the awful noise and complaining about the disgusting smell. My parents are not keen on lending me their car, anyway. Probably because I have had an unfortunate history of bad luck with cars. Due to no fault of mine. I totalled two cars in three years. So my parents consider the fact that I am embarrassed by their car as yet another advantage of diesel ownership. Why, I wonder, can't my parents be like other people's parents? Driving a nice big Buick or a comfortable Volvo? Or even a compact that runs on normal gasoline and doesn't sound as if it's about to explode every time you turn the key in the ignition? And, most important, doesn't smell like the exhaust system of an 18-wheel transport truck? My parents are so inconsiderate. Never thinking of others. Always thinking only of themselves.

EXERCISE 6.14

Although I had been well-trained by my parents in the arts of dishwashing and kitchen clean-up. When I moved away from home to go to college and began to keep house for myself. My roommate and I somehow let things slide in this department. Every dish we used found its way into the sink or onto the kitchen counter. Without being washed or even rinsed. Naturally, as the days and weeks went by, and the food hardened. Eventually bonding to the surface of the dishes. The prospect of cleaning up became less and less appealing. We made trips to junk shops and lawn sales. Where we added to our collection of chipped and mismatched dinnerware. Anything to avoid tackling the piles of food-encrusted plates that filled our kitchen. Then, one day, my roommate looked out of the window of our apartment. Just in time to see my parents drive up to surprise us with one of their rare visits. A moment of paralyzing panic and indecision. My roommate began piling dirty dishes in a closet. While I opted for stashing them under the bed and in the oven. In a frenzy of activity, while my parents were innocently parking their car and unloading the care packages of home-baked goodies they always brought us. We managed to dispose of most of the evidence of our laziness. After taking us out for dinner and before heading back home. My mother even commented on how tidy our apartment seemed to be. This nerve-shattering experience teaching us a lesson, however. My roommate and I resolved to wash dishes at least once a week. But first we had to get them out of the closet, out from under the bed, and out of the oven.

EXERCISE 6.15

As a final test of your skill in correcting sentence fragments, try this exercise. Put an S before each item that contains only complete sentences. Put an F before each item that contains one or more sentence fragments. Then make each fragment into a complete sentence. No answers are provided for this exercise.

1. ____ In terms of both qualifications and experience, absolutely perfect for the job.

2. ____ On the few occasions that your timetable has you scheduled for two classes in a row. You can count on their being located in buildings at opposite ends of the campus.

3. ____ In the next decade will see more changes in methods of food production than have occurred in the last thousand years. Thanks to advances in biotechnology.

4. ____ When I read a description of the computer game, Doom, I couldn't believe what I was reading. Then discovering that my children had been playing it happily for months.

5. ____ While in the Industrial Age, progress depended on physical strength. In the Information Age, progress will depend on intellect and imagination.

6. ____ Better late than never? No. Better never than late. (Frank Ogden)

7. ____ In the past ten years, science having learned more about how the brain functions than in all of humankind's previous history.

8. ____ Although she reads the "Companions Wanted" column faithfully, Drusilla has yet to find a man who fulfils her requirements. One who is sensitive, well-educated, cuddly, and rich.

9. ____ One of George Orwell's most famous sentences from *Animal Farm* being "All animals are created equal, but some animals are more equal than others."

10. ____ As a general rule, it is best to avoid writing sentence fragments. Until you are an experienced, skilful, and confident writer. Even then, fragments appropriate only in informal writing.

CHAPTER 7

Solving Run-On Sentence Problems

Some sentences lack essential elements and thus are fragments. Other sentences contain too many elements, or elements that are incorrectly linked together. A sentence with too much in it or with inadequate punctuation between clauses is a **run-on.** Run-ons tend to occur when you write in a hurry, without taking time to organize your thoughts first. If you think about what you want to say and punctuate carefully, you shouldn't have any problems with run-ons.

Let's look at the three kinds of run-on sentences: the comma splice, the fused sentence, and the true run-on.

Comma Splices and Fused Sentences

As its name suggests, the **comma splice** occurs when two complete sentences (independent clauses) are joined together with only a comma between them. Here's an example:

Our dog is obedient, he has been well trained.

A **fused sentence** occurs when two complete sentences are joined together with no punctuation between them. For example:

Our dog is obedient he has been well trained.

There are three ways you can fix a comma splice or fused sentence.

> 1. Use a semicolon to separate the independent clauses.

For example:

Our dog is obedient; he has been well trained.

(If you are not sure how to use semicolons, see Chapter 18.)

> 2. Add an appropriate linking word between the two clauses.

Two types of linking words will work.

1. You can add one of these words: *and, but, or, nor, for, so,* or *yet.* These words should be preceded by a comma. Here is an example:

Our dog is obedient, for he has been well trained.

2. You can add one of the dependent clause cues listed on p. 62. For example:

Our dog is obedient because he has been well trained.

> 3. Make the independent clauses into two separate sentences.

Our dog is obedient. He has been well trained.

Note that all three solutions to comma splices and fused sentences require you to use a word or punctuation mark strong enough to come between two independent clauses. A comma by itself is too weak, and so is a dash.

The sentences in the following exercises will give you practice in fixing comma splices and fused sentences. Correct the sentences where necessary, then check your answers, beginning on p. 328. Since there are three ways to fix each sentence, your answers may differ from our suggestions. If you're confused about when to use a semicolon and when to use a period, be sure to read p. 193 before going on.

EXERCISE 7.1

1. I hate computers they're always making mistakes.
2. Snowboarding is lots of fun, but it isn't as fast as skiing.
3. Stop me if you've heard this one there was this cab driver on her first day at work.
4. Rudolf is bone lazy, Dwight isn't much better.
5. Chocolate is Ninik's weakness she cannot resist a Toblerone bar.
6. I'll probably be going out tonight Gretta offered to take me to a movie.
7. Efficiency is what most consumers look for in a new car, high performance isn't as important as it used to be.
8. I have a 3000-word assignment due tomorrow if it weren't for that, I'd love to teach you to play solitaire.
9. It bothers me to see Krystal and Sparkle playing cards all the time they could easily fail the term.
10. Anand was transformed overnight he had changed from a normal-looking student into a fashion plate.

EXERCISE 7.2

1. A fine mess this is; I'll never forgive you for getting me into this situation.
2. Let's take the shortcut; we need to get there as quickly as possible.
3. No one in the department supports her she's both arrogant and indolent.
4. I want to play the banjo, the only thing stopping me is a complete lack of musical talent.
5. Of course, it would also help if I owned a banjo.
6. I'd rather be lucky than good, on the other hand, I'd rather be good than unlucky.
7. Many environmentally aware people are heating their homes with woodstoves nowadays the result is "ecologists' smog."
8. The snow is turning into freezing rain we'll be lucky to get home before dawn if these conditions persist.
9. When you are looking for a new car, there are many factors to consider, the most important is probably price.

10. Many good films are made in both Canada and the United States, I wish I could tell which ones they were before paying my admission to a movie theatre.

EXERCISE 7.3

1. The largest dog in the world is the Irish Wolfhound; the strongest dog in the world is the Newfoundland; the stupidest dog in the world is my Afghan.
2. Please go to the door and see who's there, I'm on the phone.
3. Early Canadian settlers saw the Americans as a constant menace, even Ottawa—miles from anywhere and hardly a threat to anyone—was not considered safe.
4. They can crawl on their knees and beg that's the only way they'll ever get any more money from me!
5. Think carefully before you answer, a great deal depends on what you decide.
6. Cooking is my favourite pastime I don't enjoy it nearly so much when I have to do it as when I choose to do it.
7. There is a great deal to be said for woodcutting as a career, much of it bad.
8. My chiropractor has given me a sheet of exercises that he says will make my back stronger, he has convinced me that if I do these exercises daily, my pain will disappear.
9. Karin was given the choice of joining her father's firm as a driver or continuing her education at college knowing Karin, I think she's sure to take the job.
10. There are two students in this class named Xan; one is from China, the other from Russia. The latter's name is a nickname it is a short form of Alexandra.

EXERCISE 7.4

1. When our team travels to Moncton, we always stay at the same motel, it's not expensive, but it is centrally located and well-maintained.
2. I don't know whose boots those are; they were left here after our party, probably they belong to one of your friends.
3. With his huge, brown, adoring eyes and his obedient disposition, my dog is the most important creature in my life I know I'll never find a man so good-natured and well-trained.
4. Cats are wonderful creatures, they are often more sensitive than humans, as any true cat lover will tell you.
5. Lucy said she'd love to help me sort through the answers to my ad in the Personals column, but she had her own problems to worry about.

6. Backing the car off the shoulder and onto the highway. Krystal neglected to check her rearview mirror; as a result, she produced a significant alteration to the front end of a Honda.
7. I completely understand his feelings of rejection after discovering that his family had moved to another city while he was out getting a pizza for supper.
8. Appraising Rudolf's progress is difficult, when you realize that he has submitted none of the assignments, written none of the tests, and attended only about a third of the classes, you can see why I despair.
9. Fast food is generally less nutritious than home-cooked meals; although I know of some home cooking that rates below cardboard in nutritional value, I still prefer it as a rule.
10. The biggest drawbacks to keeping tropical fish are that you get soaked whenever you pet them, and they take a long time to grow big enough to eat.

In the exercises that follow, correct the comma splices and fused sentences any way you choose. This would be a good time to review the three ways of fixing these errors. Your goal should be to produce paragraphs in which the sentences are both correct and effective.

EXERCISE 7.5

Last year, an exchange student from the south of France came to live with us, her name was Simone and she came to Canada to practise her English and to experience something of our culture. Simone was amazed by our fondness for fast food; she found it inedible. Another cultural difference she observed was the emphasis many Canadian women place on their appearance, they often applied fresh makeup between classes, they dressed as if they were going out to a fashionable restaurant instead of school. As everyone exposed to the international media knows, no women in the world are better groomed, dressed, and coiffed than the French, Simone was no exception. She loved to dress up, she delighted in showing off the designs, both subtle and dramatic, that the French are famous for, she wore them only on special occasions, however. The emphasis on multiculturalism in Canada, the relative newness of our towns and cities, and the vast size of our country all impressed her during her stay with us, the huge expanses of untouched wilderness she found a little intimidating. Though she was homesick, especially in the first few weeks, Simone enjoyed her year with us, when she was packing up to return to her home in Provence, she was already planning her next visit to Canada—a camping holiday in Banff.

EXERCISE 7.6

An acquaintance of mine recently became a Canadian citizen, when she told me about her citizenship hearing, however, I couldn't bring myself to offer her the congratulations she was obviously expecting. In preparation for the hearing, she had been told to study a small book containing basic facts about Canada: its government, history, and people, and she was told the judge who interviewed her would ask questions based on the information in this book, she neglected to study, or even to read the book. At the hearing, the judge asked her to identify the name of the current governor general, to explain some of the advantages of being a Canadian citizen, and to tell him whether health care was a federal or a provincial responsibility. Unable to answer any of these questions, my friend just giggled and shrugged then she listened while the judge gave her the answers. She expected to be told to come back when she had learned more about her adopted country, she was astonished when the judge congratulated her for successfully completing the interview and set a date to confirm her citizenship. I find the judge's decision appalling for three reasons, first, my friend's failure even to open the book she was given suggests she doesn't have much respect for Canadian citizenship, second, her low opinion of our citizenship process was reinforced when the judge passed her, third, I can't help but feel that she was passed because she is an attractive blonde woman, a university professor, and speaks with a polished, upper-class English accent. If she had been a man or woman of colour, or spoken little or no English, or had a less impressive job, I cannot help but think she would have been rejected. she deserved to be.

The True Run-On Sentence

In the true **run-on sentence,** too many words or too many clauses are crowded together into one sentence. There is no hard-and-fast rule about how many independent clauses you may have in a sentence, but more than two can result in a sentence that is hard to read and even harder to understand.

> There were still a dozen or so guests who remained at the party, not counting the host, but after Raoul and Su Mei left, we decided it was time to go, so we collected our coats and said goodbye to the others, and then, after driving home very cautiously at speeds not exceeding 50 km/h, we sat up drinking coffee until three o'clock in the morning discussing our host's terrible taste in friends.

Clearly, the writer who created this monster got carried away with enthusiasm and just scribbled down everything that came to mind without thinking of the reader's tolerance or patience. If you take your time and remember your readers, you probably won't make this error. If you do find run-on sentences in your writing, however, you can correct them by following these steps:

1. Cut out all unnecessary words.
2. Apply the three solutions to comma-splice and fused-sentence problems: semicolons, linking words, and sentence breaks.

To turn a monster sentence into a correct and civilized one, first read through your sentence and identify any words or phrases that are not essential to its meaning.

> *There were still* a dozen *or so* guests *who* remained at the party, *not counting the host,* but after Raoul and Su Mei left, we decided *it was time* to go, so we collected our coats and said goodbye *to the others,* and then, after driving home *very* cautiously at *speeds not exceeding* 50 km/h, we sat up drinking coffee until three o'clock *in the morning* discussing our host's terrible taste in friends.

Run-on sentences are often made worse by **wordiness** (see Chapter 29 for hints on how to eliminate unnecessary words from your writing). In this example, the words in italics are unnecessary or redundant and should be eliminated. Here's how the sentence reads without them:

> A dozen guests remained at the party, but after Raoul and Su Mei left, we decided to go, so we collected our coats and said goodbye, and then, after driving home cautiously at 50 km/h, we sat up drinking coffee until three o'clock discussing our host's terrible taste in friends.

This version is an improvement, but it is not as clear and concise as it could be. Let's move on to step 2:

> A dozen guests remained at the party, but after Raoul and Su Mei left, we decided to go. We collected our coats and said goodbye. Then, after driving home cautiously at 50 km/h, we sat up until three o'clock drinking coffee and discussing our host's terrible taste in friends.

This version is both concise and clear.

In the following exercises, first eliminate all unnecessary words. Then use semicolons, linking words, or sentence breaks to correct what is left. There is more than one right way of fixing these sentences. Just make sure your corrections make sense and are easy to read. The answers we've provided, which begin on p. 330, are only suggestions.

EXERCISE 7.7

1. Special effects have been the focus of sci-fi movies since Stanley Kubrick made a computer and a space ship the stars of *2001: A Space Odyssey* and George Lucas continued the trend with the *Star Wars* trilogy, and movie makers ever since have been employing increasingly more powerful computers to generate increasingly more spectacular effects.

2. A great many films have been made about Count Dracula, from *Buffy the Vampire Slayer* to *Nosferatu,* Dracula has been portrayed as a completely depraved monster, a legendary warrior, and even a misunderstood social outcast and so many different versions of his story have been told that fact and fiction are now inseparable.

3. For more than thirty years, Clint Eastwood has held the Hollywood record for successful films and while others have had longer careers, and though Clint is still going, no one has nearly equalled his record in producing box-office winners, and furthermore, he is widely acclaimed internationally as a director as well as an actor.

4. Each year an annual poll is taken among film critics to determine the best movies ever made and every year one film ranks first on top of the poll and this movie didn't even win the Academy Award as best picture for its year. Shot in black and white, it is the story of a newspaperman who is driven to succeed and it was made in 1941 and this film is *Citizen Kane.*

5. Some of the worst movies ever made have become big money-makers, thanks to the industry's practice of describing all movies as "the best," "the biggest," and "not-to-be-missed," no matter how mediocre or even downright bad they may be and a good example is the work of Edward D. Wood, Jr., the man known as the world's worst director, and if you want to see a couple of sensationally dreadful films, check your local video store for Wood's truly awful *Bride of the Monster* and *Plan 9 from Outer Space.*

6. Animated features have always had a special place in the hearts of their audiences, even though most of them were designed for children, this doesn't mean that adults don't find cartoon characters just as moving and affecting as live actors, indeed, William Goldman, the well-known author and writer of *Butch Cassidy and the Sundance Kid* and *The Princess Bride,* claims that the most traumatic moment in any movie, animated or live, produced before 1960, is the death of Bambi's mother.

7. One of Hollywood's all-time favourite subjects is sports, we have baseball films, such as *Bull Durham, Field of Dreams,* and *A League of Their Own,* glorifying both the game and the men and women who play it then we have films such as *The Longest Yard* and *Knute Rockne, All American* celebrating the heroism of the football field, and even hockey has attracted the attention of a few filmmakers, though films like *Slapshot* and *The Mighty Ducks* have not done much to enhance the image of Canada's favorite game.

8. Some of the most successful television series started life as movies, among them is one of television's longest running shows, *M*A*S*H,* which began as a huge hit on the big screen in 1970, and more recently, the movie *The Last of the Mohicans* was reworked into a weekly TV show called *Chingachook* and both these examples began their popular life as best-selling books, interestingly enough.

9. Horror films have been with us since the very beginning of cinema, but they have undergone drastic changes since 1931 when *Franken-stein* first lumbered across the screen in the 50s, Alfred Hitchcock, the master of psychological suspense, turned a generation of people off showers with his masterpiece, *Psycho,* and more recently, in the 80s, horror films became "butcher films," and today's directors seem to be competing to see who can show the most blood spilled by totally deranged maniacs wielding a mind-boggling array of weapons.

10. Documentaries, though less popular and certainly less lucrative than feature films, are often more interesting thematically and technically because they deal with real-life situations and explore the thoughts and actions of real people and documentaries require a completely different technique from fiction features because the story is factual, the director has limited control over the actions of the people in the film and only in the editing room can the director shape the movie, deciding what to use and what to discard, and how to sequence scenes to achieve a particular effect. Canadians are recognized as being among the best documentary filmmakers in the world, in this field, as in so many others, we give ourselves too little credit.

EXERCISE 7.8

Having decided to spend two weeks canoeing in La Verendrye Park, northeast of Ottawa, Chantal and Yoko began to make plans, but it didn't take them long to realize that they had some problems to overcome because, while Chantal was an experienced canoe tripper and even owned her own kevlar canoe, Yoko had only been in a canoe once before and she could not imagine what two people would eat for two whole weeks in the wilderness with no nearby local convenience store to supply such necessities as potato chips and soft drinks. Chantal took charge of the planning, and she drew up a list of supplies and equipment that they would have to buy or borrow and together they worked out a menu that would be nutritious, tasty, and easy to pack and prepare. Planning and preparing for the trip brought them closer together and made both a little more confident that the trip might prove to be a lot of fun, nevertheless, when they arrived at the park and registered with the park officials before loading up the canoe, each still had some doubts, Yoko was worried about whether they would run out of food, and Chantal was still uncertain about her friend's canoeing ability.

Despite a constant drizzle and a 500-metre portage that got them soaked up to the knees and dampened their spirits as well as their clothes, they managed to survive the first day, and their camp that night was a huge success because Yoko turned out to have a real talent for fishing and they ate fresh-caught trout and the weather cleared and they sat around the campfire watching the moon come up, but eventually the mosquitoes became a nuisance, forcing them into the protection of their tent. The two weeks flew by, and back home, when they reflected on the trip, they agreed that their fears had been needless Yoko had gained 2 k, and Chantal confessed that she had never canoed with a better bow paddler, in fact, they had had such a good time they decided to make it an annual event.

EXERCISE 7.9

American gun laws are a mystery to most Canadians, we look at the annual death toll south of the border and compare it to our own more modest statistics and it seems obvious that our restrictive regulations are responsible for our relatively few gun incidents and we wonder at the blind prejudice of Americans that they cannot see that open access to firearms leads to more deaths and one statistic clearly supports our point of view for every intruder killed by a privately owned handgun in the United States, two hundred innocent people are killed in domestic disputes and accidents, and this figure does not take into account those killed in incidents related to drugs or organized crime.

In using these figures to question the wisdom of our southern neighbours, we overlook the reason for their insistence on free access to firearms, that their country was born out of a revolution against a despotic king, and that what made their revolution successful was that every household had at least one gun and at least one person who knew how to use it, armed civilians were responsible for the founding of America, a fact that led directly to the provision in their Constitution that every citizen has the right to bear arms. (I know a couple of people who assume this means that every American has the constitutional right to wear short-sleeved shirts.) To argue against the right to bear arms is to be un-American in the minds of many U. S. citizens it makes no difference to them that the right to own a gun to protect the United States of America is an almost comically archaic concept in the age of nuclear missiles.

EXERCISE 7.10

As a final test of your ability to identify and correct sentence errors, supply the appropriate sentence breaks to make this garble into a grammatically correct paragraph. No answers have been provided for this exercise.

Since cats can't read, I wonder why the companies that make cat food pay advertising agencies millions of dollars to create packages for their products the labels proclaim the box or can contains "irresistible morsels of delectable goodness" with a "rich, meaty taste" of course the answer is that people buy cat food, and people are apparently easily persuaded that what a package says on the outside is a reliable indicator of what is to be found inside, but the fallacy of this assumption is easily proved just open a can of cat food and examine the contents for any sign of the qualities advertised on the label I speak from experience I recently bought a case of cat food, or "premium feline dinner," as the manufacturer calls it, because of the enticing description of the contents in particular the words, "scrumptious, succulent chunks of real chicken in a gourmet sauce," caught my attention and made me long for Chef Antoine's specialty at my favorite French restaurant but the sticky, grey mess inside the tin was a bit of a letdown but, undeterred, I emptied the muck onto a plate and probed it with my fork, hoping for a glimpse of the "tender, savory, prime cuts of real beef" or a whiff of the "aromatic, taste-tempting flavours of real liver," but the more closely I examined my cat's intended dinner, the more certain I became that the label's insistent repetition of the word "real" with respect to every ingredient was a deliberate attempt to delude the consumer and it certainly required a great deal more faith in the manufacturer's integrity than I could muster after a close visual and olfactory examination of the evidence.

CHAPTER 8

Solving Modifier Problems

The thieves were caught before much of the loot could be disposed of *by the police.*

Stamping her feet and switching her tail to brush away flies, Josée led the mare out of the barn.

For sale: A complete set of first-year accounting texts *by a needy student in almost perfect condition.*

These sentences show what can happen to your writing if you aren't sure how to use modifiers. A **modifier** is a word or group of words that adds information about another word in a sentence. In the examples above, the italicized words are modifiers. Used correctly, modifiers describe or explain or limit another word, making its meaning more precise. Used carelessly, however, modifiers can cause confusion or, even worse, amusement. Few things are more embarrassing than being laughed at when you didn't mean to be funny.

You need to be able to recognize and solve two kinds of modifier problems: **misplaced modifiers** and **dangling modifiers**.

Misplaced Modifiers

Modifiers must be as close as possible to the words they apply to. Usually, a reader will assume that a modifier modifies whatever it's next to. It's important to remember this, because, as the following examples show, changing the position of a modifier can change the meaning of your sentence.

Only I love you. (No one else loves you.)

I only love you. (I don't have any other feelings for you.)

I love only you. (You are the only one I love.)

I love you only. (You are the only one I love.)

> To make sure a modifier is in the right place, ask yourself, "What does it apply to?" and put it beside that word.

When a modifier is not close enough to the word it refers to, it is said to be misplaced. A **misplaced modifier** can be *a single word in the wrong place:*

The supervisor told me they needed someone who could use a word processor badly.

Is some company really hiring people to do poor work? Or does the company urgently need someone familiar with word processing? The modifier *badly* belongs next to *needed:*

The supervisor told me they badly needed someone who could use a word processor.

> Be especially careful with these words: *almost, nearly, just, only, even, hardly, merely, scarcely.* Put them right before the words they modify.

Misplaced: I almost ate the whole pie.
Correctly placed: I ate almost the whole pie.

Misplaced:	When he was a defenceman for the Boston Bruins, Bobby Orr (nearly) had knee surgery in the off-season every year he played.
Correctly placed:	When he was a defenceman for the Boston Bruins, Bobby Orr had knee surgery in the off-season (nearly) every year he played.

A misplaced modifier can also be *a group of words in the wrong place:*

(Scratching each other playfully,) we watched the monkeys.

The modifier, *scratching each other playfully,* is too far away from the word it is supposed to modify, *monkeys.* In fact, it seems to modify *we,* making the sentence ridiculous. We need to rewrite the sentence:

We watched the monkeys (scratching each other playfully.)

Look at this one:

I worked for my aunt, who owns a variety store (during the summer.)

During the summer applies to *worked* and should be closer to it:

(During the summer,) I worked for my aunt, who owns a variety store.

Notice that a modifier need not always go right next to what it modifies; it should, however, be as close as possible to it.

Occasionally, as in the examples above, the modifier is obviously out of place. The writer's intention is clear, and the sentences are easy to correct. But sometimes modifiers are misplaced in such a way that the meaning is not clear, as in this example:

Mara said (on her way out) she would deliver the package to Julio.

Did Mara *say* it on her way out? Or is she going to *deliver the package* on her way out? To avoid confusion, we must move the modifier and, depending on which meaning we want, write:

(On her way out,) Mara said she would deliver the package to Julio.

or:

Mara said she would deliver the package to Julio (on her way out.)

In the following exercises, rewrite the sentences that contain misplaced modifiers, positioning the modifiers correctly. Check your answers to each set before going on. Answers begin on p. 332.

EXERCISE 8.1

1. Fernando has almost insulted everyone he's gone out with.

2. The boss told me on Friday I was being let go.

3. They nearly decided to pay me $850 a week.

4. I will ask you only one more time.

5. My sister only could pray to win the lottery.

6. I hate parties where the food is served to the guests who are all standing around on tiny paper plates.

7. Elmo bought a cigarette lighter for his girlfriend costing $29.95.

8. The angry hippo chased me toward the exit in a rage.

9. Unless they are poodles or terriers, most pet owners don't bother having their dogs professionally groomed.

10. I appreciate a car designed for the safety and comfort of the driver with an air bag and soft seat.

EXERCISE 8.2

1. In Minoan Crete, there are wall paintings of boys jumping over bulls with no clothes on.

2. Two suitable jobs were only advertised.

3. This course can be completed by anyone who has learned English grammar in six weeks.

4. The obituary column lists the names of people who have died recently for a small fee.

5. Alice discovered a mushroom walking through Wonderland.

6. She only ate one bite and found herself growing larger.

7. Every week they told me to come back and check the notice board.

8. Parents want to know what their children are doing in school, for their own satisfaction.

9. The cause of the accident was a little guy driving a small car with a big mouth.

10. The salesperson told me once I bought the VCR I would need an instruction manual to learn how to operate it.

EXERCISE 8.3

1. People who shoplift frequently get caught.

2. Stan almost watched television all night.

3. Dolly tried to convince the members of her fan club to wear two or three sets of false eyelashes enthusiastically.

4. Melted in a saucepan, stir the sifted flour into the butter.

5. As someone who is concerned about fitness, you really should stop smoking.

6. No one is allowed to dump any pollutants except petrochemical company executives into the river.

7. He took a stand against a tree while waiting for the bear with an old black-powder rifle.

8. Rosa passed the security guard and two workmen walking to school.

9. I am pleased to meet with student representatives from all of our colleges here in Petawawa.

10. Perhaps you're on your own in Vancouver, with a sparkling city to explore and a couple of tickets to an event at the covered stadium in your pocket. (B.C. travel flyer)

Dangling Modifiers

A **dangling modifier** occurs when there is no appropriate word in the sentence for the modifier to apply to. That is, the sentence does not contain a *specific word* or *idea* to which the modifier can sensibly refer. With no appropriate word to refer to, the modifier seems to apply to whatever it's next to, often with ridiculous results:

> (After a good night's sleep,) my teachers were impressed by my alertness.
>
> (This sentence seems to say that the teachers had a good night's sleep.)
>
> (Cycling close to the curb,) a minivan swerved and nearly hit me.
>
> (The minivan was cycling close to the curb?)

Dangling modifiers are trickier to fix than misplaced ones; you can't simply move danglers to another spot in the sentence. There are two ways to correct them. One way requires that you remember this rule:

> When a modifier comes at the beginning of a sentence, it modifies the subject of the sentence.

This rule means that you can avoid dangling modifiers by choosing the subjects of your sentences carefully. All you have to do is make the subject an appropriate one for the modifier to apply to. Applying this rule, we can correct both examples simply by changing the sentences' subjects:

> (After a good night's sleep,) I impressed my teachers with my alertness.
>
> (Cycling close to the curb,) I was nearly hit by a swerving minivan.

Another way to correct a dangling modifier is to change it into a dependent clause:

> After I had had a good night's sleep, I impressed my teachers with my alertness.
>
> While I was cycling close to the curb, a minivan swerved and nearly hit me.

Sometimes a dangling modifier comes at the end of a sentence:

> A picnic would be a good idea, not having much money.

Can you correct this sentence? Try it; then look at the suggestions at the bottom of the page.[1]

Here is a summary of the steps to follow in solving modifier problems:

> 1. Ask "What does the modifier apply to?"
> 2. Be sure there is a word or word group *in the sentence* for the modifier to apply to.
> 3. Put the modifier as close as possible to the word or word group it applies to.

Most of the sentences in exercises 8.4 and 8.5 contain dangling modifiers. Correct them by changing the subject of each sentence to one the modifier can appropriately apply to. There is no one "right" way to correct each sentence; our answers are only suggestions.

EXERCISE 8.4

1. As a college English teacher, dangling modifiers are annoying.

2. When writing, a dictionary is your best friend.

3. Driving recklessly, the police stopped Sula at a roadblock.

4. Because they don't shed their hair, our neighbours love their Cornish Rex cats.

5. The surface must be sanded smooth before applying the varnish.

6. Upon entering, the store was empty.

7. Attempting to hotwire a '95 Mercedes 318, the police were called and made an arrest.

---

[1]Here are two suggestions:
 1. Add a subject: Not having much money, *I* thought a picnic would be a good idea.
 2. Change the dangler to a dependent clause: *Since I didn't have much money,* I thought a picnic would be a good idea.

8. Having rotted in storage, the farmers could not sell their grain for the profit they were counting on.

9. In very cold weather, the engine should be thoroughly warmed up before attempting to drive.

10. Driving through the desert, our mouths became drier and drier.

EXERCISE 8.5

1. After changing the tire, the jack should be released.

2. The next question is whether to order beer or wine, having decided on pizza.

3. After waiting for you for an hour, the evening was ruined.

4. Jogging through Stanley Park, a cluster of totem poles came into view.

5. Most of the spare keys, after spending nine dollars on them, have been lost.

6. Having set the microwave on automatic, the turkey was quickly cooked to perfection.

7. Having completed the beginning, the ending is the second most important part of the essay.

8. Convicted of aggravated assault, the judge sentenced her to two years in Kingston.

9. After scoring the goal in overtime, a huge victory parade wound through the city.

10. It was a great moment: after making the speech of a lifetime, the election put him in the leader's office.

EXERCISE 8.6

Correct the dangling modifiers in exercise 8.4 by changing them into dependent clauses.

EXERCISE 8.7

Correct the dangling modifiers in exercise 8.5 by changing them into dependent clauses.

Correct the misplaced and dangling modifiers in exercises 8.8 through 8.10 in any way you choose. Our answers are only suggestions.

EXERCISE 8.8

1. Being made of very thin crystal, the dishwasher breaks the glasses as fast as I can buy them.

2. Driving through Yellowstone, a buffalo blocked the road.

3. As a college student constantly faced with stress, the pressure is intolerable.

4. A Geo is the car to get, looking for both style and economy.

5. Stewed in wine, my guests loved the coq au vin.

6. We were impressed as she rode by on a horse in a bikini.

7. After deciding whether the wine should be blended, sugar is added.

8. The sign in the restaurant window read, "Our Establishment Serves Tea in a Bag Just Like Mother."

9. Peering out of the office window, the Goodyear Blimp sailed past.

10. Having broken its wing, they took the seagull to the SPCA.

EXERCISE 8.9

1. Although he lives more than 50 km away, he nearly manages to come to every class.

2. The sign said that students are only admitted to the pub.

3. The lion was recaptured before anyone was mauled or bitten by the trainer.

4. While asleep, the blankets were kicked off the bed.

5. I saw the Queen and her entourage arrive through a plate-glass window.

6. Having ruled out the other two Japanese imports, the Mazda is the one we chose.

7. Swimming isn't a good idea if polluted.

8. The man wore a hat on his head which was hideous.

9. I learned about Joan's having a baby in last week's letter.

10. The counsellor who admitted he was not familiar with the college's harassment policy recently has alienated the students.

EXERCISE 8.10

1. Gnawing on a bone, Joe found his dog.

2. He said on Tuesday we would have a test.

3. Left over from last week's party, our guests didn't find the food very appetizing.

4. Employees who are late frequently are dismissed without notice.

5. Having forgotten to pick me up twice this week, I'm quitting Jim's car pool.

6. Although badly bruised, Maria turned the avocados into great guacamole.

7. Before going to bed, the alarm should be set for 6:00 A.M.

8. Though drunk daily, many people don't trust Lake Ontario water.

9. It is traditional to pay one's respects to friends and relatives after they have died in a funeral parlour.

10. After completing the study of staffing requirements, an assistant to the personnel manager will be hired.

EXERCISE 8.11

To test your mastery of modifiers, try this final exercise, for which no answers are provided.

1. While still in kindergarten, my parents moved me to Red Deer.

2. After finishing high school, college seemed like a good idea.

3. Having been overfertilized, my sister thinks our cactus may not survive.

4. A person who blacks out while drinking nine times out of ten is an alcoholic.

5. Hiking out into the wilderness, the weather grew ominous.

6. Elmo asked Dee Dee to marry him during the evening.

7. If caged, you can bring your Great Dane on the flight.

8. Being overinflated, Roderick thinks the inner tube will burst.

9. Weighing at least 80 kg, even Bettina couldn't move the baggage.

10. One morning I shot an elephant in my pajamas. How he got into my pajamas, I don't know. Then we tried to remove the tusks but they were embedded so firmly that we couldn't budge them. Of course, in Alabama the Tuscaloosa. But that's entirely irrelephant. . . . (Groucho Marx)

CHAPTER 9

The Parallelism Principle

When writing about items in a series, you must be sure all the items are **parallel;** that is, they must be written in the same grammatical form.

> I like camping, fishing, and to hike.

The items in this sentence are not parallel. Two end in *ing,* but the third *(to hike)* is the infinitive form of the verb. To correct the sentence, you must make all the items in the series take the same grammatical form—either

> I like to camp, to fish, and to hike.

> *or*

> I like camping, fishing, and hiking.

> Correct faulty parallelism by giving all items in a series the same grammatical form.

One way to tell whether all the items in a series are parallel is to write the items in list form, one below the other. That way, you can make sure that all the elements are the same—that they are all words, or all phrases, or all clauses.

NOT PARALLEL	PARALLEL

NOT PARALLEL

Sula is pleasant,
      attractive and
  likes to help.

I support myself by delivering pizza,
            poker,
              and
    shooting pool.

Kheeran is neat,
    polite, and
  an obnoxious person.

Claude tries to do what is right,
      different things, and
    make a profit.

With his sharp mind,
by having the boss as his uncle, and
    few enemies,
        he'll go far.

PARALLEL

Sula is pleasant,
      attractive, and
  helpful.

I support myself by delivering pizza,
        playing poker, and
      shooting pool.

Kheeran is neat,
    polite, and
    obnoxious.

Claude tries to do what is right,
      what is different, and
      what is profitable.

With his sharp mind,
    the boss as his uncle, and
    few enemies,
      he'll go far.

or

Having a sharp mind,
    the boss as his uncle, and
    few enemies,
      he'll go far.

As you can see, achieving parallelism is partly a matter of developing an ear for the sound of a correct list. Practice and the exercises in this chapter will help. Once you have mastered parallelism in your sentences, you will be ready to develop ideas in parallel sequence and thus to write clear, well-organized prose. Parallelism, far from being a "frill," is a fundamental characteristic of good writing.

In the following exercises, correct the sentences where necessary. As you work through these exercises, try to spot faulty parallelism and correct it from the sound of the sentences before you examine them closely for mistakes. Check your answers to each set of ten before going on. Answers begin on p. 335.

EXERCISE 9.1

1. The three main kinds of speech are demonstrative, informative, and

the kind persuading someone of something.

2. The single mother faces many problems. Two of the most difficult are supporting her household and sole parent to her child.

3. She advised me to take two aspirins and that I call her in the morning.

4. Books provide us with information, education, and they're entertaining to read.

5. To make your court appearance as painless as possible, prepare your case thoroughly and maintaining a pleasant, positive attitude.

6. The apostrophe is used for two purposes: contraction, and it shows possession.

7. Swiftly and with skill the woman gutted and scaled the fish.

8. I am overworked and not paid enough.

9. You need to develop skill and strategy and be agile to be a good tennis player.

10. The two main responsibilities of a corrections officer are security and controlling the inmates.

EXERCISE 9.2

1. A part-time job can develop your decision-making skills, your sense of responsibility, and you feel more self-confident and independent.

2. The three keys to improving your marks are study, you must work hard, and bribing the teacher.

3. I couldn't decide whether I should become a chef or to study data processing.

4. The recent increase in teenage suicides can be attributed primarily to two causes: the widespread lack of strong religious beliefs and there are no strict moral codes either.

5. A course in logical reasoning will help us evaluate what we read and making sound decisions.

6. My supervisor told me that my performance was generally satisfactory but to improve my writing.

7. Ms. Hencz assigns two hours of homework every night, and we're expected to do an essay each week.

8. The two most important characteristics of a personal work space are how neat and well organized it looks and the privacy.

9. Playing with small construction toys is beneficial to young children because it develops their fine motor skills, encourages concentration and patience, and their creative imagination is stimulated.

10. When you're buying a new car, you should look at more than just the size, style, and how much it costs. The warranty, how much it costs to run, and trade-in value, should also be taken into consideration.

EXERCISE 9.3

1. The role of the health instructor is to teach preventive medicine, care of the sick, and how to go about rehabilitating the injured.

2. The most common causes of snowmobile accidents are mechanical failure, the weather conditions might be poor, and the driver careless.

3. The portable classrooms are ill-equipped, poorly lighted, and there isn't any heat.

4. The advantages of a thesis statement are that it limits your topic, the contents of the paper are made very clear, and you show how your paper will be organized.

5. Unemployment deprives the individual of purchasing power, and the country's national output is reduced.

6. A good nurse is energetic, tolerant, sympathetic, and can be relied upon.

7. The money spent on space exploration should be used to provide aid to underdeveloped countries, and medical research could be funded.

8. The best house cats are quiet, clean, affectionate, and should be somewhere else.

9. Springtime brings out some interesting emotions along with the flowers and leaves: a new appreciation for the beauty of nature, and members of the opposite sex are newly admired.

10. You can conclude a paper with a summary of main points, by posing a question, or you could end with a quotation.

EXERCISE 9.4

1. Our winter has not been very pleasant: we've had vicious ice storms, followed by heavy snowfalls, followed by freezing rain that is dangerous.

2. Baseball is a game that requires a high level of skill with natural talent in large measure.

3. Many foreigners see conservatism, a pride in our country, and an interest in being orderly as characteristic of Canadians.

4. Patience and dexterity will make you a good person who plays the piano, or cutter of meat, or Lego builder.

5. Being a dutiful son, loyal husband, and treating his children with affection made Jason so stressed that he took up boxing as an outlet for his aggression.

6. There are some parents who think that rock music is dangerous and causes an addictive reaction.

7. Selena has three passions in her life: to dance with her boyfriend, listening to Charlie Major's music and fast cars.

8. After this year at school, I intend to go into nursing or I'll become a teacher.

9. After nine years of making up faulty sentences for students to fix, Brian can no longer write properly or correctly express himself.

10. Both those in management positions and workers must make compromises if this joint committee is to succeed.

EXERCISE 9.5

1. I'm looking for a sitter who is patient, intelligent, and who is basically a kind person.

2. Be sure your report is comprehensive, clear, readable, and that it records everything accurately.

3. Health care workers must be objective but sympathetic, and they must also be able to understand people's problems.

4. We were told to study the report carefully and that we should make our recommendations in writing.

5. Dwight's chances for a lasting relationship with Krystal aren't good, considering their goals are extremely different, their temperamental differences, and their different religious backgrounds.

6. Her small build, quick temper, and the fact that she has a criminal record will disqualify her from becoming a corrections officer.

7. Anand is everything a girl could want: handsome, highly intelligent, quite successful, and he's even considerate to his mother.

8. The designer kitchen, the fully equipped spa, and a security system that was burglar-proof were what sold us on our condominium.

9. The location, design, and the people who work there make the UBC hospital a more pleasant place to recuperate than most.

10. Darla explained that, through constant repetition and quietly being firm, she had trained her gerbil to be obedient and to demonstrate affection.

EXERCISE 9.6

Make the following lists parallel. In each case there's more than one way to do it, because you can make your items parallel with any item in the list. Therefore, your answers may differ from ours. Here's an example:

wrong:	stick handling . . .	score a goal
right:	stick handling . . .	goal scoring
also right:	handle the stick . . .	score a goal

1. *wrong:* mechanically   by using your hands
   right:

2. *wrong:* nursing   being a pilot
   right:

3. *wrong:* achieve her goals   finding true happiness
   right:

4. *wrong:* sense of humour   wealthy   intelligent
   right:

5. *wrong:* daily exercise   wholesome food   getting a checkup regularly
   right:

6. *wrong:* a good cigar   drinking a glass of brandy   catching up on friends' news
   right:

7. *wrong:* speed   comfortable   good manoeuverability
   right:

8. *wrong:* look for bargains   quality should be chosen   value comes first
   right:

9. *wrong:* security   valuable   safety
   right:

10. *wrong:* tanned golden brown   skimpy bathing suit   big boyfriend
    right:

EXERCISE 9.7

Create a sentence for each of the parallel lists you developed in exercise 9.6. Example: His stick handling was adequate, but his goal scoring was pitiful.

EXERCISE 9.8

Correct the faulty parallelism in the following paragraph.

When they buy a car, most people consider a number of factors, such as safety, style, how fast they go, whether or not they are reliable, how much they cost. For some buyers, the most important consideration is the impression their new car will make on their relatives and people they like. Unfortunately, these would-be buyers often make an unfavourable impression on their loans officer or the manager of their bank by choosing a vehicle that is beyond their means. Another kind of car buyer will settle for nothing less than the loudest, flashiest vehicle available with loads of power. As I plug along in my aged, rusted out, underpowered Ford, I console myself with the thought that people who drive flashy sports cars with too much power are trying to make up for other inadequacies.

EXERCISE 9.9

As a test of your ability to correct faulty parallelism, fix the errors in the sentences below. No answers are provided for this exercise.

1. My cat is noisy, smells, and suffers from arthritis, but the whole family loves her anyway.

2. Tonight's show has all the ingredients of a successful television series: lots of sex, greedy characters, and it's violent.

3. The computer is helping me write faster, I find it easier, and it is certainly more accurate.

4. Anna is trying to decide whether she wants to be an actress, to practise medicine, or playing golf professionally.

5. When I'm canoeing, I value the silence most, but catching fish and bird-watching, and taking pictures are important to me, too.

6. As I watched the Commonwealth Games, I found I could classify the athletes into three categories: the able-bodied, those who were physically challenged, and the chemically enhanced.

7. Jean is comfortable with her decision to be a wife, a mother, and pursue a career.

8. Rudolf's being selfish, unkind to others, and a cheapskate are the reasons why everyone dislikes him.

9. Travel teaches us to be tolerant of others, patient, how to be resourceful, and independence.

10. Forests are to British Columbia what grain is to the Prairies, their language is to the people of Quebec, and fish to Newfoundland—a battleground for competing economic interests and the interests of politicians.

EXERCISE 9.10

For each of the topics below, list five descriptive features in grammatically parallel form. Here is an example for the topic "insurance sales representative":

SINGLE WORD	PHRASE/CLAUSE
talkative	talks incessantly
aggressive	won't take "no" for an answer
knowledgeable	knows the insurance business
enthusiastic	is full of energy
inflexible	refuses to consider another opinion

1. Shania Twain (or another popular musician)

2. a trip to the supermarket

3. your local police force

4. the college cafeteria

5. a stepmother (*or* stepfather)

CHAPTER 10

Refining by Combining

To reinforce what you've learned about sentence structure, try your voice and your hand (preferably with a pencil in it) at sentence combining. You've rid your writing of fragments; you've cast out comma splices; you're riding herd on run-ons. But you may still find that your sentences, although technically correct, are choppy or repetitious. And you may be bored with conveying the same idea in the same old way. Sentence combining will not only confirm your mastery of sentence structure but also enable you to refine and polish your writing.

What is sentence combining? Sometimes called sentence generating or embedding, **sentence combining** is a technique that enables you to avoid a choppy, monotonous style while at the same time producing correct sentences.

Let's look at an example of two short, technically correct sentences that could be combined:

Our paperboy collects on Fridays.

Our paperboy delivers the *Winnipeg Free Press* on Saturdays.

There are several ways of combining these two statements into a single sentence.

> 1. You can connect them with an appropriate linking word, such as *and, but, or, nor,* or *for.*

Our paperboy delivers the *Winnipeg Free Press* on Saturdays <u>and</u> collects on Fridays.

> 2. You can change one of the sentences into a subordinate clause.

Our paperboy, <u>who delivers the *Winnipeg Free Press* on Saturdays,</u> collects on Fridays.

On Fridays, our paperboy collects for the *Winnipeg Free Press*, <u>which he delivers on Saturdays.</u>

<u>Although he delivers the *Winnipeg Free Press* on Saturdays,</u> our paperboy collects on Fridays.

> 3. You can change one of the sentences into a modifying phrase.

(Having collected his money on Friday,) our paperboy delivers the *Winnipeg Free Press* on Saturday.

On Fridays, our paperboy collects for the *Winnipeg Free Press,* (a Saturday paper.)

> 4. Sometimes it is possible to reduce one of your sentences to a single-word modifier.

On Fridays, our paperboy collects for the (Saturday) *Winnipeg Free Press.*

In sentence combining, you are free to move parts of the sentence around, change words, add or delete words, or make whatever other changes you find necessary. Anything goes: just make sure you don't drastically alter the meaning of the base sentences. Keep in mind that your aim in combining sentences is to make effective sentences—not long ones. Clarity is essential and brevity has force. Here's another example for you to consider.

Correct but stilted sentences conveying an idea:

Malcolm X was an influence.
He influenced American culture.
His influence was strong in the 1960s.

Correct and smooth sentences conveying the same idea:

Malcolm X had a strong influence on American culture in the 1960s.
Malcolm X strongly influenced American culture in the 1960s.
In the 1960s, American culture was strongly influenced by Malcolm X.

The skills that you learn by combining sentences identify you as a perceptive and sensitive writer. They are useful not only in writing and speaking, but also in reading, listening, and problem solving.

In the following exercises, try out your answers aloud before you write them. (You may want to scan the punctuation information in Unit 4 before you tackle these exercises.)

EXERCISE 10.1

Combine the following sentences, using the cues in parentheses as your guide to linking the sentences. Answers begin on p. 338.

1. The picketers left the streets.
   The police arrived. (when)

2. The angry bystanders knocked down the assassin.
   The angry bystanders tore him limb from limb. (-ing)

3. Maria is forty-one years old.
   She looks about twenty. (but)

4. He always quits.
   You need him. (just when)

5. Leonard Sly made much money in cowboy movies.
   Roy Rogers was known as Leonard Sly. (who)

6. Football is violent.
   North Americans love football. (even though)

7. Newspapers distort facts.
   Politicians charge this. (that)

8. Television manipulates feelings.
   Many people are not aware of this fact. (that)

9. Vesna hates zucchini.
   She planted zucchini anyway.
   She planted zucchini to please her husband. (although)

10. Scientists in the ancient world looked to the stars for guidance.
    Modern scientists may travel to the stars. (whereas)

EXERCISE 10.2

Using dependent clause cues (see p. 62) and the transitions listed on pp. 193 and 194, combine the following sentences into longer, more interesting units. (*Hint:* Read each set of statements through to the end before you begin to combine them, and try out several variations aloud or in your head before writing down your preferred solution.)

1. I don't get there by noon.
   Come looking for me.
   I may be in trouble.

   _____

   _____

   _____

2. The moon was full.
   We sat huddled under sleeping bags.
   The sleeping bags were full of down.

The sleeping bags were warm.
It was time to turn in for the night.

_____

_____

_____

3. The student begged for mercy.
   The student threw herself at her instructor's feet.
   The student had been caught plagiarizing.

_____

_____

_____

4. Jamie was lonely.
   Jamie was disillusioned.
   Jamie was bitter.
   Jamie stumbled into the rest room.
   Her shoulders were sagging.
   Her school books were heavy in her hand.

_____

_____

_____

5. The moose sensed danger.
   The moose lifted its head.
   Its ears were stiff and straight.
   Its body was tense.
   It was ready to explode into action at the slightest sound.

_____

_____

_____

6. The old train station was once the hub of the city.
   The old train station is now the dilapidated refuge of rats.

_____

_____

_____

7. Key glanced at first base.
    He went into his windup.
    Then he threw a hanging curve up in the strike zone that Murray, anticipating, unloaded over the right field wall.

    _____

    _____

    _____

8. Matthew stumbled down the stairs.
    He gasped for air.
    He was horrified by the sight.
    Sadik and two of his friends were wrestling in the living room.

    _____

    _____

    _____

9. The chocolate sauce was rich.
    The chocolate sauce was dark.
    The chocolate sauce was unbelievably sweet.
    The chocolate sauce covered my Death by Chocolate dessert.
    The chocolate sauce was like a thick blanket.

    _____

    _____

    _____

10. Philosophy 101 is Monika's favourite course.
    Few students register for philosophy.
    Students think philosophy is a tough course.

    _____

    _____

    _____

EXERCISE 10.3

This set of exercises is more challenging. In some questions you may need to combine the given statements into two or more sentences. Again, be sure to read through all the statements in each question to identify related ideas before you begin revising. Turn to p. 338 to compare your sentences with our suggested revisions.

1. The City of Toronto boasts about the CN Tower.
   The CN Tower has a record.
   It is 555 metres high.
   It is the world's tallest freestanding structure.

2. Nursing is a discipline.
   The discipline is concerned with promoting the well-being of the individual in society.
   A good nurse respects the dignity of each human being.
   A good nurse respects the autonomy of each human being.
   A good nurse respects the individuality of each human being.

3. Lawyers are professionals.
   Doctors are professionals.
   Businesspeople are professionals.
   These professionals constitute fewer than 10 percent of the Canadian work force.
   These professionals occupy almost three-quarters of the seats in the House of Commons.
   These professionals occupy two-thirds of the offices in local party organizations.

4. There are blue-collar workers too.
   They comprise nearly 50 percent of the population.
   They hold fewer than 10 percent of the positions in local parties and Parliament.
   Women are underrepresented in Canada's political and economic institutions.
   Native people are underrepresented in Canada's political and economic institutions.
   Minorities are underrepresented in Canada's political and economic institutions.
   Such underrepresentation calls into question our nation's commitment to democracy.

5. Citizenship is an abstract term.
   For most, it means loyalty.
   For most, it means obedience.
   For most, it means conformity.
   Citizenship is often used as a passive term.

It means to play one's part.
That part is in the existing scheme of things.
That part means no questions asked.
For a few, it means thinking for themselves.
For a few, it means acting independently.
For a few, it means taking control of their own lives.

6. The new Exclusiva is a luxury automobile.
It is the ultimate in luxury automobiles.
It is priced for the successful executive.
It is engineered for safety.
The new Exclusiva is built for comfort.
It is powered by a state-of-the-art, 6-cylinder engine.
The engine has 24 valves.
The new Exclusiva is eye-catching.
Its design is sleek and sophisticated.

7. Tiananmen Square is in Beijing.
Beijing is in China.
Three thousand students began a hunger strike in the square on May 13, 1989.
The students erected a homemade, 10-metre-high replica of the Statue of Liberty.
They called it the "Goddess of Democracy."
This largely peaceful occupation of the square lasted for four weeks.
Thousands of armed troops descended on the square.
The troops first fired off tracer bullets and tear gas.
Loudspeakers urged the students to leave.
The soldiers opened fire directly on the crowds and charged them with bayonets.
Hundreds of demonstrators were killed and hundreds were wounded.
It was a Sunday morning, June 4, 1989.
It was a massacre.

8. Canada has some unusual place names.
These names appear all across the country.
These place names are often amusing to people who don't live there.
Saskatchewan has a particularly large number of peculiar place names.
Cut Knife is an example.
Moose Jaw is an example.
Cudworth is an example.
Climax is perhaps the most famous example.
Newfoundland is also rich in peculiar place names.
Jerry's Nose is an example.
Fogo is an example.

Bumble Bee Bight is an example.
Come-by-Chance is an example.
These names often sound strange to outsiders.

9. Computer help-line personnel get some very strange calls.
These calls come from new computer owners.
They are often confused about their new purchase.
They call the help line to get assistance with their computer problems.
One woman had just bought a laptop computer.
She called to ask how to install the battery.
The technician told her the directions were on page one of her manual.
The customer retorted that she had just spent $2000 on her computer.
She wasn't about to read a book to tell her how to use it.
Another caller complained that he couldn't get his computer to turn on.
The technician asked him to check if it was plugged in.
The technician asked if the customer had pressed the power switch.
The customer said he kept pressing on the foot pedal.
Nothing happened.
The technician was puzzled.
"What foot pedal?" asked the technician.
The "foot pedal" turned out to be the mouse.

10. Culture shock can occur anywhere.
It can occur in one's own country.
It can occur even in one's own city.
Rudi was an advertising executive.
He wanted to find out more about multimedia.
He thought his company should be exploring multimedia.
Multimedia combines computers with television.
Multimedia is interactive.
Rudi put on his best blue suit.
He chose a conservative tie.
He put on his black, wing-tip shoes.
He went to a conference on multimedia programming.
Everyone at the conference was under 30.
Most of the men wore their hair long.
Some of the men had ponytails.
All of the men wore earrings.
Most of the women had very short hair.
Most of the women wore heavy black boots.
These men and women were the multimedia programmers.
These men and women were the best people in Canada.
These men and women were the most creative people in multi-media
programming.
Rudi watched and listened to their presentations.
He experienced culture shock.

After you have combined a number of sentences, you can evaluate your work. Read your sentences aloud. How they *sound* is important. Test your work against these six characteristics of successful sentences:

1. MEANING — Have you said what you mean?
2. CLARITY — Is your sentence clear? Can it be understood on the first reading?
3. COHERENCE — Do the parts of your sentence fit together logically and smoothly?
4. EMPHASIS — Are the most important ideas either at the end or at the beginning of the sentence?
5. CONCISENESS — Is the sentence direct and to the point? Have you cut out all redundant or repetitious words?
6. RHYTHM — Does the sentence flow smoothly? Are there any interruptions in the development of the key idea(s)? Do the interruptions help to emphasize important points, or do they distract the reader?

If your sentences pass all six tests of successful sentence style, you may be confident that they are both technically correct and pleasing to the ear. No reader could ask for more.

_____ UNIT THREE

Grammar

CHAPTER 11

Choosing the Correct Verb Form

Errors in grammar are like flies in soup: most of the time, they don't affect meaning any more than flies affect flavour. But they are both distracting and irritating. You must eliminate grammar errors from your writing if you want your readers to pay attention to what you say rather than to how you say it.

Good writers pay particularly careful attention to verbs. A verb is to a sentence what an engine is to a car; it is the source of power and a frequent cause of trouble.

Every verb has four forms, called its **principal parts:**

1. The **base** form: used by itself or with *can, may, might, shall, will, could, should, would, must*
2. The **past tense** form: used by itself
3. The **present participle** (the **-ing**) form: used with *am, is, are; was, were; will be; have been,* etc.
4. The **past participle** form: used with *have, has, had*

Here are some examples:

BASE	PAST TENSE	PRESENT PARTICIPLE	PAST PARTICIPLE
dance	danced	dancing	danced
learn	learned	learning	learned
play	played	playing	played
seem	seemed	seeming	seemed

To use verbs correctly, you must be familiar with their principal parts. Knowing three facts will help you. First, you won't have trouble with the present participle, the *-ing* form. It is always made up of the base form of the verb + *ing*. Second, your dictionary will give you the principal parts of all **irregular** verbs. Look up the base form, and you'll find the past tense and the present and past participles given beside it, usually in parentheses. For example, if you look up "sing" in your dictionary, you will find *sang* (past tense), *sung* (past participle), and *singing*, (present participle) listed immediately after the verb itself. If the past tense and past participle are not given, the verb is **regular.** So, the third thing you need to know is how to form the past tense and the past participle of regular verbs: add *-ed* to the base form. The examples listed above—*dance, learn, play, seem*—are all regular verbs.

Unfortunately for native speakers and EFL speakers alike, many of the most common English verbs are **irregular.** Their past tenses and past participles are formed in unpredictable ways. The verbs in the list below are used so often that it is worth your time to memorize their principal parts. (We have not included the *-ing* form because, as we have noted above, it never causes any difficulty.)

The Principal Parts of Irregular Verbs

BASE (Use with *can, may, might, shall, will, could, would, should, must*)	PAST TENSE	PAST PARTICIPLE (Use with *have, has, had*)
awake	awoke/awaked	awaked/awoke
be (am, is)	was/were	been
bear	bore	borne
beat	beat	beaten
become	became	become
begin	began	begun
bid (offer to pay)	bid	bid
bid (say, command)	bid/bade	bid/bidden
bite	bit	bitten
bleed	bled	bled
blow	blew	blown
break	broke	broken
bring	brought (*not* brang)	brought (*not* brung)
broadcast	broadcast	broadcast
build	built	built

BASE (Use with *can, may, might, shall, will, could, would, should, must*)	PAST TENSE	PAST PARTICIPLE (Use with *have, has, had*)
burst	burst	burst
buy	bought	bought
catch	caught	caught
choose	chose	chosen
come	came	come
cost	cost	cost
cut	cut	cut
deal	dealt	dealt
dig	dug	dug
dive	dived/dove	dived
do	did (*not* done)	done
draw	drew	drawn
dream	dreamed/dreamt	dreamed/dreamt
drink	drank (*not* drunk)	drunk
eat	ate	eaten
fall	fell	fallen
feed	fed	fed
feel	felt	felt
fight	fought	fought
find	found	found
fling	flung	flung
fly	flew	flown
forget	forgot	forgotten/forgot
forgive	forgave	forgiven
freeze	froze	frozen
get	got	got/gotten
give	gave	given
go	went	gone (*not* went)
grow	grew	grown
hang (suspend)	hung	hung
hang (put to death)	hanged	hanged
have	had	had
hear	heard	heard
hide	hid	hidden
hit	hit	hit
hold	held	held
hurt	hurt	hurt
keep	kept	kept
know	knew	known

BASE (Use with *can, may, might, shall, will, could, would, should, must*)	PAST TENSE	PAST PARTICIPLE (Use with *have, has, had*)
lay (put or place)	laid	laid
lead	led	led
leave	left	left
lend	lent (*not* loaned)	lent (*not* loaned)
lie (recline)	lay	lain (*not* layed)
light	lit/lighted	lit/lighted
lose	lost	lost
mean	meant	meant
meet	met	met
pay	paid	paid
raise (to lift up, increase, bring up)	raised	raised
ride	rode	ridden
ring	rang	rung
rise	rose	risen
run	ran	run
say	said	said
see	saw (*not* seen)	seen
sell	sold	sold
set (put or place)	set	set
shake	shook	shaken (*not* shook)
shine	shone	shone
sing	sang	sung
sink	sank	sunk
sit	sat	sat
sleep	slept	slept
slide	slid	slid
speak	spoke	spoken
speed	sped	sped
steal	stole	stolen
stick	stuck	stuck
strike (hit)	struck	struck
strike (affect)	struck	stricken
swear	swore	sworn
swim	swam	swum
swing	swung (*not* swang)	swung
take	took	taken
teach	taught	taught
tear	tore	torn

BASE	PAST TENSE	PAST PARTICIPLE
(Use with *can, may, might, shall, will, could, would, should, must*)		(Use with *have, has, had*)
tell	told	told
think	thought	thought
throw	threw	thrown
wake	woke/waked	waked/woken
wear	wore	worn
weave	wove	woven
win	won	won
wind	wound	wound
wring	wrung	wrung
write	wrote	written

EXERCISE 11.1

In the blanks, write the correct form (past tense or past participle) of the verb shown to the left of the sentence. Do not add or remove helping verbs. Answers begin on p. 340.

1. bear   Politely, we _____ Biff's complaining until we could not have _____ it another minute.

2. ride   Having _____ a cow once, I wouldn't mind if I never _____ one again.

3. tear   Alberto _____ the sheet into strips; then he tied the _____ strips together and escaped through the window.

4. lie   The cat _____ defiantly right where the dog had _____ all morning.

5. shake   After I had _____ the money out of the envelope, I _____ the envelope thoroughly to be sure I had got it all.

6. freeze   I _____ the meat, as you asked me to, but I'm sure it's been _____ before.

7. lay   Rajiv _____ his passport on the official's desk where all the others _____ .

8. lend   I _____ Maria the money she asked for, even though I had _____ her ten dollars already this week.

9. rise   Juliet _____ from her bed to see if the sun had _____ .

10. swim, dive   After not having _____ or _____ for years, we _____ and _____ all afternoon in our neighbors' new pool.

EXERCISE 11.2
Choose the correct verb forms for each of the following sentences.

1. When I (raised rose) the issue of a salary increase, my supervisor (raised rose) from her desk without a word and pointed to the door.
2. After Kareem became tired of (lying laying) in the sun, he (swam swum) thirty lengths of the pool.
3. I was happy that my bike, which had been (stole stolen), was found, but I wasn't happy to find that it had been (broke broken).
4. After we (paid payed) our admission, we were (gave given) free pop-corn and soft drinks, probably to keep us from demanding our money back after we'd seen the dreadful movie.
5. A feather (laying lying) on the carpet and a fat cat (laying lying) con-tentedly on the windowsill were the only clues in the case of the miss-ing canary.
6. Only hours after I had (bought boughten) my new lawn ornaments, they were (stole stolen) from my yard.
7. My roommate insists on listening to a nauseating call-in show that is (broadcast broadcasted) every day at noon, just as I am (setting sit-ting) down for lunch.
8. Frank had (brought brung) some European beer to the party for everyone to taste, but before anyone could try it, Frank had (drank drunk) it all himself.
9. I was so (shook shaken) by the incident that I took off my jacket and (hanged hung) it in the refrigerator, then poured myself a tall, re-freshing glass of floor wax from the cupboard.
10. After the judge had sentenced my uncle to be (hanged hung), my father removed his brother's portrait from our living room, where it had (hanged hung) for years.

EXERCISE 11.3
Find and correct the verb errors in the following sentences.

1. After Mildred had wrote one final letter to the editor, she retired from

   public life, confident that she had did her duty to the community.

2. We seen what we had came to see and done what we had came to do.

3. Lori should have knew better than to challenge me at pogs because I

   have never been beat.

4. The final scene in the play has shook the audience so badly that they

   have all went to a bar to argue over the meaning of the ending.

5. I don't mind so much that they have stole my honour and wounded my pride, but they should never have took my coffee mug.

6. After laying around all day watching TV, Kim had no time to write her essay so I loaned her mine.

7. Harvey thought that he had wrote a masterpiece, but he begun to realize that perhaps it wasn't all that great when his mother throwed it in the garbage.

8. The tornado had tore a path right through the centre of town, but luckily it hadn't stricken the hospital or hit any schools as it speeded by.

9. We have forgave Sparkle for ruining our project, but none of us was unhappy to learn that she was chose "least likely to succeed" by her Poise and Personality class.

10. "Strike three!" yelled the umpire as soon as I swang the bat, but I run around the bases anyway.

EXERCISE 11.4
Find and correct all verb errors in the following sentences.

1. If Tanya had read the weather report and knew it was going to rain, she would have wore a raincoat and a hat.

2. We laid in the grass for over an hour, completely hid from the other players.

3. Revenue Canada has not forgave my uncle who claimed for three years that he had no income; meanwhile, he had took frequent trips to the Caribbean and had boughten a sports car.

4. Dwight's jacket is wove from camel hair and would be very attractive if it weren't for the hump that has arose in the back.

5. As soon as I opened my mouth, I wished I had sang a song I was familiar with instead of having chose "Mon Futon" from the list of karaoke tunes.

6. The rookie slided into first base, despite the fact that the coach had told him again and again that he should run right across the base to avoid being threw out.

7. I have spoke on the phone to the sales manager, wrote to the personnel director, and saw the president in person, but none of them will agree to consider my application because they say I am illiterate.

8. The elbows on my old sweater are just about wore through and it is tore at the shoulder, but it is still my favourite because it was gave to me by my first love.

9. We seen that the goldfish laid on the bottom of the pond once it had froze, so they would survive the winter.

10. After the students had got the assignment from Ms. Critelli, several claimed that they had not been gave a due date, so Ms. Critelli sended all students an e-mail message to remind them of the date she had set at the beginning of term.

EXERCISE 11.5

As a final test of your mastery of verb forms, try this exercise. No answers have been provided.

1. It must not be forgotten that, while capital punishment is no longer practise in Canada, in some states of the United States, you can be hung if you have broke certain laws.

2. The telephone rung and rung, but no one answered because they had all went out for pizza.

3. Darryl was struck with remorse after he struck out in the ninth and lost us the game.

4. After we sung every campfire song we could remember, we laid down in our sleeping bags and snored happily until the sun raised.

5. The lake had froze in a clear, even sheet, so, after we had ate, we put on our skates and spend most of the night on the ice.

6. We had deliberately went camping late in the season to avoid the bugs; unfortunately, there was a long summer that year and we were practically bit to death by black flies.

7. By about three-quarters of the way through the semester, Biff and Eugene were stricken by the fact that if only they had went to class and did the homework, they would probably have managed to pass their courses.

8. I loaned Raj twenty dollars on condition that he made sure I was payed back by the end of the week.

9. On a dare, Rudolf drunk a six-pack in two hours; not surprisingly, he was suffering from a horrible hangover when he was woke up the next morning.

10. All our players shined like stars that night, but our captain was the brightest as he weaved in and out of the opposing defence until he got into a fight. Then he was throwed out of the game.

CHAPTER 12

Mastering Subject–Verb Agreement

One of the most common grammatical errors is failure to make the subject and the verb in a sentence agree with each other. Here is the rule for subject–verb agreement:

Singular subjects take singular verbs.
Plural subjects take plural verbs.

Singular and Plural

Here's an example of the singular and plural forms of a regular verb in the present tense:

	SINGULAR	PLURAL
1st person	I work	we work
2nd person	you work	you work
3rd person	*she (he, it, one, the student) works	*they (the students) work

From this example, you can figure out what the word **person** means. We have asterisked the third person singular and plural forms of the verb because these are the only forms likely to cause you trouble. In the third person, the endings of verbs and their subjects do not match. Singular verbs end in "s" *(works)*, but singular subjects do not *(student)*. Plural subjects regularly end in "s" *(students)*, but plural verbs do not *(work)*. When you are using a regular verb in the third person, remember that *either* the subject *or* the verb ends in "s," but not both.

Singular words concern one person or thing.

> The <u>phone</u> <u>rings</u>. <u>Claude</u> <u>sleeps</u>.

Plural words (and multiple subjects) concern more than one person or thing:

> The <u>phones</u> <u>ring</u>. The <u>boys</u> <u>sleep</u>. <u>Claude and Saieed</u> <u>snore</u>.

The rule governing subject–verb agreement will cause you no difficulty so long as you make sure that the word the verb agrees with is really the subject of the sentence. To see how problems can arise, look at this example:

> One of the boys write graffiti.

The writer of this sentence forgot that the subject of a sentence is never in a prepositional phrase. The verb needs to be changed to agree with the true subject, *One*:

> <u>One</u> of the boys <u>writes</u> graffiti.

If you're careful about identifying the subject of your sentence, you'll have no difficulty with subject–verb agreement. To sharpen your subject-finding ability, review Chapter 5, "Cracking the Sentence Code." Then do the following exercises.

EXERCISE 12.1
Identify the subject in each sentence. Answers begin on p. 341.

1. On TV right now is *Thriller*, your favourite video.

2. Unfortunately, large numbers of Canadians are bored by politics.

3. Where are the invoices for this last shipment of software?

4. Have you met my mother-in-law, Grace, and her husband, Morty?

5. Respect for students is an essential characteristic of a good teacher.

6. One of the most popular comic book characters of all time, Superman was the invention of a Canadian cartoonist.

7. There are many reasons for starting a fitness program right now, no matter what your age.

8. Has anyone in this class not read Anne Rice's novels?

9. Reports of sexual harassment of males by females are increasing.

10. The pressures of homework, part-time work, and nagging parents have caused many students to drop out of school.

EXERCISE 12.2

Rewrite each of the following sentences, using the alternate beginning shown.

Example: My <u>roommate</u> <u>wants</u> to make a rock video.

My <u>roommates</u> <u>want</u> to make a rock video.

1. That policy change affects our entire program.

   Those

2. He likes to work with children, so he is looking for a job in a child care centre.

   They

3. That woman is here in Canada because her husband wanted to emigrate from Poland.

   Those

4. They do their best work when they are unsupervised.

   He

5. They insist on doing things their way.

   She

6. A man who worries about baldness should consider having a hair transplant.

   Men

7. My flight has been delayed because of the storm.

   Our flights

8. Each of Cinderella's sisters was horrid in her own way.

   Both

9. They often spend the weekend at their cabin up north.

   He

10. A civil servant with an indexed pension stands to gain from future inflation.

    Civil servants

EXERCISE 12.3

Rewrite each sentence below, switching the position of its two main elements.

Example: <u>Doritos</u> <u>are</u> my favourite snack.
  My favourite <u>snack</u> <u>is</u> Doritos.

1. What Vinh spends most of his money on is clothes.

   Clothes

2. Hostess Twinkies are the only junk food Tim eats.

3. Brown rice and tofu are my least favourite meal.

4. What Canada needs now is strong leadership and more jobs.

5. The reason for Eugene's failure was too many absences from class.

6. Vince's favourite pastime is computer games, especially *Doom* and *Myst*.

7. Disputes over wages and benefits are often the cause of strikes.

8. What I find fascinating is the differences between the Chinese and the Canadian attitudes toward the elderly.

9. Something Tanh always enjoys is political discussions.

10. Garlic, a cross, and a stake through the heart are the only known protection against a vampire attack.

So far, so good. You can find the subject, even when it's hiding on the far side of the verb or buried under a load of prepositional phrases. You can match up singular subjects with singular verbs, and plural subjects with plural verbs. Now let's take a look at a few of the complications that make subject–verb agreement such a disagreeable problem.

Six Special Cases

Some subjects are tricky. They look singular but are actually plural, or they look plural when they're really singular. There are six kinds of these slippery subjects, all of them common, and all of them likely to trip up the unwary writer.

> 1. Multiple subjects joined by *or; either . . . or; neither . . . nor;* or *not . . . but.*

All the multiple subjects we've dealt with so far have been joined by *and* and have required plural verbs, so agreement hasn't been a problem. But watch out when the two or more elements of a compound subject are joined by *or; either . . . or; neither . . . nor;* or *not . . . but.* In these cases, the verb agrees in number with the nearest subject. That is, if the subject closest to the verb is singular, the verb will be singular; if the subject closest to the verb is plural, the verb must be plural, too.

Neither the <u>federal government</u> nor the <u>provinces</u> <u>accept</u> responsibility for the deficit.

Neither the <u>provinces</u> nor the <u>federal government</u> <u>accepts</u> responsibility for the deficit.

EXERCISE 12.4

Circle the correct verb.

1. Not the parents but the child (seems seem) to control the family.
2. Either "Mrs." or "Ms" (is are) fine with me.
3. Onions, sad movies, or happiness (is are) likely to make her cry.
4. Either your friend or you (is are) lying about the accident.
5. Not cheap liquor but friendly people (is are) what I miss most about the States.
6. The oil company informed me that neither they nor their representative (is are) responsible for the damage to my car.
7. Neither the practical training nor the courses I took (was were) able to prepare me for the job.
8. According to a recent survey, not sexual incompatibility but disagreements over children (cause causes) the most strain in a marriage.
9. Not high unemployment but high interest rates (remain remains) Canadians' first concern.
10. Neither the landlord nor the tenants (know knows) who is responsible for the break-in.

> 2. Subjects that look multiple but really aren't.

Don't be fooled by phrases beginning with such words as *with, like, as well as, together with, in addition to, including.* These phrases are NOT part of the subject of the sentence. Mentally cross them out; they do not affect the verb.

> My math professor, as well as my counsellor, has advised me to change my major.

Two people were involved in the advising; nevertheless, the subject (<u>professor</u>) is singular, and so the verb must be singular (<u>has advised</u>).

> All my courses, including English, are easier this term.

If you mentally cross out the phrase "including English," you can easily see that the verb (<u>are</u>) must be plural to agree with the plural subject (<u>courses</u>).

EXERCISE 12.5

Circle the correct verb.

1. Eddie Vedder, with Pearl Jam, (is are) beginning a North American tour soon.
2. Margaret Atwood, like many contemporary Canadian authors, (write writes) novels with political themes.

3. My accounting assignment, not to mention my psychology and English homework, (is are) enough to drive me to drink.
4. The whole computer package, including monitor, disk drive, printer, and software, (is are) too expensive for us.
5. In spite of the efforts of parents and educators, television, with its mix of adventure shows, comedies, and rock videos, (remain remains) the most popular pastime for young people.
6. My brother, as well as my parents, (want wants) me to move out.
7. The food he serves, along with the drinks he mixes, (is are) delicious.
8. This play, in addition to the ones she wrote in her youth, (is are) guaranteed to put you to sleep.
9. The waiter, along with two busboys and the wine steward, (expect expects) us to tip generously.
10. Full employment, like lower taxes, (has have) become an impossible dream.

---

3. Words ending in *-one, -thing,* or *-body.*

When used as subjects, the following words are always singular, and they require the singular form of the verb:

anyone	anything	anybody
everyone	everything	everybody
no one	nothing	nobody
someone	something	somebody

The last part of the word is the tip-off here: every*one*, any*thing*, no*body*. If you focus on this last part, you'll remember to use a singular verb with these subjects. Usually, these words cause trouble only when modifiers crop up between them and their verbs. For example, you would never write "Everyone are here." The trouble starts when you sandwich a group of words in between the subject and the verb. You might, if you weren't on your toes, write this: "Everyone involved in implementing the company's new policies and procedures are here." The meaning is plural: several people are present. But the subject (every*one*) is singular, so the verb must be *is*.

EXERCISE 12.6
Circle the correct verb.

1. Everybody on the fourth and fifth floors (was were) questioned by the police inspector.
2. No one who had seen the murderer (was were) found.

3. Everyone, including the victim's husband, (believe believes) the butler did it.
4. Anyone with information leading to an arrest (is are) entitled to a reward.
5. So far, no one but Jessica Fletcher (seem seems) entitled to the money.
6. Everything she had discovered, including the clue of the blood-stained Adidas, (is are) to be revealed tonight.
7. Until then, absolutely nothing in the victim's rooms (is are) to be touched.
8. Nobody (dare dares) challenge Ms. Fletcher's explanation of the crime.
9. *Murder, She Wrote* (has have) for years been one of television's most popular mystery programs.
10. Its star, Angela Lansbury, after numerous facelifts, (look looks) younger with every passing year.

---

4. *Each (of), either (of), neither (of).*

Used as subjects, these take singular verbs. (Remember, the subject is never in a prepositional phrase.)

Either <u>was</u> suitable for the job.
Each of the boys <u>dreams</u> of scoring the winning goal.
Neither of the stores <u>is</u> open after six o'clock.

EXERCISE 12.7
Circle the correct verb.

1. Neither of the singers (work works) very hard.
2. Either (is are) likely to be fired.
3. Neither of the proposals (interest interests) me.
4. Each of the contestants (hope hopes) to be chosen.
5. Either of the available seats (is are) very close to the stage.
6. I am sorry to say that neither (is are) ready to be used.
7. Each of the instructors (was were) eccentric in both method and appearance.
8. We were astonished to learn that each of them (has have) won a full-tuition scholarship.
9. If either of the candidates (answer answers) my questions honestly, then that person will get my vote.
10. Each of the leads in the *Star Trek* series, William Shatner, Patrick Stewart, and Avery Brook, (has have) played Shakespeare and other classical roles in live theatre.

---

5. Collective nouns.

A collective noun is a word naming a group. Some examples are *band, gang, orchestra, company, class, committee, team, crowd, public, family, audience, group,* and *majority*. When you are referring to the group acting as a unit, use a singular verb. When you are referring to the members of the group acting individually, use a plural verb.

> The <u>team</u> <u>is</u> sure to win tomorrow's game. (Here *team* refers to the group acting as a whole.)
>
> The <u>team</u> <u>are</u> getting into their uniforms now. (The separate members of the team are acting individually.)

EXERCISE 12.8
Circle the correct verb.

1. The nuclear family (is are) the fundamental unit of society.
2. The electorate (seem seems) to be in an ugly, vengeful mood.
3. My department (pride prides) itself on a high degree of efficiency.
4. The budget committee (fight fights) among themselves continually.
5. (Has Have) the jury reached a verdict?
6. Having waited for almost an hour, the crowd (was were) growing restless.
7. Our office (give gives) a farewell party whenever anyone leaves.
8. The majority of immigrants (find finds) Canada a tolerant country.
9. The entire gang, without exception, (is are) getting together this weekend.
10. The audience (sit sits) impatiently, waiting for the concert to begin.

---

6. Units of money, time, mass, length, and distance.

These require singular verbs.

> <u>Six dollars</u> <u>is</u> too much to pay for a hamburger.
>
> <u>Two hours</u> <u>seems</u> like four in our sociology class.
>
> <u>Five kilometres</u> <u>is</u> too far to walk.
>
> <u>Eighty kilograms</u> <u>is</u> the mass of an average man.

EXERCISE 12.9

Circle the correct verb.

1. Three hours (seem seems) to pass very quickly when I'm at the movies.
2. Patients who suffer from anorexia nervosa find that even 40 kg (seem seems) like too much weight.
3. Ninety-nine cents (seem seems) a fair price.
4. Thirty dollars (is are) all I need for a ticket to Barenaked Ladies.
5. Forty years in the desert (is are) a long time to delay one's gratification.
6. Twenty centimetres of snow in six hours (was were) enough to paralyze the city.
7. Six dollars an hour for babysitting (is are) not bad.
8. Seven hours of classes (is are) too much for one day.
9. Thirty years of working at the same job from nine to five, five days a week, fifty weeks a year, (go goes) by very slowly.
10. When you are cooking your turkey, remember that twelve kilos (take takes) about seven hours in a 170° oven.

In exercises 12.10 and 12.11, correct the errors in subject–verb agreement. Check your answers to each exercise before going on.

EXERCISE 12.10

1. A group of unbiased students and faculty are trying to solve the problem.

2. Anybody who really want to succeed will do so.

3. Over the past ten years, the number of couples living together has increased greatly.

4. Every one of the contestants thinks winning a week in Lackawanna would be wonderful.

5. You'll find that not only ragweed but also cat hairs makes you sneeze.

6. If there is no bubbles, then you have patched your tire successfully.

7. Neither Amelash nor I is a very strong swimmer.

8. The lack of things to write about causes the headaches.

9. Michael Jackson, along with his handlers, pets, and bodyguards, have

    ~~has.~~

    begun another world tour.

10. The amount of money generated by rock stars on concert tours are

    ~~is.~~

    enormous.

EXERCISE 12.11

The joys of being a disk jockey at a dance club is sometimes hard to explain. At times the DJ's job, like other public performances, result in embarrassment and stress. When someone who doesn't like your selections start to complain loudly, for example, or when the audience you are trying so hard to please don't respond, you wish you were a waiter or even a dishwasher. However, there's many positive things about the job, as well. When you hit the combination of songs that get the crowd up and dancing for number after number, you feel a real sense of satisfaction. Either your instincts or your knowledge of the dance tunes have given these people a great deal of enjoyment and have contributed to making their evening a success. Your co-workers, not to mention your boss—the bar owner—is also happy, because when everybody out on the dance floor are having a good time, more money gets spent. Another reward is people's gratitude. When someone who has enjoyed the evening because of the music—and maybe your introductions and comments—come up to you and compliment your work, that praise makes it all worthwhile. The experience you gain from dealing with people and performing in front of an audience are also a plus, as are the salary you make. Not everyone would want to be a DJ at a dance bar or night club, but it can be a rewarding and interesting part-time job.

EXERCISE 12.12

There's many good reasons for staying fit. The diminished strength, flexibility, and endurance that results from lack of exercise are very compelling factors, but everyone who joins the many health clubs in this city have individual reasons as well. The people I talked with says appearance or weight loss are their main motivation for working out. No one among the two hundred patrons of a local health club were there for the social life, according to my poll. Either weightlifting or daily aerobics was what they wanted from their club, and the intensity of the workouts were clear evidence that they were serious. The manager of the club, along with all the members of the staff, were careful to point out that supervised exercise is essential for best results, but neither she nor her staff was in favour of fad diets or sweat programs.

Complete the sentences in exercises 12.13 and 12.14 using present-tense verbs. After doing each set of ten sentences, check the answer section to see whether your verbs should be singular or plural.

EXERCISE 12.13

1. Neither my boss nor the receptionist

2. Everybody with two or more pets

3. Not the lead singer but the musicians

4. A flock of birds

5. Every one of his employees

6. Ten dollars

7. The whole family, including two aunts and six cousins,

8. The actors, as well as the director,

9. Either a Big Mac or a Whopper

10. No one among the hundreds present

EXERCISE 12.14

1. The committee

2. The bill, including tip and taxes

3. Part of the cost

4. Either Romeo or Juliet and the Nurse

5. A hike of fourteen or more kilometres

6. Each of the band members

7. A covey of birds

8. Fort Francis and Rainy River, together with Kenora,

9. The Canadian hockey audience

10. Each and every one of you

EXERCISE 12.15

Write your own sentences, choosing your subjects as indicated and using present-tense verbs.

1. Use a collective noun as subject.

2. Use a compound subject.

3. Use *no one* as your subject.

4. Use *everything* as your subject.

5. Use *neither . . . nor.*

6. Use *not . . . but*.

7. Use a collective noun as singular subject.

8. Use a collective noun as plural subject.

9. Use your own weight as subject.

10. Use a compound subject joined by *or*.

EXERCISE 12.16
Correct the following passage.

The rewards of obtaining a good summer or part-time job goes well beyond the money you earn from your labour. Contacts that may be valuable in the future and experience in the working world is a very important part of school-time employment. Even if the jobs you get while attending school has nothing to do with your future ambitions, they offer many benefits. For example, when scanning your résumé, an employer always likes to see that you know what working for other people require: arriving at the work site on time, getting along with fellow workers, following directions. Neither instinct nor instruction take the place of experience in teaching these basic facts of working life. These long-term considerations, in addition to the money that is the immediate reward, is what make part-time work so valuable. Everyone who have gone to school and worked part-time or during vacations are able to confirm these observations.

EXERCISE 12.17

As a final check of your mastery of subject–verb agreement, correct the following sentences. No answers are provided for this exercise.

1. All of Ravi's courses, including drafting and architectural history, is easier for him this term.

2. Either the class or the instructor were mistaken about the due date for the project.

3. Although you are unsure of your position on the issue, everyone else in my classes want to ban Rush Limbaugh from the airwaves.

4. A losing coach, together with his hapless players, are often abused by the media.

5. Each of those outfits give Laszlo a seedy, disreputable look.

6. There is a buxom woman and two beefy gentlemen lurking in the parking lot waiting for you.

7. Did you know that a "pride" of lions are what a group of them are called?

8. Twenty dollars seem like a lot to pay for a portrait of Elvis on velvet.

9. Everyone who fear for the life of this planet are concerned about global warming and the depletion of the ozone layer.

10. Either Ngoc or Hiang, together with the children, are going to the Galaxyland on Saturday.

CHAPTER 13

Keeping Your Tenses Consistent

Verbs are time markers. Changes in tense express changes in time: past, present, or future.

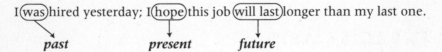

I (was) hired yesterday; I (hope) this job (will last) longer than my last one.

       past   *present*   *future*

Sometimes, as in the sentence above, it is necessary to use several different tenses in a single sentence to get the meaning across. But most of the time, whether you're writing a sentence or a paragraph, you use one tense throughout. Normally, you choose either the past or the present tense, depending on the nature of your topic. (Very few paragraphs are written completely in the future tense.) Here is the rule to follow:

> Don't change tense unless meaning requires it.

Readers like and expect consistency. If you begin a sentence with "I argued, protested, and even attempted an appeal to his masculine pride," the reader will tune in to the past-tense verbs and expect any other verbs in the sentence to be in the past tense too. So, if you finish the sentence with ". . . but he looks at me with those big blue eyes and gets me to pay for dinner," your readers will be jolted abruptly out of one time frame into another. This sort of jolting is uncomfortable, and readers don't like it.

Shifting tenses is like shifting gears: it should be done smoothly and when necessary—never abruptly, out of carelessness, or on a whim. Avoid causing verbal whiplash; keep your tenses consistent.

> *Problem:* Meiling goes into the garage and tried to start the car.
> *Solution 1:* Meiling went into the garage and tried to start the car.
> *Solution 2:* Meiling goes into the garage and tries to start the car.
>
> *Problem:* Rudolf delayed until the last possible minute, but then begins to write his paper. When he gets halfway through, he decided to change his topic.
> *Solution 1:* Rudolf delayed as long as possible, but then began to write his paper. When he got halfway through, he decided to change his topic.
> *Solution 2:* Rudolf delays as long as possible, but then begins to write his paper. When he gets halfway through, he decides to change his topic.

In the exercises for this section, most of the sentences contain unnecessary tense shifts. Use the first verb in each sentence as your time marker and change the tense(s) of the other verb(s) to agree with it. Answers begin on p. 344.

EXERCISE 13.1

1. Allan went home and tells Guljan what happened.

2. Kristi was so tired that, about ten minutes after class started, she goes right to sleep.

3. The umpire stands there, rubbing his eyes, unable to believe what he was seeing.

4. The goalie must not move from his stand until the penalty kicker makes contact with the ball.

5. When I answered the phone, there is yet another person on the line soliciting a contribution to some worthy cause.

6. First, gently fry the onion, garlic, and seasonings; then you will brown
   the meat.

7. Kyra watched TV all evening until she finally fell asleep at about
   midnight.

8. My deadline is next Thursday, by which time I had to have an outline
   and a rough draft ready for my prof's inspection.

9. I drank a half-litre of milk, then I eat two protein- and veggie-stuffed
   sandwiches, and I am ready for anything.

10. When Roch Voisine came on stage, the crowd goes crazy.

EXERCISE 13.2

1. First, backcomb your hair into spikes, then you'll coat your head with
   glue.

2. The guard walked over and punches me in the stomach.

3. The Peter Principle states that every employee will rise to his or her
   level of incompetence.

4. Amin and Mia go on their first date and it is a disaster; however, they
   decided to try again.

5. The couple living in the next apartment had a boa constrictor that
   keeps getting loose.

7. Prejudice is learned and will be hard to outgrow.

8. As usual, Professor Campbell began by asking a rhetorical question that he proceeds to answer without waiting for anyone in the class to attempt to respond.

9. Are you going to this week's game? It'll be sure to be the best one of the series.

10. Just as time runs out, Emir launched a shot at the basket from the centre line. It missed the rim by about two metres.

EXERCISE 13.3

Correct the faulty tense shifts in this paragraph. Use the italicized verb as your time marker.

As a boy, Ralph *had* a remarkable knack for making accurate predictions about the future. When he was 7, he announces to anyone who would listen that he would be a millionaire by the time he is old enough to vote. When he was 11, he predicts that he would star in a major motion picture by the time he reaches the legal driving age. At the age of 14, he prophesies that he would be elected mayor before his twenty-third birthday. Incredibly, his predictions come to pass, one after the other. At 16, he becomes the youngest person ever to play James Bond in a movie, and this role leads to other projects and a salary well into six figures. Good financial advice and careful investing make him a millionaire in two years. With all that money behind him, there will be no stopping Ralph's campaign to have become, at 22, the youngest mayor in Red Deer's history. However, his amazing early successes are not sustainable, and Ralph becomes a has-been by the time he turns 25.

EXERCISE 13.4

The paragraph below contains a number of distracting and potentially confusing tense shifts. Rewrite the paragraph, using the present tense as your base form.

The sea squirt is a tiny marine creature that will be shaped like a bottle. It is a mollusc, so when it has reached its juvenile stage, it will wander through the sea searching for a suitable rock or shell or hunk of coral to cling to. When it has found just the right solid object, it will make this object its home for life. To complete its biologically determined task, the sea squirt has been equipped with a rudimentary nervous system; however, once it has found the perfect spot and has established its roots, it no longer will have any use for its brain. So it will eat it. As Professor D. Dennett has observed in his book, *Consciousness Explained*, the process the sea squirt has gone through is much like the process of getting tenure in an academic institution.

EXERCISE 13.5

Test your mastery of tense consistency by correcting the following sentences. No answers are given for this exercise.

1. When the fax machine broke down, the whole office goes into a state of panic.

2. Lisa sat in front of the computer for two hours trying to detect the bug in her program, and when finally she sees it, she knew immediately how to correct it.

3. After school, Terry went straight to the fast-food restaurant where she is a cashier and gets into her uniform.

4. I was so sick that I go to bed and don't get up for three days.

5. The building manager agreed to rent us an apartment only after we offered her a substantial bribe.

6. We knew that Rudolf would fail math; he keeps skipping class.

7. It was not until the Constitution Act of 1982 that Canada becomes fully responsible for its own destiny.

8. Ron says there were none left, but I wanted to see for myself, so I drive to the store and find he was right.

9. The detective climbs the stairs as the music got louder and louder. Just when you can't stand it any more, the old woman leaped out at him and stabs him to death.

10. A new era was upon us. No more are we at the mercy of invisible bureaucrats and politicians. Now we are at the mercy of invisible experts and poll takers.

CHAPTER 14

Choosing the Correct Pronoun Form

After verbs, pronouns are the class of words most likely to cause problems for writers. In this chapter and the two following, we will look at the three aspects of pronoun usage that can trip you up if you're not careful: pronoun **form, agreement,** and **consistency.** We will also consider the special problems of usage that lead to sexist language.

English has eight different kinds of pronouns, but only three kinds are potentially troublesome for the writer:

> *personal pronouns: I, we, she, they,* etc.
> *relative pronouns: who, that,* etc.
> *indefinite pronouns: any, somebody, none, each,* etc.

The first thing you need to do is be sure you are using correct pronoun forms. Look at these examples of incorrect pronoun usage:

Her and me decided to rent a video.

Between you and I, I think Biff is cheating again.

How do you know which form of a pronoun to use? The answer depends on the pronoun's place and function in your sentence.

There are two forms of personal pronouns. One is used for subjects and one is used for objects. Pronoun errors occur when you confuse the two. In Chapter 5, you learned to identify the subject of a sentence. Keep that information in mind as you learn this basic rule:

> When the subject of a sentence is (or is referred to by) a pronoun, that pronoun must be in **subject form;** otherwise, use the **object form.**

SUBJECT PRONOUNS

Singular	*Plural*
I	we
you	you
he, she, it, one	they

She and *I* <u>decided</u> to rent a video. (The pronouns are the subject of the sentence.)

The lucky <u>winners</u> of the all-expenses-paid weekend in Pelvis, Saskatchewan, <u>are</u> *they.* (The pronoun refers to the subject of the sentence, "winners.")

The only <u>person</u> who handed in the assignment on time <u>was</u> *she.* (The pronoun refers to the subject of the sentence, "person.")

We serious <u>bikers</u> <u>prefer</u> Harleys to Hondas. (The pronoun refers to the subject of the sentence, "bikers.")

OBJECT PRONOUNS

Singular	*Plural*
me	us
you	you
him, her, it, one	them

Between you and *me,* <u>I</u> <u>think</u> Biff is cheating again. ("Me" is not the subject of the sentence; it is one of the objects of the preposition "between.")

<u>Karim</u> <u>asked</u> both *her* and *me* to the semiformal. ("Her" and "me" are not the subject of the verb "asked"; "Karim" is, so the pronouns need to be in the object form.)

The <u>police</u> <u>are</u> always suspicious of *us* bikers. ("Us" does not refer to the subject of the sentence, "police"; it refers to "bikers," the object of the preposition "of.")

Be especially careful with pronouns in multiple subjects or after prepositions. If you can remember these two rules, you'll be able to eliminate most potential errors in pronoun form:

---

1. A pronoun that is part of a multiple subject is *always* in subject form.
2. A pronoun that comes after a preposition is *always* in object form.

Examples:

She and *I* <u>had</u> tickets to The Tragically Hip. (The pronouns are used as a multiple subject.)

We are counting on *you* and *him* to finish the project. (The pronouns follow the preposition "on.")

Here's a practically foolproof way for native English speakers to tell which pronoun form is needed. (EFL speakers, unfortunately must rely on memorizing the rules.) When the sentence contains a pair of pronouns, mentally cross one out. Applying this technique to the first example above, you get "*She* had tickets" and "*I* had tickets," both of which sound right and are correct. In the second sentence, if you try the pronouns separately, you get "We are counting on *you*" and "We are counting on *him*." Again, you know by the sound that these are the correct forms. You would never say, "*Her* had tickets," or "*Me* had tickets," or "We are counting on *he*." If you deal with paired pronouns one at a time, you are unlikely to choose the wrong form.

EXERCISE 14.1

Choose the correct pronouns from the words given in parentheses.

1. Those videotapes belong to Patrick and (I me).
2. I can't believe that the committee would choose Bennie along with (we us).
3. Neither (they them) nor (us we) deserve to be treated like this.
4. Danny and (he him) think no one knows they smoke in the stairwell.
5. Just between you and (I me), the engagement between Yolande and (he him) is off.
6. If I have to choose between (he him) and you, I'm afraid it is (he him) who will be going to the lake with me.
7. As devoted television watchers, (us we) love it when (us we) and the program producers share similar tastes.

8. It would be preferable for (them they) to come here rather than for (us we) to go there.
9. I can't believe Chandra would break up with me after (her she) and (I me) got matching tattoos and navel rings.
10. It is likely that (us we) musicians would get more favourable reviews from the critics if we and (them they) met socially more often.

EXERCISE 14.2

Correct the errors in pronoun form in the following sentences.

1. Her and me have completely different tastes in music, though we agree on practically everything else.
2. There aren't many vegetarians besides Ettore and I who are so strict that they will not wear leather or wool.
3. It is not for you or I to decide whether they go to the game or stay home.
4. Iain and her are the best curlers on our team; if it weren't for they, we would be in last place.
5. Her and Marie took the magazines before either Tom or me had had a chance to read them.
6. Us and them were exhausted from studying all night, so we can't be blamed for the explosion.
7. Fate has put we two together and no matter what her or your father says, it is us who will live happily ever after at the end of the story.
8. Have you and him finally finished your project, or must us seniors do your work for you again?
9. It is up to you and he to piece together the clues and come up with the solution to the crime so that us innocent victims can be set free.
10. I don't need to see my doctor because I know that my chiropractor and her agree that I should not play in the championship game tonight, and they are both fans of we "Fighting Treefrogs."

Choosing the correct pronoun form is more than just a matter of not wanting to appear ignorant or careless. Sometimes, the form you use determines the meaning of your sentence. Consider these two sentences:

> Lin treats her dog better than *I*.
> Lin treats her dog better than *me*.

There's a world of difference between the meaning of the subject form: "Lin treats her dog better than *I* [do]" and the object form: "Lin treats her dog better than [she treats] *me*."

When using a pronoun after *than,* or *as well as,* or *as,* decide whether you mean to contrast the pronoun with the subject of the sentence. If you do, use the subject form of the pronoun. If not, use the object form.
    Example:

Tammy would rather listen to Jim Witter than I. (*I* is contrasted with *Tammy.*)

Tammy would rather listen to Jim Witter than me. (*Me* is contrasted with *Jim Witter.*)

EXERCISE 14.3
Correct the following sentences where necessary.

1. Nobody hates English more than me.

2. She is more frightened of being alone than him.

3. Everyone wanted to go to the movies except Yvon and I.

4. More than me, Yuxiang uses the computer to draft and revise his papers.

5. Only a few Mexican food fanatics can eat jalapeno peppers as well as him.

6. At last I have met someone who enjoys barbecued eel as much as me!

7. After our instructor handed out the papers, Rudolf and me got into a fight.

8. Since he had copied his essay from me, he shouldn't have got a better grade than me.

9. Rudolf's thinking is that since he is better looking than me, he deserves the higher mark.

10. I have a real problem with a teacher who gives good marks to they who are blessed with a winning smile and great hair.

EXERCISE 14.4

Revise the paragraph below to correct all errors in pronoun form.

You and me can both learn a lesson from a story that happened to our village priest and his curate. Them and their congregation were plagued by a colony of bats that had moved into the church. Whenever the priest began his sermon, the bats and him had to compete for the attention of we in the congregation. Unfortunately for the priest, the bats always won because they were more interesting than him. Then the curate had an idea. He suggested that every night for a week, him and the priest would go into the church and fire a blank shotgun shell. This strategy didn't bother the bats at all, but the congregation was most alarmed and asked the priest and curate if it was them who had been causing mysterious explosions in the church at night. Sheepishly, they had to admit that it had been them. The priest's next move was to ring the church bells while the curate played the organ at top volume, hoping that the racket would drive the bats away. Instead, the awful noise almost drove we parishioners to another church. The bats, who have more patience than us—or perhaps they're tone-deaf— didn't seem to mind at all.

Finally, the priest, the curate, and us had a long meeting to resolve the problem. One member of the congregation had an idea: she suggested that the priest hold a special service, to be attended by all of we parishioners, during which the bats would be baptized. The priest duly performed this service, and neither him, nor the curate, nor us ever saw bats in the church again.

EXERCISE 14.5

Correct the pronouns where necessary in the following sentences. No answers have been given for this exercise.

1. No one feels worse about your loss than my family and me.

2. I decided not to apply for the position because both Pol and Stella wanted it more than me, and I didn't want to risk losing our friendship by being selected over they.

3. Quint likes our local talk-show host better than me and often calls in to her show; my roommate and me, on the other hand, have little interest in current affairs and just listen to music all day long.

4. My mother would rather cook for my brother than I because, unlike me, he never complains when dinner is burned or raw.

5. It is foolish to suppose that both the Flyers and us will finish out of the playoffs, so you will have to meet either they or us before you can claim the cup.

6. The responsibility for the shortfall in sales this month falls on marketing and we, even though I think it's clear they were more negligent than us.

7. I enjoy talking to Rogelio more than them, but if there's no one else around, I'll endure a conversation with they.

8. The major difference between Eugene and me is that he thinks he's perfect, while I am.

9. Us full-time computer programmers are curious to know why the person who was awarded the contract for designing the new software was her, a part-timer without qualifications.

10. To increase your chances of getting the raise you want, you should speak to your supervisor first, then she, but, between you and I, it's a good idea to wait until she's had her morning coffee.

CHAPTER 15

Mastering Pronoun– Antecedent Agreement

Now that you know how to choose the correct form of pronouns within a sentence, let's look at how to use pronouns consistently throughout a sentence and a paragraph.

Pronoun–Antecedent Agreement

The name of this pronoun problem may sound difficult, but the idea is very simple. Pronouns are words that substitute for or refer to the name of a person, place, or thing mentioned elsewhere in your sentence or your paragraph. The word(s) that a pronoun substitutes for or refers to is called the **antecedent.**

Hannibal had his own way of doing things.

antecedent   *pronoun*

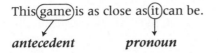

This game is as close as it can be.

antecedent   *pronoun*

Normally, as in these two examples, the antecedent comes before the pronoun that refers to it. The rule to remember is this:

> A pronoun must agree with its antecedent.

You probably follow this rule most of the time without even realizing that you know it. For example, you would never write

> Hannibal had *its* own way of doing things.
> *or*
> This game is as close as *she* can be.

You know that these pronouns don't agree with their antecedents.

There are three kinds of pronoun–antecedent agreement, however, that you need to watch out for. They involve **relative pronouns**; **indefinite pronouns ending in** *-one*, *-body*, **or** *-thing*; and **vague references**.

1. Relative Pronouns

The first potential difficulty with pronoun–antecedent agreement is how to use the relative pronouns—*who, whom, which,* and *that*—correctly. Relative pronouns can be used only to refer to someone or something already specifically mentioned in the sentence. Here is the guideline to follow:

> *Who* and *whom, whoever* and *whomever* refer to people.
> *That* and *which* refer to everything else.

The player *who* was injured had to be taken to the hospital.

The students *who* were present supported the dean's proposal.

The moose *that* I met looked hostile.

Her report, *which* is due today, will address most of the concerns *that* the union has raised.

Whether you need *who* or *whom*, *whoever* or *whomever*, depends on the pronoun's place and function in your sentence. Apply the basic pronoun rule:

> If the pronoun is acting as, or refers to, the subject, use *who/whoever*. Otherwise, use *whom/whomever*.

It was he *who* filled out the form that won us the trip to Pelvis.
(The pronoun refers to the subject of the sentence, "he.")

The trip's promoters were willing to settle for *whomever* they could get.
(The pronoun does not refer to the subject, "promoters"; it is the object of the preposition "for.")

An even simpler solution to this problem is to rewrite the sentence so you don't need either *who* or *whom*:

He filled out the form that won us the trip to Pelvis.

The trip's promoters were willing to settle for anyone they could get.

That is required more often than *which*. You should use *which* only in a clause that is separated from the rest of the sentence by commas.

The moose *that* I met looked hostile.

The moose, *which* was standing right in front of my car, looked hostile.

EXERCISE 15.1
Correct the following sentences where necessary. Answers begin on p. 347.

1. Clive is the only one that wants his picture hung in the board room.

2. Everyone that went to the party had a good time, though a few had more punch than was good for them.

3. Is this the dog which bit the mail carrier that carries a squirt gun?

4. The path led me past the home of a hermit that lives all alone in the forest which surrounds our town.

5. A filmmaker that stays within budget on every production will always have work, no matter how mediocre his movies might be.

6. The open-office concept is one which makes sense to anyone that has worked in a stuffy little cubicle all day.

7. One advantage of the open office is that it lets you see who is working hard and who is taking it easy. It also allows you to spot people that you'd like to meet.

8. The four tests which we wrote today would have defeated anyone that wasn't prepared for them.

9. Sales clerks that want to make good commissions must have good people skills as well as knowledge of the products which they are selling.

10. The winning goal, that was made with only two seconds left in the game, was scored by a player that I used to know in high school.

2. Pronouns Ending in *-one*, *-body*, *-thing*

The second tricky aspect of pronoun–antecedent agreement involves these pronouns:

anyone	anybody	anything
everyone	everybody	everything
no one	nobody	nothing
someone	somebody	something
each (one)		

In Chapter 12, you learned that when these words are used as subjects, they are singular and require singular verbs. So it makes sense that the pronouns that stand for or refer to them must also be singular.

> Antecedents ending in *-one, -body,* and *-thing* are singular. They must be referred to by singular pronouns: *he, she, it; his, her, its.*

Each of the students must buy *his* or *her* own lab coat.

Every mother deserves a break from *her* children now and then.

Everybody is expected to do *his* share of the cleaning up.

No one could say that in *his* heart *he* believed she was guilty.

But take another look at the last two sentences. Until about twenty years ago, the pronouns *he, him, his* were used with singular antecedents and referred to both men and women. Today, however, many readers are sensitive to sex bias in writing and feel that it is not appropriate to use the masculine pronoun when referring to both sexes. As a writer, you should be aware of this sensitivity. If you want to appeal to the broadest possible audience, you should avoid what some readers may consider sexist language.

In speech, it has become acceptable to use plural pronouns with *-one, -body,* and *-thing* antecedents. Although these are grammatically singular and take singular verbs, they are often plural in meaning, and in conversation we find ourselves saying

Everybody is expected to do their share of the cleaning up.

No one could say that in their hearts they believed she was guilty.

This usage is acceptable only in speech; it is not acceptable in standard written English. Writers sometimes make errors in pronoun–antecedent agreement because they are trying to write without indicating whether the person referred to is male or female. "Everybody is expected to do *their* share" is incorrect, as we have seen; however, it does avoid making "everybody" male. The writer could replace the plural *their* with the singular and nonsexist *his or her*—"Everybody is expected to do *his or her* share"—but *his or her* sounds clumsy, especially if it is used frequently.

There are two better ways to solve the problem.

1. Revise the sentence to leave the pronoun out.

Everybody is expected to help clean up.

At heart, no one really believed she was guilty.

Such creative avoidance of sex-specific language or incorrect constructions can be an interesting intellectual challenge. The results sometimes sound a little artificial, however. The second solution is easier to accomplish.

2. Revise the sentence to make both the antecedent and the pronoun plural.

   You are all expected to do your share of the cleaning up.

   In our hearts, we did not believe she was guilty.

Here are a couple of examples for you to study:

Problem:　Each of the students has been given his assignment.
Revision 1:　Each of the students has been given an assignment.
Revision 2:　All of the students have been given their assignments.

Problem:　Everyone is looking forward to seeing his or her former classmates again.
Revision 1:　Everyone is looking forward to seeing former classmates again.
Revision 2:　All the graduates are looking forward to seeing their former classmates again.

EXERCISE 15.2

Identify the most appropriate word(s) from the choices given in parentheses. Check your answers carefully before continuing.

1. Each of the women would prefer to answer the charges (herself, themselves.)
2. Would someone kindly lend (his, their, a) copy of the text to Jan?
3. Any one of us would be happy to take (his, her, his or her, their, the) time to help you.
4. I expect everyone to do (his, her, his or her, their) best in this course.
5. Everyone is expected to pay (his or her, their, a) portion of the expenses.
6. Everybody enjoys getting together with (his or her, their, the) family on Thanksgiving.
7. No one I know is willing to allow (his, her, his or her, their) name to appear on the ballot.
8. None of the pictures we took could be called great by (itself themselves), but together they make an impressive collection.
9. So far, no one on the football team has been able to get (his, their) parents to donate (his or her, their) house for the party.
10. Any man (that who) would buy an orange and purple tie should have (his, their) head examined.

EXERCISE 15.3

Correct the errors in the following sentences, being careful to avoid awkward repetition and sexist language.

1. Every child is a product of their environment as well as their heredity.

2. Anyone who would write a sentence like that last one should give up their computer.

3. The team agreed that everyone would have to show up for their practices.

4. Everybody must get in their places for the game to begin.

5. Anybody without a partner will have to try to find one approximately his height.

6. Golf is a game that is good for anyone who wants to enjoy outdoor exercise without getting their body sweaty or hurt.

7. We have asked every student with a complaint to see their instructor.

8. Do you know whether anyone in your neighbourhood wants their house painted or their grass cut this summer?

9. Few people I know enjoys himself on a squash court, but they like to play tennis whenever they can.

10. We're looking for someone whose intelligence and creativity are so outstanding that they can work unsupervised.

3. Vague Reference

Avoiding the third potential difficulty with pronoun–antecedent agreement requires common sense and an ability to put yourself in your reader's place. If you look at your writing from your reader's point of view, it is unlikely that you will break this rule:

> A pronoun must *clearly* refer to the correct antecedent.

The mistake that occurs when you fail to follow this rule is called **vague reference.**

> Jules pointed to his brother and said that he had saved his life.

Who saved whom? Here's another:

> Sabina felt that Mary should have been more careful with her car when she lent it to her because she was a good friend of her husband.

Who owns the car? Who has the husband?

In sentences like these, you can only guess the meaning because you don't know who is being referred to by the pronouns. The antecedents are not clear. You can make such sentences less confusing either by using proper names (Jules, Sabina, Mary) more frequently or by changing the sentences around. These solutions aren't difficult; they just take a little time and some imagination. Try them on our examples.

Another type of vague reference occurs when there is no antecedent in the sentence for the pronoun to refer to.

> He loves watching off-road rallies and would love to do it himself one day. (Do what?)

> Snowboarding is her favourite winter sport, so it's odd that she doesn't own one. (One what?)

How would you revise these sentences?

Make sure that every pronoun has a clear antecedent, and that every pronoun agrees with its antecedent. Both must be singular or both must be plural. Once you have mastered this principle, you'll have no trouble with pronoun–antecedent agreement.

EXERCISE 15.4

Correct the following sentences where necessary. There are several ways to fix these sentences. In some cases, the antecedents are missing and you won't know what is being referred to. In other cases, the antecedents are so vague that the meaning of the sentence can be interpreted in more than one way.

1. Max is a good skater, which he practises daily.

2. He didn't hear her cry for help, which was due to his wearing earplugs.

3. That Miss Grundy would be Betty's teacher never occurred to her.

4. Every time David looked at the dog, he barked.

5. In a rage, Biff threw his ghetto blaster on the floor and cracked it.

6. Carla told her mother she was sure to get a job soon.

7. Whenever Rudolf and Biff met, he acted in a relaxed, friendly fashion so that no one would suspect he hated him.

8. Krystal told Sparkle she was losing her looks.

9. At our college, they introduced a "no smoking" policy three years ago.

10. I am writing this letter in response to your ad for a waiter and bartender, male or female. Being both, I wish to apply for the position.

The following exercises contain all three kinds of pronoun–antecedent agreement errors. Correct each sentence any way you choose, remembering that your answers may differ from the answers we've provided and still be correct. Our suggested answers begin on p. 348.

EXERCISE 15.5

1. Did anyone that submitted their essay late get a passing grade?

2. George is the only person I know who can whistle while they eat crackers.

3. Quilting is something Becky has a real passion for, but she hasn't had time to complete one in months.

4. Is there anyone in the world so confident of success that they never contemplate an excuse for failure, just in case?

5. Each of the three cars I could afford had their drawbacks, but the '89 Honda had the best maintenance-cost record.

6. Fishermen who know this lake use only jigs when they are after walleye.

7. How can anyone, after twelve years of schooling, still misplace their modifiers?

8. I know that smoking is bad for me, but I just can't manage to give them up.

9. She'll put her to bed now because she is so overtired she can't stop crying.

10. He said he wasn't trying hard enough, and that anyone who said he was would get a punch on their nose.

EXERCISE 15.6

1. Neither the jacket nor the pants fit the way it should.

2. There's nobody around to help you since every other performer left hours ago to get their costume fitted.

3. Bernice would love to meet someone that is tall, dark, handsome, and rich; in fact, they don't even have to be tall, dark, or handsome.

4. They said they would try to find accommodation for the tourists, even though they didn't really know what they wanted.

5. I remember the old days when anyone who used computers wore thick glasses, solved calculus problems for fun, and didn't know whether their shoes were tied.

6. This is a beaten team; the players don't care any more whether he performs well or poorly.

7. Denise told Mara that she had an excellent chance of making the team if she just did everything she told her to do when she spoke to the coach.

8. Omar sat down next to Barry in the cafeteria and ate his lunch.

9. Every twelve-step program is based on the belief that nobody can rise above their dependency or addiction without faith in a higher power and the help of their friends.

10. Someone who has many friends is truly rich; friends will help them when all else fails.

EXERCISE 15.7

1. Each car in the rally must have their own mechanic and navigator.

2. Lisa and Nasreen plan to share an apartment next year, providing she gets the student loan she applied for.

3. Every time that Rudolf sat next to Dwight during an exam, he tried to copy his answers.

4. The colour television with which we are familiar will become obsolete as they are replaced by HDTV, the high resolution broadcast standard that is common in Europe.

5. Isn't anyone going to try their luck at beating the house at blackjack?

6. Medical researchers have found that some forms of it may be linked to the consumption of red meat.

7. Brandi's dream is to meet just one man that will live up to her expectations of them.

8. Akil wrote to tell Mikail that, because of the political unrest in his country, it probably wasn't safe for him to visit him this summer.

9. Can there be anyone among Canada's culture buffs so out of touch with significant cultural events that they don't know about my recent victory in the national clog dancing championships?

10. I've been told repeatedly that postsecondary education is essential to my chances of future employment, but I don't bother to go anymore, now that I've found a full-time job loading trucks.

EXERCISE 15.8

1. Every student graduating from high school should be careful to choose a college or university program designed to prepare them for the career they are interested in.

2. Before they buy vitamins, drugs, or any over-the-counter medication, a woman should get a pharmacist's advice.

3. Fishing is a sport I have enjoyed for many years, but I have never caught even one of record size.

4. My mother's constant nagging would make anyone lose their mind.

5. Rick and Clement agreed that they could go camping on the weekend, so long as they left early enough to be sure he got back in time to get to work.

6. Everybody I know is going, even though they have to rent a tux.

7. Anyone that has finished all their homework so quickly can't possibly have done them properly.

8. In this company, everyone is encouraged to find their own path to success, according to their own definition of success.

9. I have never advocated banning fighting in hockey because I think a good one now and then releases tensions which might otherwise result in much worse violence, among the fans as well as the players.

10. Professor Chan, obviously annoyed, told Kathy and Tamara that she had thought she would have known better than to copy her friend's homework assignment.

EXERCISE 15.9

Correct the problems in the following paragraph, which contains all three kinds of pronoun–antecedent agreement errors. Part of the challenge in this exercise is to make the paragraph not only grammatically correct, but also free of sexist language.

Anyone that has competed in a triathlon (a three-part race consisting of swimming, cycling, and running) knows that proper training is an absolute necessity, not only to their success, but also to their survival. Swimming is one of the toughest contests, because it demands cardiovascular fitness as well as strength, and it makes demands on the whole body. While each of the three segments has their own challenges, the cycling part of the triathlon is the event which separates serious athletes from part-time fitness buffs. Here, he will find he can't summon enough energy after his swim to stay close to his opponent if he has trained harder than he. The serious athlete will begin to assert their dominance now, and by the end of the bike ride, anyone that has achieved a high level of physical efficiency through their training will still have a chance of a high placing. For the competitor in a triathlon, survival is often the primary goal. The body's reserves are called on, and only the dedicated, well-trained athlete will be able to do it. For most, reaching the finish line is a personal test, and the only competition is against one's previous finish times. The person that still has winning in mind after the swim, the cycle race, and the run has physical and mental reserves beyond the ordinary.

EXERCISE 15.10

Check your mastery of pronoun–antecedent agreement by correcting the errors in the following sentences. No answers have been provided for this exercise.

1. Each of the boys tried their best, so it was difficult for them to decide who should receive the "most enthusiastic player" award.

2. When it comes to snacking, Sharon can't resist those which are loaded with butter and sugar.

3. His scoring is the reason he was added to the team, but he hasn't got one in the last six games.

4. Anyone that wants to understand the Internet needs to have lots of time on their hands to spend exploring and experimenting.

5. The disagreement between Karin and Marie has finally gone too far; if she doesn't ask her to go, the rest of us will have to leave.

6. Attila is the one that asked all those at a party to divulge his or her most personal fantasies, and then wrote a movie script based on their stories.

7. "Is there *anyone* in the class that has finished their experiment yet?" Professor Bunsen asked testily.

8. We want to thank everyone that was so kind to us with their good wishes and generous wedding gifts, and also to inform them that, in spite of the recent divorce, we do sincerely appreciate their thoughtfulness.

9. Since I discovered the efficiency and fun of computing, all I dream about is getting one with a CD-ROM, a colour laser printer, and about three hundred games.

10. The lawyers directed the accountants to get their books in order so that, when the tax auditors checked their records, they could prove they had suffered substantial business losses during the past year.

CHAPTER 16

Maintaining Person Agreement

So far, we have focussed on using pronouns correctly and clearly within a sentence. Now let's turn to the problem of **person agreement,** which means using pronouns consistently throughout a sentence or a paragraph. There are three categories of person that we use when we write or speak:

	SINGULAR	PLURAL
First person:	I; me	we; us
Second person:	you	you
Third person:	she, he, it, one; her, him *and all pronouns ending in* -one, -thing, -body	they; them

Here is the rule for person agreement:

> Do not mix "persons" unless meaning requires it.

In other words, be consistent. If you begin a sentence using a second-person pronoun, you must use second person all the way through. Look at this sentence:

If *you* wish to succeed, *one* must work hard.

This is the most common error—mixing second-person *you* with third-person *one*.

Here's another example:

> *One* can live happily in Vancouver if *you* have a sturdy umbrella.

We can correct this error by using the second person throughout:

> *You* can live happily in Vancouver if *you* have a sturdy umbrella.

or by using the third person throughout:

> *One* can live happily in Vancouver if *one* has a sturdy umbrella.
> *or*
> *One* can live happily in Vancouver if *he or she* has a sturdy umbrella.

These last three sentences raise two points of style that you should consider.

1. **Don't overuse *one*.** Although all three revised sentences are correct, they affect the reader differently. The first sentence, in the second person, sounds the most informal and natural—like something you would say. It's a bit casual for general writing purposes. The second sentence, which uses *one* twice, sounds the most formal—even a little stilted. The third sentence falls between the other two in formality and is the one you'd be most likely to use in writing for school or business. It's grammatically correct and nonsexist, but it raises another potential problem.

2. **Don't overuse *he or she*.** If this construction occurs frequently, the reader cannot help shifting focus from what you're saying to how you're saying it. The best writing is transparent—that is, it doesn't call attention to itself. If your reader becomes distracted by your style, your meaning gets lost. Consider this sentence:

> A student can easily pass this course if he or she applies himself or herself to his or her studies.

Awkward, isn't it? Imagine being the unfortunate reader who has to struggle through a whole paragraph filled with this clumsy construction!

The solutions to this problem are the same as those for making pronouns ending in *-one, -body,* or *-thing* agree with their antecedents. You can either change the whole sentence to the plural:

> Students can easily pass this course if they apply themselves to their studies.

or you can rewrite the sentence without using pronouns:

> A student can easily pass this course by applying good study habits.

EXERCISE 16.1

Choose the correct word(s) from the parentheses for each of the following sentences. Answers begin on p. 350.

1. You mustn't annoy the instructor if (one wants, you want, he or she wants) to leave class on time.
2. Any woman will be irresistible if (you, one, she) uses our line of Beautifem products!
3. If you do the homework regularly and hand in all assignments on time, the chances are (one, you) will do well in the course.
4. You'd do better if (one, she, you) were to try harder.
5. When we came up for air, (one, we, you) couldn't see the boat!
6. If you want to avoid the winter flu, (one, you, they) should get a flu shot in the fall.
7. (One, You) mustn't push Biff too far, because he will either lose his temper or become hysterical, and that isn't what you want.
8. When we analyzed the situation, (one, they, we) realized that the problem would never have arisen if (one, they, we) had been more careful in (our, their) planning.
9. When you're bright and talented, (one doesn't, you don't, they don't) have to try very hard to impress (ones, your, their) elders, especially if (one is, you are, they are) also handsome.
10. You can't really enjoy a sport unless (one knows, you know) the basic rules. How can (one, you) understand the game unless (one knows, you know) what's going on?

Correct the following sentences where necessary. Check your answers to each set of ten before going on.

EXERCISE 16.2

1. A great worry is lifted from one's mind when you learn your application has been accepted.

2. If only one had read the instructions carefully, I wouldn't have messed up the answer on the test.

3. If any of you are planning to go to the class party, they can pick up their tickets now.

4. Men who don't think women are their equals may have to get used to living on your own.

5. It has taken most Canadians far too long to recognize the seriousness of our debt and deficit problems.

6. If one is convicted on that charge, a fine is the least of your worries.

7. After we had driven about 400 km, the lack of sleep made it hard to keep your eyes open.

8. If you can't cope with the pressure, one must expect to be replaced by someone who can.

9. The penalties for plagiarism are severe, but one doesn't usually think about penalties until after you are caught.

10. It's very difficult for a 14-year-old to control his or her temper when you feel frustrated or angry.

EXERCISE 16.3

1. When one has completed all the sentences in an exercise, don't forget to check your answers in the back of the book.

2. In this country, you receive more acclaim, not to mention more money, as a hockey player than one does as a symphony conductor.

3. Can you really blame me for getting so tired of picking up after one's messy children all day long?

4. Anyone who rides a motorcycle and does not wear a helmet should be aware of the risk you're taking.

5. When we left the comfort of the air-conditioned hotel, the heat was enough to knock you over.

6. I wonder why people always long for what they don't have, even when you have more than you need?

7. I enjoy living in the country, because there one doesn't have to deal with traffic or pollution, and you can always get to the city if you want to.

8. Ken collects art because, if one knows something about it, you can always get your money back on his investment, and one can sometimes make a killing.

9. An expert wine taster will find this a very acceptable vintage, and even one who knows little about wine will enjoy yourself with a bottle or two.

10. Canadian history may seem dull if you don't know much about it, but to someone who is fascinated by the unusual and the eccentric, it is a goldmine of wonderful stories.

EXERCISE 16.4

Rewrite the following paragraph, changing the third-person pronouns to second-person pronouns.

How can one fight the common cold? If one had the energy to research the subject, he or she would find books, television programs, and thousands of articles in newspapers and magazines advising one how to cope with a cold. A cold cannot be prevented or cured since it is not known what organism actually causes it. However, one's research will not be wasted: one will find no shortage of folk remedies and "personally guaranteed" cures, most of which do nothing more than make one feel better while he or she waits for the cold to go away. Advertisements for pharmaceutical companies promise their pills, syrups, lozenges, and capsules will relieve one's symptoms, but no one claims to offer a cure. There is something strangely comforting in this fact. Since the only thing one can do for a cold is wait for it to go away, one need not spend any of his or her energy or effort visiting a doctor or seeking a miraculous remedy. One might as well relax, spend a day or two indulging himself or herself snuggled up in bed, and enjoy whatever restorative one finds most to his or her liking. One might discover, for example, that chicken soup is his or her treatment of choice. Or one might prefer a large hot rum, with brown sugar and lemon. (Most medical practitioners agree that, when suffering from a cold, one needs additional Vitamin C.) Whatever one's preferred treatment, one should indulge and enjoy oneself! This is one of the few times in one's life when he or she can pamper himself or herself not just without guilt, but in the knowledge that self-indulgence is good for one.

EXERCISE 16.5

Now rewrite the paragraph above by changing the whole thing from third person singular to third person plural.

In the following paragraphs, choose the correct pronouns from those given in parentheses.

EXERCISE 16.6

   People who get married while (they're, one is) still in college may have an especially hard time completing (your, their, one's) studies. If both spouses are in school, (they, he or she, one) may not have enough money for an apartment, and they may have to live with (one's, your, their) parents for a while. Students whose spouses work may find (oneself, themselves, himself) studying on weekends while (their, his or her, one's) spouses rest or socialize. The wife who supports a student husband, along with the husband who supports a student wife, may find that the responsibility weighs heavily on (him, her, them). People in such situations are likely to feel at the end of (their, your) wits sometimes, so students whose marriages are shaky may find that (one is, they are, you are) having a very hard time of it and that (you, their, one's) schoolwork is suffering. On the other hand, these various demands may strengthen a marriage, and a student who marries may find that (their, one's, his or her) motivation to succeed at school has increased. Some married students may even find (themselves, himself, oneself) studying more, spending on schoolwork the time (they, he, one) would otherwise have spent dating.

EXERCISE 16.7

   A woman who enjoys baseball may have difficulty explaining (their, one's, her) passion to those who find the game a bore. Each February, the die-hard fan begins to sharpen (their, one's, her) listening and watching skills by tuning in to spring training games. If you have ever seen one of these fanatics watch a baseball game, (one, you, he) can't help but notice the alertness and intensity with which (one, they, she) follows the play. It is this single-minded dedication that the nonfan finds (himself, themselves, yourself) unable to comprehend. How can one be so interested in something that (one, they, you) must watch for three hours to see almost nothing take place? How can (one, they, you) get excited by a no-hitter, which, by definition, means that nothing has happened during the game? Baseball fans maintain that the game to which (one is, they are) addicted has many more pleasures than mere action. They cite fielding plays and the strategy of pitcher-versus-hitter matchups in defence of the game that (he, one, they) would rather watch than any other. Those for (which, whom, who) these pleasures hold little appeal might enjoy watching golf or lawn bowling.

EXERCISE 16.8

As a final test of your mastery of person consistency, correct the errors in the following paragraph. No answers are provided for this exercise.

(1) When students arrive at college, it is often apparent to your teachers that many lack the study, writing, note-taking, and scheduling skills necessary for one to succeed at the post-secondary level. (2) Much of college work is independent, and you have to be able to function on one's own. (3) It is not unusual for students to be given an assignment at the beginning of term and be expected to hand it in weeks or even months later without your being reminded repeatedly of the deadline. (4) This requires students to schedule your time effectively. (5) College study requires concentration and organization skills that students often have to develop for him or herself. (6) Having been given notes in handouts or on the board throughout high school, many students find it difficult to take notes from the lectures and seminars one encounters at college. (7) Students who are weak in any of these skills are at risk of failing your year. (8) Fortunately, at many colleges, help is available: you can sign up for study skills and mastery programs, sometimes for course credit. (9) Part of success at college depends on one's level of preparation. (10) To acquire the knowledge and skills to do well academically, all of us first have to know how to budget our time, take notes, study, and write.

EXERCISE 16.9

Think of a significant experience you've had since coming to college. (If you don't like "significant," try embarrassing, enlightening, or frightening.) Write an account of this experience, telling your story in the third person: that is, instead of using *I*, use *he* or *she*. When you have finished your paper, reread it carefully. Check your sentence structure. Check your spelling. Check the agreement of your subjects and verbs, and of your pronouns and antecedents. And finally, check to be sure you have maintained consistency of verb tense and pronoun person in each paragraph of your paper.

_____ UNIT FOUR

Punctuation

CHAPTER 17

The Comma

The comma is the most frequently used—and misused—punctuation mark in English. Leaving out a necessary comma can distort the meaning of your sentence. Including unnecessary commas can distract the reader and give your sentences a jerky quality. Perhaps nothing is so sure a sign of a competent writer as the correct use of commas, so it is very important that you master them. This chapter presents four comma rules that will give you a good indication of when you should use a comma. If you apply these four rules faithfully, your reader will never be confused by missing or misplaced commas in your writing. And if, as occasionally happens, the sentence you are writing is not covered by one of our four rules, remember the first commandment of comma usage: when in doubt, leave it out.

Four Comma Rules

Here are the four essential rules that cover most instances in which you need to use a comma.

> 1. Use commas to separate items in a series of three or more.

The required subjects in this program are math, physics, and English.

Drive two blocks north of Main, turn left, go past two traffic signals, and turn right.

Tom went to the movies, Jan and Yasmin went to play pool, and I went to bed.

The comma before the *and* at the end of the list is optional; use it or leave it out, but be consistent.

EXERCISE 17.1

Insert commas where necessary in the following sentences, then check your answers on p. 352.

1. Does anyone remember John, Paul, George, and Ringo?
2. Goldfish and gerbils make the best pets. *Correct.*
3. Krystal thinks she wants to get married, but she can't decide whether Dwight, Rudolf, or Eugene should be the lucky man.
4. Fans of rock, folk, and ska all enjoyed the Days of You concert.
5. MacDonald, Laurier, Borden, and Pearson are four dissimilar men who have one thing in common.
6. Arnold is an all-round athlete; he enjoys skating, skiing, cycling, tobogganing, and showering.
7. Marieke has strong ambition, a cool head, good health, and an inquiring mind; everyone hates her.
8. Careful investment of time and money can lead to a luxurious lifestyle, international fame, and early retirement.
9. Mowing the lawn, shopping for groceries, and doing my teenagers' homework are my least favourite activities.
10. Most of the world sees Canada as a land where French is spoken, ice and snow are year-round hazards, and violent hockey is the natives' favourite pastime.

> 2. Use comma(s) to separate from the rest of the sentence any word or expression that is not essential to the sentence's meaning *or* that means the same as something else in the sentence.

To find out whether a word, phrase, or clause is essential to the meaning of the sentence, try crossing it out. If the sentence remains complete and still makes sense, the crossed-out expression is *nonessential*, and should be set off by commas. Study the following four examples.

Writing a good letter of application isn't difficult, ~~if you're careful~~.

The phrase "if you're careful" is not essential to the meaning of the sentence, so it's separated from the rest of the sentence by a comma.

Writing a letter of application ~~that is clear and concise~~ is a challenge.

If you take out "that is clear and concise," the meaning of the sentence is completely changed. Not all letters of application are a challenge to write: only clear and concise ones. Writing vague and wordy letters is easy; anyone can do it. The words "that is clear and concise" are therefore essential to the meaning of the sentence, and so they are *not* set off by commas.

> ~~One of Canada's best-known novelists~~, Alice Munro spends the summer in Clinton, Ontario, and the winter in Comox, B.C.

The phrase "one of Canada's best-known novelists" means the same as "Alice Munro." The two expressions refer to the same person, so the first is set off by commas. When a nonessential word or phrase occurs in the middle of a sentence, rather than at the beginning or the end, be sure to put commas both before and after it.

> In *Selling Illusions*, ~~published in 1994~~, Neil Bissoondath explains why he thinks Canada's multiculturalism policy has done more harm than good.

Deleting "published in 1994" does not change the meaning of the sentence, so it is set off by commas.

EXERCISE 17.2

Insert commas where necessary in the following sentences. Check your answers before going on.

1. My mother's favourite singer is Gordon Lightfoot, the former Elvis imitator from Orillia.
2. The winner of the 1994 Yorkton Film Festival Jury Award was Janis Lundman's documentary, *Lawn and Order.*
3. The underlying message of the film is that, whether you like it or not, your lawn says a lot about who you are.
4. Listening to music is a perfect way to relax, after a tough day at school.
5. Despite her reputation as an air head, Leticia is, we have discovered, fairly bright.
6. To no one's surprise, Professor Lam, a popular mathematics instructor, won the distinguished teacher award again this year.
7. No one who has seen Patrick Roy play can doubt that he is a superstar. *Correct.*
8. In a radical departure from tradition, the bride wore a bright red gown and matching veil.
9. One of the wedding guests remarked, rather cattily, I thought, that the bride looked like a Tomato Festival Queen.
10. Not surprisingly, a recent study of driver stress shows that aggressive behaviour such as flashing high beams at other drivers, increases during high-congestion traffic.

> 3. Put a comma between independent clauses when they are joined by these transition words:
>
> | | | |
> |---|---|---|
> | and | nor | for |
> | or | but | yet |
> | so | | |

I like Céline Dion, but I prefer Sarah McLachlan.

We shape our tools, and our tools shape us. (Marshall McLuhan)

I knew I was going to be late, so I went back to sleep.

I hope I do well in the interview, for I really want this job.

Be sure that the sentence you are punctuating contains two independent clauses rather than one clause with a single subject and a multiple verb.

We <u>loved</u> the book but <u>hated</u> the movie. (<u>We</u> is the subject, and there are two verbs, <u>loved</u> and <u>hated</u>. Do not put a comma between two or more verbs that share a single subject.)

We both <u>loved</u> the book, but <u>Kim</u> <u>hated</u> the movie. (This sentence contains two independent clauses—<u>We</u> <u>loved</u> and <u>Kim</u> <u>hated</u>—joined by *but*. The comma is required here.)

EXERCISE 17.3

Insert commas where they are needed in the following sentences. Check your answers when you're done.

1. He and I are good friends, yet we often disagree.
2. We have a choice: we could try bribery, or we could resort to force.
3. We can't win this game, nor can we afford to lose it.
4. The car swerved wildly, and just missed the crossing guard.
5. Mona tried and tried to pass her driver's test, and her persistence finally paid off.
6. My wife and I would like to buy a house, but we don't have enough money for a down payment.
7. I'm bored and underpaid at work, so I'm going back to school next fall.
8. Ravi and Denis are travelling to Whitehorse this summer, and Sandy is going to St. John.
9. This is Bambi's last semester, so she's concentrating on school for a change.
10. Please pay close attention, for the instructions are a little complicated.

> 4. Put a comma after a word or group of words that comes before an independent clause.

Biff, you aren't paying attention.

No matter how hard I try, I will never be able to forget you.

Exhausted and cranky from staying up all night, I staggered into class.

If that's their idea of a large pizza, we'd better order two.

Until she got her promotion, she was quite friendly.

EXERCISE 17.4

Insert commas where they are needed in the following sentences. Check your answers when you have finished all ten.

1. In the end, quality is what counts.
2. Second, our department is required to cut costs by fifteen percent.
3. If there were any justice in this world, I'd have been rewarded for my performance.
4. Moved beyond words, the victorious candidate was able only to gesture his thanks to his supporters.
5. Carefully placing one foot in front of the other, she managed to walk along the white line for several metres.
6. Where a huge hardwood forest had once stood, only acres of tree stumps remained.
7. Finally, it is clear that we must make our decision today.
8. While Rudolf may be short on brain, he's long on brawn.
9. As her fortieth birthday approached, Drusilla met the challenge by trading in her sedan for a sports car and her husband for a boyfriend ten years her junior.
10. When the first robin heralds the return of spring, I begin to dream of lazy summer days lying beside the pool with a cool drink in my hand and a ball game on the radio.

The rest of the exercises in this chapter require you to apply all four comma rules. Before you begin, write out the four rules on a sheet of paper. Refer to them frequently as you punctuate the sentences that follow. After you've finished each exercise, check your answers and make sure you understand any mistakes you've made.

① Seperate items on a list.

② Word(s) that only add to the sentence but are not essential.

③ Before a transition word: but, yet, or, nor, for, so, and

④ After word(s) that comes before an idependant clause.

EXERCISE 17.5

1. Despite some excellent action sequences the movie was a failure because of the terrible script.
2. Your fall order which we received last week has been shipped.
3. These cold wet grey days are not good for the crops.
4. If starvation and lack of recognition made great artists Canada would be a land of Picassos.
5. What you hear what you read and what you experience all help to form your cultural background.
6. A few days after we sailed the boat sprang a leak.
7. Inside the band was playing at full blast.
8. The letter of application is one of the most important documents you will ever write yet you have spent only an hour composing it.
9. Despite some early problems Ottawa's National Gallery has become the home of one of the most interesting collections in North America.
10. Doing punctuation exercises is tedious work but is cleaner than tuning the car.

EXERCISE 17.6

1. There is something wrong with this proposal but I haven't yet figured out what it is.
2. Our hope of course is that the terrorists will be caught and punished.
3. George Washington the first president of the United States was an officer in the British army before he was engaged in the American Revolution.
4. Charlottetown Quebec and Kingston were the sites of the conferences that eventually led to Confederation in 1867.
5. If you can cope with overloaded logging trucks passing you at high speeds on narrow mountain roads you'll enjoy the spectacularly scenic drive from Hope to Princeton.
6. The Great Lakes form an inland passageway through which huge seagoing ships reach the heart of the North American continent. *Correct*
7. A good dictionary consulted frequently is probably the most important resource for any student who wishes to develop a mature vocabulary.
8. While I respect your opinion and your right to express it that doesn't mean that I necessarily agree with you.
9. After our guests had gone home we discovered that they had drunk all the beer but had left most of the food so we'd be dining on leftovers for the next two weeks.
10. If there were any point in protesting the president's decision I would have complained long ago but I don't think anything will change her disastrous course of action.

EXERCISE 17.7

1. My world includes: gorgeous men, fast cars, loud music, expensive clothes, and other dreams.

2. After carefully wrapping the watch in a handkerchief the magician produced a hammer and smashed the expensive timepiece to smithereens, or so it appeared.

3. The retirement of Bobby Orr from hockey was the end of an era for the game, but those who saw him play will never forget it.

4. A 25 m heated pool is available for those who like to swim, and for those who play golf, there is a beautiful eighteen-hole course.

5. Ever since, I have been a regular theatre-goer.

6. Antonio's grandmother was very short and extremely thin. *Correct.*

7. When you enter the store, go to the counter on your immediate left, ask for Ms. Seth and tell her you would like to see samples of the new shipment.

8. Flattery, the old saying goes, will get you nowhere, but this has not been my experience.

9. The head of our physics department Professor Vector, despite his vast theoretical knowledge of his subject, couldn't change a light bulb if his life depended on it.

10. Before he was asked to leave, Rudolf managed to offend the host, insult the hostess, and humiliate the guest of honour.

EXERCISE 17.8

One of the psychologists in our department, a mild-mannered man under most circumstances, burst into my office one day last spring and spent twenty minutes pouring out his frustration. It seemed that just as he was about to enter his classroom to teach a lesson on stress management he had been confronted by a student who asked whether he was going to do anything important in class that day. This is a question teachers are often asked and every teacher I know finds it infuriating. Most, however, are able to control themselves and respond politely. But our psychologist obviously had been asked this question once too often. He ranted, raved and roared despite my best efforts to reason with him, and calm him down. Finally, he ran out of steam and collapsed into a quivering blob. When I could see that he was more or less under control, I suggested he try some of the time-honoured defence mechanisms teachers have developed in response to students' insensitivity. For example, one response to The Question the one that happens to be my personal favourite, is to ask why today's class should be any different from any other class in the term. Some students take this as sarcasm but others assume that I'm giving them permission to skip. The beleaguered psychologist found my recommendation helpful, I think, because he was smiling as he left my office on his way to teach another class on stress management.

EXERCISE 17.9

Over the past couple of decades young people have adopted a number of strange novel and inexplicable fads. How can one explain the popularity among adolescents of "Docs" footwear which was originally designed by a Dr. Marten for therapeutic use? Why wear a baseball cap with the visor which is supposed to protect one's eyes from the sun facing backward? Why on earth given the initial pain and the continuing risk of infection would young people choose to pierce sensitive parts of their anatomy for the purpose of inserting rings and studs? These contemporary fashion statements however are no more peculiar than some of the fads of the 60s and 70s such as bouffant hairdos bell-bottomed pants or platform shoes which unfortunately seem to be making a comeback. All these design horrors make me shudder but my mother's experiment with permanent false eyelashes probably wins the prize for fashion idiocy. Long thick curled lashes were *de rigueur* for the chic 50s matron. While most of my mother's contemporaries were content to glue their false eyelashes to their lids each day my mother was not. A fashion slave from her four-inch spike heels to her beehive hairdo my mother decided to make her "eyelash enhancement" permanent. So off she went to her local beauty salon an establishment in which she spent hours each week and submitted to the torture of having individual hairs inserted one by one into her eyelids. Triumphant though in considerable pain she emerged with thick luxuriant black eyelashes that Elizabeth Taylor would die for. Unfortunately my mother's beauty transformation did not have a happy ending. A few weeks after her "enhancement" she gave a dinner party. Moments before her guests were to arrive she opened the oven to check on her roast and her eyelashes melted into black blobs bonding themselves to her eyelids. The salon had not thought to warn her that her "permanent" lashes were made of nylon and could not therefore be exposed to extreme heat. The surgery my mother had to endure to have her "permanent" lashes removed is another story.

EXERCISE 17.10

This paragraph contains many comma errors that are often found in student writing. Your task is to remove all unnecessary commas and insert commas where they belong, according to the four comma rules.

The Canadian appetite, for sports entertainment, seems insatiable. In the past, three sports dominated the year for the sports fan but now thanks to specialty television, some very unusual and exotic competitions are finding fans, in this country. Australian-rules football a game that belies its name by seeming to have no rules is gaining in popularity, though purely as a spectator sport. Triathlons, biathlons, marathons, mini-marathons, and a host of similar endurance events, are now avidly watched, by the armchair athlete and enthusiastically entered, by the physically fit. Sumo wrestling while not accessible to most of us as a participatory activity, seems to have a devoted following and even darts and lawn bowling, have their supporters. And then there is, golf. To some watching golf on television, is as exciting as watching paint dry, but during inclement weather when golf addicts can't be on the course themselves, they follow their heroes' every televised step and agonize with them, over every shot for hours. The challenge, for Canadian jocks of both sexes, and all ages is to tear themselves away from these various spectator entertainments in order, to play their favourite sports.

EXERCISE 17.11

Insert commas where they are needed in the following sentences. No answers are provided for this exercise.

1. As long as you're prepared relaxed and confident you'll find that an employment interview is not necessarily a terrifying prospect.
2. Some people believe it or not actually enjoy interviews.
3. Others on the other hand are absolutely terrified at the prospect of confronting an interviewer or even worse a whole group of interviewers.
4. The first thing you should do to prepare yourself for an interview is to find out as much information as you can about the company. *Correct*
5. Among the things you absolutely need to know are the title of the job you are applying for the name of the person or persons who will be conducting the interview the address of the company how long it will take you to get there and where the washrooms are.
6. Many employment consultants recommend that you visit the office of the firm to which you've applied to confirm how long it will take you to get there to check out the physical layout and to be sure you know where the interview room—and the washrooms—are located.
7. On your advance scouting trip you can also glean valuable information about the company's working conditions employee attitudes and even the dress code.
8. On the day of the interview be sure to show up ten or fifteen minutes in advance of your scheduled appointment. *Correct*
9. When the interviewer greets you be sure to identify yourself and extend your hand. Your handshake should be brief and firm not limply passive or bone-crushingly aggressive.

10. And finally as one who has conducted hundreds of applicant inter-
    views my advice to you is this: don't smoke even if you are invited to
    and say "No thank you" to an interviewer's offer of coffee or juice.
    There is nothing more embarrassing than dropping a lighted cigarette
    a hot cup of coffee or a bottle of grape juice into one's lap during the
    course of an interview.

CHAPTER 18

The
Semicolon

The colon and semicolon are often confused and used as if they were interchangeable. They serve very different functions, however, and their correct use can dramatically improve a reader's understanding of your writing. Here is one function of the semicolon:

> A semicolon can replace a period; in other words, it can appear between two independent clauses.

You should use the semicolon when the two clauses (sentences) you are joining are closely connected in meaning or when there is a cause-and-effect relationship between them.

I'm too tired; I can't stay awake any longer.

There's a good movie on tonight; it's a Canadian film called *Exotica*.

A period could have been used instead of the semicolon in either of these sentences, but the close connection between the clauses prompted the writer to use a semicolon.

Certain connecting or transition words are sometimes put between independent clauses to show a cause-effect relationship or the continuation of an idea. Words or phrases used in this way must be preceded by a semicolon and followed by a comma:

; also,	; furthermore,	; nevertheless,
; as a result,	; however,	; then,
; besides,	; in addition,	; therefore,
; consequently,	; in fact,	; thus,
; finally,	; instead,	
; for example,	; moreover,	

We had hiked for three hours; consequently, we were glad to rest.

There are only two of us; however, we're both pretty big.

The sun was very hot; therefore, we stopped for a drink and a swim.

In other words, *a semicolon + a transition word/phrase + a comma* = a link strong enough to come between two related independent clauses.

Note, however, that when the words and phrases listed in the box are used as *nonessential* expressions rather than as connecting words, they are separated from the rest of the sentence by commas (Comma Rule 2, p. 184).

However hard I try, I just can't seem to master particle physics.

Ten years from now, however, I'm sure I'll have no difficulty with the subject.

> To make a COMPLEX LIST easier to read and understand, put semicolons between the items instead of commas.

Here's an example:

> We need to pack several things: matches to start a fire; an axe or hatchet to cut wood; cooking utensils and eating implements; and, of course, food.

In exercises 18.1 and 18.2, put a check mark (√) next to the sentences that are correctly punctuated. Consult the answers on p. 356 before continuing.

EXERCISE 18.1

1. ___√___ He sat down in a convenient bar; he was very thirsty.

2. _____ He sat down near a refreshing stream, for he was very tired.

3. ✓ My cats get along fine with the dog; it's each other that they hate.

4. ✓ It's a beautiful day; just right for a long walk.

5. ✓ Six of the Indian nations joined together in a loose union, they were called Iroquois.

6. ✓ The lawn, a little ragged, needs to be cut; the hedge, shrubs, and ivy need to be trimmed; the flowers need to be watered, and, most important, the gardener needs to be paid.

7. ✓ I'd like to help; however, I'm supposed to rest all day.

8. ✓ We reached Canoe Lake in time to meet the others; in fact, we arrived a little ahead of schedule.

9. ✓ Halifax is my favourite city; someday I'm going to move there.

10. ✓ Winter is something only Canadians really understand; it has shaped this country more than the railways, the politicians, and even the founding peoples.

EXERCISE 18.2

1. ✓ It's far too expensive; besides, we really don't need one.

2. ____ There are only a few who could catch him; and I'm sure she isn't one of them.

3. ✓ Coffee prices are ridiculous, yet I still must have my morning cup or three.

4. ✓ Ninik wants to be an Olympic gymnast; consequently, she spends at least six hours a day in training.

5. ____ We'll have to go soon; for it's getting late.

6. ✓ The weather is bad; I have a cold; the electricity is out; and, to top it all off, my in-laws are coming for dinner.

7. ____ If ever there were a time to act; it is now.

8. ✓ Some people are skilled in many fields; Kumari, for example, is both a good plumber and a great cook.

9. _____ She disobeyed the rules; so, she will have to be punished.

10. _____ Krystal is always late, however, she's worth waiting for.

EXERCISE 18.3
Correct the faulty punctuation in exercise 18.1.

EXERCISE 18.4
Correct the faulty punctuation in exercise 18.2.

EXERCISE 18.5
Insert commas and semicolons where necessary in these sentences. Then check your answers carefully.

1. There seems to be no end to the work that must be done furthermore there isn't enough time in which to do it.
2. There must be a way or we're finished before we've even begun.
3. I can't afford a Porsche therefore I drive a Neon.
4. Jana is one of my favourite people she can always cheer me up.
5. There will be ample opportunity to finish your homework but right now I need your help.
6. The floor was knotty pine the furniture and walls were designed and finished to complement it.
7. Brock was killed early in the morning but the Americans were driven from Queenston Heights by nightfall.
8. Canada's history is not a very violent one however we've had several rebellions of note.
9. Jon has gone away to become a teacher Marta now has twin baby girls Kevin is unemployed Julie is a lawyer or stockbroker (I forget which) and Pavel is as usual drifting from job to job.
10. When the rain started they were trapped in the open nevertheless they stayed where they were until it let up and then made their way to the nearest shelter.

EXERCISE 18.6
Correct the punctuation in these sentences by changing commas to semicolons where necessary. Then check your answers carefully.

1. The entire town is in an uproar it seems Rudolf has been missing since Tuesday.
2. Of course, everyone knows Rudolf is a bit wacky he's been very strange since his close encounter of the fourth kind.

3. Rudolf's story is that a hamburger-shaped, chrome-coloured, smoke-belching UFO pinned him under its wheels; its inhabitants, he claims, kept him prisoner for several hours.
4. The creatures spoke to him through little slits; however, Rudolf says he got a good look at them.
5. According to him, the aliens looked like a cross between Arnold Schwarzenegger and Barney.
6. These creatures told Rudolf many secrets; for example, they told him they had searched the universe for a perfect specimen like him.
7. Rudolf considered this overture a friendly gesture; he immediately felt more kindly toward the aliens.
8. In fact, as Rudolf later confessed, he is under the aliens' control; perhaps this explains why he talks like Donald Duck.
9. But now people are beginning to worry; there's an unexplained burned spot in Rudolf's backyard, and he's been gone since Tuesday.
10. Is it possible, do you think, that aliens have whisked him away for a tour of the galaxy?

EXERCISE 18.7

Correct the punctuation in these sentences by inserting commas and semi-colons where necessary.

1. Alicia and Eddie are both very shy; therefore, they dread being called upon to speak in class.
2. We wondered what Ninik was scribbling so furiously; it turned out to be a letter to the dean.
3. I think you need to put the matter in perspective; therefore, I suggest you consider carefully what it is you want to accomplish.
4. Nancy wants to be helpful; in fact, she is always the first to volunteer.
5. Banish the thought of defeat from your mind; concentrate, instead, on victory.
6. If I could push defeat out of my mind, there would be only a vast emptiness left; victory is impossible when you play on this team.
7. Buying a house involves enormous responsibilities, not to mention enormous debt; consequently, I plan to live with my parents until I'm 40 or so.
8. For reasons I do not understand, my parents are not as enthusiastic about my plan as I am; in fact, they're downright hostile.
9. Turn left when you come to the fork in the road; otherwise you'll end up at the nuclear waste-disposal site and come out all aglow.
10. I'm sure you understand that I would like nothing better than for you to pass this course; however, there may be a small fee involved.

EXERCISE 18.8

Correct these sentences where necessary.

1. Please leave dinner in the oven for a little while I'll eat when I've finished this exercise.
2. Taking the corner at 90 kph, the police car swerved into the oncoming lane fortunately no one was coming.
3. The chair called the meeting to order however it quickly became apparent that none of us had done the background reading.
4. One of the products of the computer age is increased leisure this, in turn, has led to increased opportunities for physical fitness.
5. A glance at the calendar will reveal that there are only 212 shopping days left until my birthday that's just enough time for you to find the present I deserve.
6. Computers are marvellous tools they are fast efficient and accurate but they can't think. They remind me of a secretary I used to know she's now my boss.
7. The Four Horsemen of the Apocalypse are Conquest, Slaughter, Famine, and Death.
8. Some Biblical figures are familiar to people from many different cultures for example the stories of Samson, and Delilah, and of David, and Goliath are widely known.
9. We're unhappy about our instructor's evaluation procedures in fact we think they are irrational, arbitrary and often unfair.
10. Every year at tax time, I am faced with the same problem: assembling my bills and receipts figuring out my gas mileage trying to recall which expenses were business-related and which were personal finding my T4s T5s, and other T forms and organizing this mess so my accountant can attempt to keep me out of jail for another year.

EXERCISE 18.9

Correct these sentences as necessary.

1. I played squash, went jogging, and even tried weight-lifting this weekend; in addition I signed up for a six-month satisfaction-guaranteed fitness program.
2. I have mixed memories of my tour of Europe for example, while I think fondly of gorgeous little towns like Gordes and Orvieto, I think less fondly of Venice, where I was robbed.
3. As I was buying a gelato at a little stand across from our hotel a man slipped his hand into my purse grabbed my passport and was promptly seized by two plainclothes detectives who had been keeping an eye on him.
4. I was required to fill out a complaint which took hours since it had to be translated from English to Italian and back to English, consequently

the only view of Venice's famous canals that I got was from a police boat.

5. For my birthday last year, my husband gave me a dozen roses. This year he gave me a shovel; as a result I'm wondering if the romance has gone from our relationship.

6. For years, students complained that the English teachers couldn't calculate grades accurately, finally the Math Department offered to give a seminar to introduce the English Department to the mysteries of addition and subtraction.

7. Louis Riel led a Métis rebellion in Manitoba in 1885 but he was defeated, tried and executed the same year his death caused a deep rift between English and French Canada.

8. The Canadian political scene has become much less interesting since the departure of men like Pierre Trudeau and Brian Mulroney; whether you liked them or not, they both provoked a lot of public debate over political issues.

9. In preparation for the final exam, please bring your text and any notes you may have taken in class at least two pens, a scientific calculator lots of scrap paper on which to work out the problems and a drafting set.

10. Reading spy novels is I admit, a waste of time, but it beats sitting in front of the tube being bombarded with ads for products I don't need, learning intimate even embarrassing details about the lives of people I don't know, will never meet, and would never want to know and being subjected to the so-called humour that is characteristic of the average American sitcom.

EXERCISE 18.10

This exercise is designed to review your mastery of commas and to challenge your mastery of semicolons. Using commas and semicolons where they are appropriate, correct the following passage. No answers are provided for this exercise.

The original shaggy dog story, the tale that gave the long-winded joke its name began on a dark and stormy night. Many years ago a young knight had been left behind when his father and his older brothers rode off with their loyal men-at-arms retainers yeomen pages and serfs leaving Sir Feckless to guard the castle the womenfolk and children. The men were passionately keen to go off on their warlike adventure thus they took with them all the horses mules and donkeys to carry their tons of arms and supplies. No livestock were left for the use of the castle's abandoned inhabitants in fact they were left with nothing but a sheepdog. Poor Sir Feckless uninvited to participate in his father's warlike enterprise sunk into a terrible depression. Then just as he was thinking of hurling himself from the closest parapet a messenger rode up to the castle to sound the dreaded alarm: "The Goths are attacking!" Pausing long enough to tell his terrified audience that they had only a couple of days before the savage hordes descended, the messenger galloped off to warn the other castles in the neighbourhood.

What should they do, where should they go? The castle's inhabitants all turned to Sir Feckless, who pledged to ride after his father and bring him back to defend the castle. Unable to find a horse, donkey, or even a mule to carry him on his mission of mercy, Sir Feckless saddled up the huge shaggy sheepdog and galloped off into the storm. The tempest worsened as the night wore on. Finally, Sir Feckless knew he could go no further, he would have to rest before resuming his ride in the morning. Luckily, he spotted an inn just ahead and he and his steed staggered up to the door. Sir Feckless knocked and knocked; his faithful steed barked and barked. The innkeeper awakened by this uproar, stuck his head out of the window, and demanded to know what was going on. Sir Feckless pleaded to be let in, but the innkeeper refused to leave his warm bed. They argued for several minutes, meanwhile the storm grew even worse.

At last the innkeeper threw up his hands and said, "All right, all right! I wouldn't leave a knight out on a dog like this!" and, so the shaggy dog story was born.

CHAPTER 19

The Colon

The **colon** functions as an introducer. When a statement is followed by a list or by one or more examples, the colon between the statement and what follows alerts the reader to what is coming.

> We have two choices: to go or to stay.

> Try to imagine yourself like me: young, gorgeous, brilliant, and rich.

> One person is responsible for your happiness in life: you.

The statement that precedes the colon must be a complete sentence (independent clause). Therefore, a colon can never come immediately after *is* or *are*. Here's an example of what *not* to write.

> Three things I am violently allergic to are: cats, ragweed, and country music.

This is incorrect because the statement before the colon is not a complete sentence.

The colon, then, follows a complete statement and introduces a list or example(s) that defines or amplifies something in the statement. The information after the colon often answers the question "what?" or "who?"

> I am violently allergic to three things: (what?) cats, ragweed, and country music.

> Business and industry face a new challenge: (what?) the global marketplace.

> The evil queen gazed into the mirror to admire the reflection of the fairest woman of them all: (who?) herself.

And finally, the colon is used after a complete sentence introducing a quotation.

> Stephen Leacock did not think very highly of his readers' tastes in literature: "There are only two subjects that appeal nowadays to the general public: murder and sex; and, for people of culture, sex-murder."

The uses of the colon can be summed up as follows:

> The colon follows an independent clause and introduces one of three things: examples, a list, or a quotation.

EXERCISE 19.1

Put a check mark (√) next to the sentences that are correctly punctuated, then turn to p. 359 to check your answers.

1. ✓ Two of the most common causes of failure are laziness and lack of self-discipline.

2. ____ Only one thing was missing the boat.

3. ✓ He tried three different tactics: phone calls, flowers, and flattery.

4. ✓ On the list we must include: chips, mix, ice, and peanuts.

5. ✓ The instructor's first words were not encouraging: "Half of you are going to fail, and the other half won't get jobs."

6. ____ Three qualities of a good quarterback are: leadership, intelligence, and physical strength.

7. ✓ There are two things that every ambitious person strives for: money and power.

8. ____ The lake is: deep and cold.

9. ✓ Dogs have many qualities that make them superior to cats: loyalty, intelligence, working ability, and friendliness.

10. ✓ Let me give you an example, Louis Riel.

EXERCISE 19.2

Put a check mark (√) next to the sentences that are correctly punctuated.

1. _____ I'd like to help, but I can't.

2. _____ I'll take the following volunteers: Marie, Susan, Ngoc, and Lewis.

3. _____ We'll have to go back to get tent poles, matches, and paddles.

4. __√__ Two very good centres were Beliveau and Apps.

5. __√__ The debate will be lively if they choose a certain topic: religion.

6. _____ No one wants to go with him, for two very good reasons: money and time.

7. __√__ He's involved in all types of athletics: skiing, hiking, hockey, and football, to name a few.

8. _____ My boss is so mean she must be bitter or crazy.

9. __√__ She won more medals at the Games than we expected: two golds and a bronze.

10. __√__ They were unlucky twice: when they bought that car and when they sold it.

EXERCISE 19.3

Insert colons in the following sentences where necessary, and then check your answers. If you find you've made any mistakes, review the explanation, and be sure you understand why your answers were wrong.

1. You'll succeed only if you win the lottery or marry money.
2. They finally realized there was only one course open to them: obedience.
3. Gary had trouble with his canoe: it tipped and sank.
4. There is someone who can save us, though: Captain Canuck!
5. He tossed and turned all night and found the same images recurring in his dreams: a river and a wolf.
6. Her body was beyond the point of exhaustion, but she tried to force herself on by thinking of one thing: victory.
7. They tried to make ends meet by making their own candles, soap, and butter.
8. I have a large garden, but it grows only two things: weeds and worms.
9. Two issues remained to be settled: wages and benefits.
10. She has one goal that she is determined to achieve: the world record.

EXERCISE 19.4
Correct the incorrectly punctuated sentences in exercise 19.1.

EXERCISE 19.5
Correct the incorrectly punctuated sentences in exercise 19.2.

EXERCISE 19.6
As a test of your ability to use colons, correct the errors in the following sentences. No answers are given for this exercise.

1. There is only one thing worse than getting old; the alternative.
2. If I had unlimited amounts of money, the two things I would most like to do are: first, to sail around the world in a luxury yacht, and, second, to do it again.
3. According to my parents, I am: lazy, selfish, careless, and ignorant, but what do they know?
4. Since it's clear our essays will be late, we have three choices: to beg for an extension, claim our computer malfunctioned, or forge a doctor's note.
5. One of the most interesting essay titles I've encountered in the past twenty years was a paper called: "How to Suck Seed in Starting You're Own Buisness."
6. After watching a program on genealogy, I began to trace my own family's history; however, I soon discovered that my family tree is a shrub best left unexamined.
7. Having listened faithfully to the CDs you recommended, I can now say without hesitation that toxic thrash does nothing for me.
8. This course requires an enormous amount of work, but when we've finished, our rewards will be: a diploma, the chance of interesting employment, and a very valuable skill.
9. With astonishing speed, computers all over the globe are being linked into one network that will become the world's primary environment for communication, research, commerce, and entertainment: the Internet.
10. In 1995, fisheries minister Brian Tobin secured his place in Canadian history with an immortal comment: "We're down to one, lost, lonely, unloved, unattractive little turbot, clinging by its fingernails to the Grand Banks of Newfoundland."

CHAPTER 20

Quotation Marks

Quotation marks (" ") are used to set off direct speech or dialogue, short passages of quoted material, and some titles. They are a signal to the reader that the words in quotes are not your words, but someone else's. Quotation marks come in pairs; there must be a set to show where the dialogue, quotation, or title begins and a set to show where it ends. You must be absolutely sure that whatever you put between them is stated *exactly* as it is in the source you are using. The only other thing you need to know about quotation marks is how to punctuate what comes between them.

Dialogue

When you quote direct speech, include normal sentence punctuation. If the speaker's name or a comment about the speaker is included in your own sentence, set it off with commas. A comma or the end punctuation mark comes *inside* the final set of quotation marks.

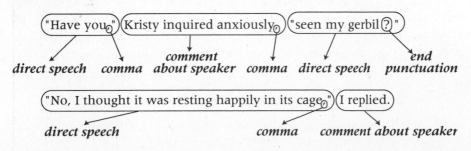

Be careful to put quotation marks only around direct speech (someone's exact words). Don't use quotation marks with indirect speech (a paraphrase of someone's words).

> Kristy inquired anxiously whether I had seen her gerbil. (These are not Kristy's exact words, nor is the sentence a question.)

A quotation *within* a quotation is punctuated by single quotation marks:

> "Diana," whined Charles, "I really do think it unkind of you to call poor Camilla 'The Rottweiler.'"

Quoted Material

When you quote a ***short*** passage (three lines of print or less), you can work it into your own sentence. Use a comma to introduce a quotation of one or more sentences, and include normal sentence punctuation within the quotation marks.

> According to Margaret Atwood, "If you like men, you can like Americans. Cautiously. Selectively. Beginning with the feet. One at a time."
>
> "As you grow old," wrote Richard Needham, "you lose your interest in sex, your friends drift away, your children ignore you. There are other advantages, of course, but these would seem to me the outstanding ones."
>
> "My idea of long-range planning is lunch," confesses Frank Ogden, Canada's foremost futurist.

If your own introductory words form a complete sentence, use a colon to introduce the quotation:

> Frank Ogden, Canada's foremost futurist, confesses that he has little respect for traditional business planning cycles: "My idea of long-range planning is lunch."

If the passage you are quoting is a couple of words, a phrase, or anything less than a complete sentence, do not use a comma or a colon to introduce it.

> Woody Allen's one regret in life is that he is "not someone else."
>
> Neil Bissoondath argues that racism is based on "willful ignorance and an acceptance of—and comfort with—stereotype."

All the lines of a ***long*** quoted passage (more than three lines of print) should be indented ten spaces from the left margin. Long quotations are not enclosed in quotation marks. The block indentation indicates to the reader that the words set off in this way are not yours, but some other writer's. (Turn to Chapter 25 to find examples of the treatment of long quotations.)

College writing normally requires that you indicate the source of any material you quote. The easiest way to do this is to give the author's surname, if it's not already included in your sentence, and the page reference in parentheses at the end of the quote.

For example,

> In the 18th century, a lifelong bachelor observed, "Marriage has many pains, but celibacy has no pleasures" (Johnson 214).

> According to Dr. Samuel Johnson, "Marriage has many pains, but celibacy has no pleasures" (214).

These source identifications are called parenthetical citations.

Some instructors prefer footnotes or endnotes to parenthetical citations. Find out what format your instructor requires and follow it. In any library or bookstore, you will find a variety of style guides and handbooks that explain different styles of documentation. Your instructor will be happy to recommend one.

Titles

Unless you are using a word processor that prints *italics*, titles of books or other entire works should be <u>underlined</u>. Titles of parts of those books or works should be put in quotation marks. Thus, titles of books, magazines, pamphlets, newspapers, plays, films, and albums should be italicized or underlined. Titles of single articles, essays, stories, poems, or songs should be placed in quotation marks.

On page 208 you will find an example of a bibliography (a list of works consulted or cited in a research paper) showing how titles of different kinds of publications are punctuated.

essay in an anthology	Atwood, Margaret. "Canadians: What Do They Want?" <u>The Act of Writing</u>. Ed. Ronald Conrad. 3rd ed. Toronto: McGraw-Hill, 1993. 302–305.
speech reprinted in a book	Brown, Rosemary. "Overcoming Sexism and Racism— How? <u>Racism in Canada</u>. Ed. Ormond McKague. Saskatoon: Fifth House, 1991. 163–177.
song lyric reprinted in an anthology	Cohen, Leonard. "Suzanne Takes You Down." <u>An Anthology of Canadian Literature in English</u>. Eds. Donna Bennett and Russell Brown. 2 vols. Toronto: Oxford, 1983. 2:350.
book review in a periodical	Conway, J. F. "The Good, The Bad, The Ugly." <u>The Literary Review of Canada</u> April 1995:17–19.
article in a newspaper	Delacourt, Susan. "Losing Interest." <u>The Globe and Mail</u> 1 April 1995: D1.
encyclopedia entry	"Flag Debate." <u>The Canadian Encyclopedia</u>. 2nd ed. Edmonton: Hurtig, 1988. 2:789.
novel	Findley, Timothy. <u>Headhunter</u>. Toronto: HarperCollins, 1993.
article in a magazine	McMurdy, Deirdre. "Drugstore Cowboy." <u>Maclean's</u> 2 Dec.1991: 74.
chapter in a book	Norton, Sarah, and Brian Green. "Cracking the Sentence Code." <u>The Bare Essentials, Form A</u>. 4th ed. Toronto: Harcourt, 1996. 43–66.

In the following exercises, place quotation marks where they are needed and insert any necessary punctuation before and after each quote. The answers for this chapter begin on p. 360.

EXERCISE 20.1

1. Three thousand is a bargain for that coat said Drusilla, eyeing the floor-length mink.
2. Simone inquired whether Canadian trains were always late.
3. Put that gun down, shouted the officer or I'll shoot!
4. The time has come the Walrus said, to talk of many things.

5. Canada's national anthem, O Canada, was written by Calixa Lavallée.
6. My father likes to remind me of John F. Kennedy's words: Too often we enjoy the comfort of opinion without the discomfort of thought.
7. In his novel, Generation X, Douglas Coupland warns, Less is a possibility.
8. Two singles from Sheryl Crow's first album, Tuesday Night Music Club, became hits All I Wanna Do and Strong Enough.
9. The Guinness Book of Records claims that the world's most-married man is former Baptist minister Scotty Wolfe, who got married 27 times.
10. When asked how many children were born of these marriages, Mr. Wolfe replied I think I had 41.

EXERCISE 20.2

1. Roman said that he'd like to meet you.
2. After his best player suffered another injury, the coach pleaded with him Please, Marcel, wear a face mask!
3. Our professor asked who had announced that today's class was cancelled.
4. Brian inquired, When are we going to eat?
5. When you cook dinner Val replied.
6. Marshall McLuhan's insight, The medium is the message appears in his most famous book, Understanding Media.
7. The headline in today's Winnipeg Free Press is Canada's dollar sinks to new low.
8. We've decided to rent a video this evening, but we can't decide between The Lion King and Priscilla, Queen of the Desert.
9. This is the second time you've been thrown out of class, the dean told Biff. I'm inclined to suspend you for a week.
10. Say you love me he pleaded. OK, she replied, You love me.

EXERCISE 20.3

1. Rust Hills wrote a very funny essay with a very boring title, How to Wash and Wax Your Car, which appears in his recent book, How to Do Things Right.
2. Pierre Elliott Trudeau made many memorable statements during his years in office, but he is probably best known for two The state has no business in the nation's bedrooms, and Fuddle-duddle.
3. Television is a vast wasteland complained Newton Minnow and is largely responsible for the fact that people today can't read.
4. For tomorrow's class, we are supposed to read the chapter called Hunger March to Edmonton in Myrna Kostash's book, All of Baba's Children.

5. According to Robertson Davies The world is burdened with young fogeys.

6. I suggest that the victim then tried to defend himself with this feather, cried the prosecuting attorney dramatically.

7. There was an uproar in the courtroom. How could he defend himself with a feather? was the question on everyone's lips.

8. Well, suggested the prosecutor, since he couldn't reach the banana in time, the feather was the best he could do.

9. At this, the defendant leaped to his feet and admitted that he was, indeed, guilty. How did you know about the banana? he muttered as he was led away.

10. Elementary, my dear Winston laughed the prosecutor, misquoting the great Sherlock Holmes.

EXERCISE 20.4

1. Lights! Camera! Action! These three words, so often used by Hollywood directors, have entered the language as a synonym for an exciting beginning.

2. Quietly and deliberately, A.J. turned to his tormentor and spoke. I don't want to play this game anymore.

3. If I had to choose one song from The Tragically Hip's Fully Completely, I'd pick Hundredth Meridian.

4. One of my favourite Canadian actors is Saul Rubinek who, after a shaky beginning in The Littlest Hobo, moved on to guest spots on The Equalizer and then to major roles in mega-hits such as Unforgiven, True Romance, and Wall Street.

5. City employees recently received guidelines for dealing with phoned-in bomb threats. Be calm, the instructions advise the lucky call-taker. Be courteous, listen carefully, and do not interrupt.

6. In addition, staffers are encouraged to ask potential bombers their name, address, and telephone number.

7. We are all immigrants to this place, wrote Margaret Atwood, even if we were born here.

8. In his poem, Keine Lazarovitch, Irving Layton sums up the experience of aging as the inescapable lousiness of growing old.

9. Political correctness has moved abroad: the headmistress of an English secondary school refused to allow her students to attend a performance of Romeo and Juliet because, she said, The play is blatantly heterosexual.

10. In another part of England, Beatrix Potter's children's classics Benjamin Bunny and The Tale of Peter Rabbit were banned from use in public schools. These stories, explained the Curriculum Council, portray only middle-class rabbits.

EXERCISE 20.5

Now test your understanding of quotation marks and the punctuation that goes with them. There are no answers provided for this exercise.

1. In the movie Forrest Gump, Mrs. Gump has a few words of wisdom for her son Life is like a box of chocolates. You never know what you're going to get.
2. At a go-kart track near Courtenay, B. C., a large sign warns drivers No Wreckless Driving Allowed.
3. Now I understand, said Minnie, as she strapped on her safety helmet, why the track is next to the hospital.
4. Foster Hewitt's words have echoed down through the years as the ultimate expression of hockey achievement He shoots! He scores!
5. Krystal isn't a big winter sports fan, but she says that there is one activity she really enjoys: aprés-ski.
6. After his first date with Rudolf's sister, Gordon swore Never again!
7. Our production of King Lear will be set in contemporary London, and the references will be updated to the 1990s our director told us in the first production meeting.
8. Frank magazine, the viciously satiric publication from Ottawa, refers to our prime minister as Jean Crouton.
9. Movie critic Dennis Dermody's article Sit Down and Shut Up or Don't Sit by Me will be reprinted in his forthcoming collection of essays on contemporary films entitled How to Cook and Eat Macauley Culkin.
10. In Pure Punnishment, her article on wordplay, Professor Banerjee recounts the following example of a pun. A husband forgot to buy his wife her favourite flowers, anemones, for her birthday, and the florist had only some ferns left. When the husband presented the ferns, his wife remarked With fronds like these, who needs anemones?

CHAPTER 21

Question Marks, Exclamation Marks, and Punctuation Review

The Question Mark

Everyone knows that a **question mark** follows an interrogative, or asking, sentence, but we all sometimes forget to include it. Let this chapter serve as a reminder not to forget!

> Put a question mark at the end of every interrogative sentence.

The question mark gives your readers an important clue to the meaning of your sentence. "There's more?" means something quite different from

212

"There's more!", and both are different from "There's more." When you speak, your tone of voice conveys the meaning you intend; when you write, your punctuation tells your reader what you mean.

The only time you don't end a question with a question mark is when the question is part of a statement.

QUESTION	STATEMENT
Are you going?	I asked whether you were going.
Do you know them?	I wonder if you know them.
Is there enough evidence to convict him?	The jury deliberated whether there was enough evidence to convict him.

Supply the correct end punctuation for these sentences, then check your answers on p. 362.

EXERCISE 21.1

1. What more could I possibly do to help
2. Val asked Biff whether he was absolutely positive he had paid the bill
3. Why is there always a cop around when I'm speeding but never when I need help
4. Have you checked the weather forecast to see when the weather is expected to clear
5. I will always wonder whether Rhonda handed in my essay
6. Is it true that voters will act rationally only when all other possibilities have been exhausted
7. Did the committee consider all the options carefully before making this decision
8. I don't understand why sociology is so important in a business program
9. Eugene is still asking the math teacher to raise his mark to at least a pass
10. The question isn't whether there is intelligent life on Mars, it's whether there's intelligent life on earth

EXERCISE 21.2

1. I'm not sure whether there is a game tonight or not
2. Is there life after long days of boring classes, followed by long nights of homework
3. If we can't complete the project on time, will we be penalized
4. Our question was what to do after the boss had burst into tears and gone home

5. What good will it do if I continue to be pleasant to people who take such delight in making me look foolish

6. How can anyone just stand by while some innocent person is being attacked

7. Whoever would have thought that the Canadian dollar would fall below the U.S. seventy-cents mark

8. I am surprised and hurt that you would question my motives in asking you for help with my studying

9. Please take a look at these tests and tell me whether you think these two students were cheating

10. Why can't the sports fans who yell so loudly at players' mistakes try to put themselves in the same position as those they criticize and be a little more forgiving

The Exclamation Mark

Consider the difference in tone between these two sentences:

There's a man behind you.
There's a man behind you!

In the first sentence, information is being supplied, perhaps about the line of people waiting their turn at a grocery-store checkout counter. The second sentence might be a shouted warning about a mugger.

Use an **exclamation mark** as end punctuation in sentences requiring extreme emphasis or dramatic effect.

Note that the exclamation mark will have "punch" or dramatic effect only if you use it sparingly. If you use an exclamation mark after every other sentence, how will your readers know when you really mean to indicate excitement? Overuse of exclamation marks is a technique used in comic books. The writers of comics use an exclamation mark after practically every sentence to try to heighten the impact of their characters' words. Instead, they rob their exclamation marks of all meaning.

   Practically any sentence could have an exclamation mark after it, but remember that the punctuation changes the meaning of the sentence. Read the following sentences with and without an exclamation mark, and picture the situation that would call for each reading.

They've moved   Don't touch that button
The carriage was empty   Listen to that noise

EXERCISE 21.3

Supply appropriate end punctuation in these sentences.

1. Take that, you monster
2. Ready, aim, fire
3. I can't believe it, We've got the winning number
4. That's the last straw, I quit
5. There's a fly in my soup
6. Run It's right behind you
7. "Slide " The whole team was screaming in unison
8. I can't believe it The thing actually flies
9. Turn the heat up. I'm freezing
10. The girls descended on the mall waving their plastic and crying, "Charge "

EXERCISE 21.4

Correct the end punctuation in the following sentences.

1. The question was whether we would spend the night in Abbotsford or push on to Vancouver?
2. Just think!! We have two glorious weeks free of English class!!!
3. Bruce thought he looked absolutely irresistible (?) in his new leather pants.
4. If you think you're confused, just imagine how I must feel?
5. If I ever hear him tell that joke again, I swear I'll hit him.
6. Katy asked Ramon if he'd like to stay over?
7. My Ph.D. didn't impress my co-workers at the doughnut shop.
8. Today we read a poem by Irving Layton, who was born in Rumania, I think?
9. After seeing your test results, I wonder if you even bought the text, let alone read it?
10. Congratulations. You've just mastered end punctuation marks.

EXERCISE 21.5

Supply the appropriate end punctuation and capitalization for the following passage. In many cases, the punctuation marks you choose will depend on how you want the sentence to be read. When you've completed the exercise, compare your answers with ours on p. 363.

When Ricky Henderson, the lead-off hitter, came to the plate, I was ready. my first pitch, a slow curve, caught the outside corner "Strike one!" howled the umpire, why was I pitching to Ricky what was an English teacher doing on the mound in the Baseball All-Star game who was that rag-tag collection of players surrounding me the answers make one of the strangest chapters in baseball history undefeated in our recreational league, we had challenged the semi-pro team in our community, defeated it, and gone on to beat three other professional teams from nearby cities then *Sports Illustrated* printed a story about our exploits it was inevitable that major league teams would want to take advantage of the publicity we were getting, so they invited us to play at the All-Star break before the regular National League versus American League game they even paid our transportation to New York

I struck out Henderson with my slider, took care of Ruben Sierra on three pitches, and got Ken Griffey, Jr. with an overpowering fast ball hey this was easy the second and third innings were repeats of the first all nine batters struck out my teammates were getting restless, so in the fourth and fifth, I allowed a couple of easy ground balls and gave the outfielders their turn with a couple of easy fly balls in the sixth then I went back to work and struck out the side in the seventh, eighth, and ninth meanwhile, I had driven in the only run with a hard-hit double down the first-base line the crowd went berserk "Sar-ah " they chanted over and over after the game the Yankees, Dodgers, Blue Jays, and Marlins began a bidding war for my services as a free agent, but when they reached twelve million for a single season, I smiled and said, "Thanks, but grammar is my game."

EXERCISE 21.6

Supply appropriate end punctuation for the sentences in the following paragraph. No answers are given for this exercise.

I wonder why it is that I cannot dance My girlfriend would go out dancing every night of the week if she didn't have morning classes And can she ever dance When she is really into the music, I've seen her receive applause from an entire club as she leaves the dance floor They applaud me, too, but it's because they're glad to see me sit down Why is it that every part of my body moves to a different rhythm When my hips find the beat, my feet are a half a beat behind, and my shoulders move around on their own as if I had some horrible nervous disorder If I kept it up for very long, I suspect my body would tear itself apart Is it because I'm tall, and nerve impulses have to travel a long way to get from one part of my frame to another I've been told that, when dancing, I look like a stork with an uncontrollable itch in a vital part of its anatomy Talk about embarrassing "What can I do " I ask myself. Should I subject myself to weeks of torture and take dancing lessons when I suspect they wouldn't help in the least Is there no medical cure for my condition I must have been born without a rhythm gene I wonder whether it's too late to get a transplant

Punctuation Review

The next five exercises will test your mastery of all punctuation studied in Unit 4. Go through them carefully and check your answers to each set before going on to the next. If you make a mistake, go back to the chapter dealing with that piece of punctuation and review the explanation and examples.

EXERCISE 21.7

1. Enjoy the view we called out as they left for the mountaintop, we had wisely decided to wait for them in a meadow halfway up.
2. To be a millionaire by the time you are thirty, you will have to: take large risks, be lucky, and have creative ideas.
3. High School was indeed the best time of my life because I met the friends there that I would continue to see for many years and I learned the principles that were to guide me through later more difficult years.
4. The question of whether evolution is a fact or a myth doesn't worry most of the people in my class, they're more concerned about whether there's a dance on Friday night.
5. Why won't he listen Marsha whispered tearfully.
6. With the crowd chanting Out Out the referee had a hard time justifying his decision: a ten-minute misconduct.
7. Typing as though his life depended on the completion of the assignment, Ted managed to get through the first chapter before supper, this left him with Chapter Two The Next Day to complete before bedtime.
8. The rain looked as though it would never let up so Gary and the two girls packed up to go home their vacation plans ruined.
9. Don't go, Angela fell to her knees and begged her friend to stay. Why must you leave now she asked just when we're about to succeed.
10. You'll find he has just one fault my friend, he snores.

EXERCISE 21.8

1. Jump. It's the only way out she cried.
2. Since there is so much time left why don't you go for a swim or have a sauna.
3. If you keep this behaviour up, you'll certainly go a long way, all the way to jail.
4. Within minutes of the blast pushing past the horrified onlookers the police officers entered the building and encountered: chaos.
5. The Montreal Expos like the Toronto Blue Jays before them are winning friends among baseball fans in the United States.
6. Don't go near the water warned the twins' mother however they were far too busy playing with the alligators to hear her.

7. My computer is a big improvement on the old typewriter I used to use, it still makes the same number of spelling errors though.

8. You'll never make it Stella we've got the whole building surrounded the detective yelled through his bullhorn, you might as well come out with your hands up.

9. Her lips curling into a sneer she replied you'll have to come in and get me copper.

10. The director his patience at an end screamed Cut that scene is too long too boring and too bad. We'll have to take it again.

EXERCISE 21.9

For having saved the leprechaun's life Devin was granted three wishes, the first he squandered on a mere one hundred dollars because he didn't believe the little man when he told Devin that his wishes would come true. After more careful consideration Devin wished again.

I want a bank account in a Swiss bank he shouted and enough money so that I will never run out.

The leprechaun frowned and looked very disappointed in Devin's wish but he screwed up his face went very red for a minute and then announced It's done but under his breath he muttered Greedy young cub he needs a lesson.

Devin was all ready with his next wish it was his greatest desire. He stared sternly at the leprechaun and in a loud voice said My last wish is the most important I want to live for one thousand years.

The tiny old man grinned then he screwed up his face and went very, very red for a minute. Finally he relaxed sighed a deep satisfied sigh and very pleased with himself walked twice around the young redwood tree that had just sprouted in front of him.

EXERCISE 21.10

All too often it seems that the Canadian national pastime is complaining about the weather! Our summers are criticized because they're too hot while our springs are too wet our autumns too cool and our winters too long. If the climate is so bad here why does anyone live north of the U.S. border. Perhaps the problem is not that Canadians don't like living in Canada but that they love to complain.

Two of the most popular sports teams in Canada were at one time those with the worst records; the Argonauts and the Maple Leafs. Could this popularity be due to the ample opportunity and scope they gave to their fans for complaint. Not only do we bemoan the record of such teams when they lose but when they win we dwell with glee on the possibilities of disaster for next year.

The same syndrome can be seen in our attitude toward Canadian heroes, it has often been said that we are a nation without heroes but I suspect that we have plenty of candidates: it's just that we enjoy complaining so much we try to find fault wherever we can and prefer to focus on clay feet rather than great works. One cannot help but wonder how Canadians fare in heaven where everything is perfect. I suspect they must be desperately unhappy?

EXERCISE 21.11

This is the last test of your punctuation skills. Supply any missing punctuation and correct any punctuation errors in the following sentences. No answers are provided for this exercise.

1. The early bird gets the worm as the old saying goes and I have always used this proverb as encouragement to get up as late as I can often holding out until after 11 A.M.
2. That my friend is the way of the world birth life death.
3. A warm bath and a cold drink are second to only one thing in my opinion, barbecued steak well done and covered in mushrooms onions steak sauce and garlic.
4. It was Charlotte Whitton former mayor of Ottawa who first said To succeed a woman must be twice as good as a man, fortunately that isn't difficult.
5. The Telefest Award ceremony is held each year to honour excellence in student productions of television film and radio, last year the winner in the best long drama category was a film called: The Absolution.
6. Running Krystal said is bad for the knees weight-lifting puts strain on the back. I'd rather die in my bed with all my parts working than wear out my body bit by bit wouldn't you.
7. It's time to pack up the homework shut down the computer make some popcorn pull up the old easy chair and park myself in front of the TV set, the world series is on.
8. The professor cleared his throat to get the class's attention then told them "to read the chapter entitled The Principle of Space Flight in their textbook The Wonders of the Twentieth Century."
9. When I told him on first meeting him that he sure was tall he replied You certainly have a firm grasp of the obvious. But in spite of that bad beginning we gradually became friends!
10. This Wednesday I have English French and math but I'll gladly skip them if you'll take me to see Night of the Ghouls and Plan Nine from Outer Space two films by the famously bad moviemaker Ed Wood that are playing at our local theatre.

EXERCISE 21.12

Write a paper of approximately two pages explaining how to do or make something or how to get somewhere. When you've finished, review your paper carefully, checking spelling, sentence structure, and grammar. Pay particular attention to punctuation. Be sure you have put a question mark at the end of every interrogative sentence and used exclamation marks only when necessary, for emphasis. Here are some topics you might explore:

1. how to shave (your chin, head, etc.)
2. how to choose a good bar (tattooist, hair stylist, professor, spiritual adviser, etc.)
3. how to dance (play golf, tend bar, care for impossible children, etc.)
4. how to survive winter (unemployment, a family reunion, etc.)
5. how to educate parents (a lover, a teacher, a younger brother or sister, etc.)
6. how to win (or lose) an argument
7. how to prepare for a job interview (a parental interrogation, an interview with the dean, etc.)
8. how to cure a cold (the blues, insomnia, an addiction, etc.)
9. how to choose a lover (college, career, apartment, roommate, etc.)
10. how to raise a family while going to school

Organizing Your Writing

CHAPTER 22

Finding Something to Write About

Everybody knows that content is important in writing. Not so many writers seem to know that form is just as important. In fact, you can't really separate the two: *what you say is how you say it*. Writing a paper (or an essay, or a report, or a letter, or anything else) is like doing a chemistry experiment: you need the right amount of the right ingredients, put together in the right proportions and in the right order. There are five steps to follow:

1. Choose a satisfactory subject
2. Select the main points of your subject
3. Write a thesis statement *or*
   Write an outline
4. Write the paragraphs
5. Revise the paper

If you follow these steps faithfully, in order, we guarantee that you will write clear, organized papers.

Note that when you get to step 3, you have a choice. You can choose to organize your paper by means of a thesis statement or by means of an outline. The thesis-statement approach works well for short papers—those no longer than about 500 words. An outline is necessary for longer papers and is often useful for organizing shorter papers. Ideally, you should learn to use both methods of organizing your writing; in fact, your teacher may require that you do so.

Steps 1, 2, and 3 make up the planning stage of the writing process. Be warned: done properly, these three steps will take you at least as long as steps 4 and 5, which involve the actual writing. The longer you spend on the preliminary steps, the less time your writing will take, and the better your paper will be.

Step 1: Choose a Satisfactory Subject

Unless you are assigned a specific subject by a teacher or supervisor, choosing your subject can be the most difficult part of writing a paper. Apply the following guidelines carefully, because no amount of instruction can help you write a good paper on something you don't know anything about or on something that is inappropriate for your audience or purpose. Your subject should satisfy the **4-S test:**

A satisfactory subject is SIGNIFICANT, SINGLE, SPECIFIC, and SUPPORTABLE.

---

1. Your subject should be **significant.** Write about something that your reader needs to know or might want to know. Consider your audience and choose a subject that will be significant to that audience. This doesn't mean that you can't ever be humorous, but, unless you're another Stephen Leacock, an essay on "How I Deposit Money in My Bank" will probably be of little significance to your reader. The subject you choose must be worthy of the time and attention you expect your reader to give to your paper.

2. Your subject should be **single.** Don't try to do too much in your paper. A thorough discussion of one topic is much more satisfying to read than a skimpy, superficial treatment of several topics. A subject like "The Problems of League Expansion in Hockey and Other Sports" includes too much to deal with satisfactorily in one paper. Limit yourself to a single topic, such as "The Problems of League Expansion in the NHL."

3. Your subject should be **specific.** This requirement is closely tied to the "single" requirement. Given a choice between a broad, general topic and a narrow, specific one, you should choose the latter. In a short paper, you can't hope to say anything new or significant about a very large topic: "Employment Opportunities in Canada," for example. But you could write an interesting, detailed discussion on a more specific topic, such as

"Employment Opportunities in Nova Scotia's Hospitality Industry." You can narrow a broad subject by applying one or more **limiting factors** to it. Try thinking of your subject in terms of a specific *kind*, or *time*, or *place*, or *number*, or *person* associated with it. To come up with the hospitality topic, for example, we limited the subject of employment opportunities in Canada in terms of both place and kind.

4. Your subject must be **supportable.** You must know something about the subject (preferably, more than your reader does), or you must be able to find out about it. Your discussion of your subject will be clear and convincing only if you can include examples, facts, quotations, descriptions, anecdotes, and other details. Supporting evidence can be taken from your own experience or from the experience of other people. In other words, your topic may require you to do some research.

EXERCISE 22.1

Test the following subjects against the guidelines we've given. Can you tell what's wrong with them? Check your answers on p. 365.

1. Employment equity
2. The theory of evolution
3. The five senses
4. Caring for your cuticles
5. Career possibilities in accounting and management
6. Television is both good and bad
7. Child care 50 years from now
8. My cat Fluffy
9. Democracy is good
10. The dangers of skin diving and sky diving

EXERCISE 22.2

Consider the following subjects in terms of the 4-S guidelines. Some are possibilities for satisfactory papers. Others are hopeless. Make good subjects out of all of them by revising to make them significant, single, specific, and supportable.

1. Air is necessary to life
2. Some people are intelligent
3. The censorship of books and movies
4. The economy in other countries
5. Famous Canadian women
6. How to use a pencil sharpener
7. Predicting the future
8. Today's teenagers have a hard time
9. Taking out the garbage
10. The disabled

EXERCISE 22.3

List five subjects that you might choose to write about. Be sure each subject is *significant, single, specific,* and *supportable.*

Step 2: Selecting the Main Points of Your Subject

Now that you have an appropriate subject for your paper, give some thought to the approach you're going to take to develop it. There are many possible ways of thinking and writing about a subject. In a short paper, you can deal effectively with only a few aspects of your topic. How do you decide which aspects of your subject to discuss, what **main points** to make and explain? One way is to make a list of everything you can think of that you might want to say about the subject. Some preliminary research may help, too. You may discover some points about the subject that you hadn't thought of.

Another way—especially useful if you find you're stuck for ideas—is to ask yourself questions about your subject. Run your subject through this list of questions and see which one "fits" it best. (The symbol S stands for your subject.)

---

1. How is S made or done? (What are the main steps to follow in accomplishing S?)
2. How does S work?
3. What are the main parts or components of S?
4. What are the main functions of S?
5. What are the important features or characteristics of S?
6. What are the main kinds or types of S?
7. What are some significant examples of S?
8. What are the causes of S?
9. What are the effects or consequences of S?
10. What are the main similarities and/or differences between S and _____ ?
11. What are the main advantages (or disadvantages) of S?
12. What are the reasons for (or against) S?

These questions suggest some of the various ways of looking at or thinking about a subject. Most subjects will yield answers to more than one of these questions. Focus on the question that produces the answers that are closest to what you want to say about your subject. The answers to that question are the main points you will discuss in your paper.

Here's how the procedure works. Assume you've been forced to accept as your subject "Writing Good Business Letters." Don't despair. Run down the list of questions until you find the one you can answer best. The process might go something like this:

1. ***How is a business letter written?***

   No answer comes to mind. Scratch that question.

2. ***How does a business letter work?***

   Silly question; it doesn't make sense.

3. ***What are the main parts of a business letter?***

   Well, there are the inside address, the body, the salutation, and the complimentary close, but you don't know enough about these to write anything intelligent or original on them.

4. ***What are the main functions of the business letter?***

   You can think of three: to request information, to place an order, and to complain about some product or service. This has possibilities, but you're not wildly enthusiastic about these aspects of your subject, so you go on.

5. ***What are the important characteristics of a good business letter?***

   At last! Here's one you can answer satisfactorily. You know that a business letter should be clear, brief and to the point, and courteous. Assuming that you know or can find out some pertinent and interesting information about these characteristics, you're all set. *Clarity, conciseness,* and *courtesy* are the points you will discuss in your paper. (Before you go any further, though, it's a good idea to apply the remaining questions in the box to your subject, just to be sure there isn't another question that yields answers you like even better.)

Selecting the main points to write about isn't a difficult process, but it is time-consuming. Don't rush. Take the necessary time. This is a crucial stage in the writing process.

Here are a few sample subjects, together with some main points that were discovered by applying the list of questions in the box on p. 226. Study the chart below until you're sure you understand how to find suitable main points for any subject.

SUBJECT	SELECTED QUESTION	MAIN POINTS
A good teacher	5. What are the important characteristics of a good teacher?	• knowledge of one's field • ability to communicate this knowledge • respect for one's students

SUBJECT	SELECTED QUESTION	MAIN POINTS
Running for fitness	12. What are the reasons for people's interest in running?	• improvement of one's physical condition • improvement of one's mental condition • low-cost approach to fitness
Common-law relationships	11. What are the main disadvantages of common-law relationships?	• possible lack of commitment between partners • possible legal problems, should separation occur • possible lack of security for children born into such an arrangement
Mental retardation	8. What are the causes of mental retardation?	• genetic defects • brain damage • early environmental deprivation
A successful party	1. How do you hold a successful party?	• by inviting the right mix of people • by planning the entertainment carefully • by preparing the food ahead of time • by providing a relaxed, friendly atmosphere
The accounting profession	6. What are the main kinds of accountants?	• Chartered Accountant • Registered Industrial Accountant • Certified General Accountant

As a general rule, you should try to identify between *two* and *five* main ideas for your subject. If you have only one main idea, you have a subject suitable for a paragraph, not an essay. If you have more than five, you have too much material for a short paper. Select the most important aspects of the subject, or take another look at it to see how you can focus it more specifically.

EXERCISE 22.4

In this exercise, select a question from the box on p. 226 and generate good main points for each subject.

SUBJECT	SELECTED QUESTION	MAIN POINTS
1. My preparation for college		•
		•
		•
		•
2. My part-time/ full-time job		•
		•
		•
		•
3. My family's immigration to Canada		•
		•
		•
		•
4. Leaving home		•
		•
		•
		•
5. Pop music		•
		•
		•
		•

EXERCISE 22.5

For each of the five subjects you chose in exercise 22.3, list two to five main points. If suitable main points do not immediately come to mind, apply to your subject the twelve questions in the box on p. 226, one at a time, until you find the one that fits best. The answers to that question are your main points.

Testing Your Main Points

Now take a close look at the main points you've chosen in exercise 22.5. It may be necessary to revise some of them before going any further. Are some points really too minor to bother with? Do any of the points overlap in meaning? Are there any points that are not directly related to the subject?

Main points must be SIGNIFICANT, DISTINCT, and RELEVANT.

To be completely satisfactory, the main points you have chosen to write about must all be **significant:** worth writing a paragraph or more on. You shouldn't have any trivial ideas mixed in with the important ones.

Second, each of the main points you've chosen must be **distinct.** That is, it must be different from all the others. There must be no overlap in meaning. Check to be sure you haven't given two different labels to what is really only one aspect of the subject.

And finally, each main point must be **relevant**; it must be clearly **related** to the subject. It must be an aspect of the subject you are writing about, not some other subject. For example, if you're writing about the advantages of a subject, cross out any disadvantages that may have appeared on your list.

EXERCISE 22.6

Here is a list of subjects, each of which is followed by some possible main points. Circle the unsatisfactory point(s) in each group.

1. Reasons for teenage drug abuse
   - peer pressure
   - school pressure
   - alcohol
   - boredom

2. How homemade bread is made
- prepare dough
- large bakeries
- kneading dough
- saving money
- bake loaves

3. The advantages of being physically fit
- improved muscle tone
- improved appearance
- improved stamina
- improved looks
- improved social life

4. Characteristics of sharks
- tiny brains
- white shark
- tough and durable beasts
- several sets of needle-sharp teeth
- hammerhead shark
- not all are dangerous to humans

5. The functions of a travel counsellor
- plan a client's itinerary
- book the required arrangements
- make travel plans
- get a passport
- ensure the client is satisfied

6. Popular fad diets
- the Scarsdale diet
- the Pritikin diet
- may be dangerous
- the Powter regime
- weight is often gained back

7. The main kinds of daytime television
- talk shows
- quiz shows
- soap operas
- largely female audience
- game shows

8. Effects of the postwar baby
- growth of postsecondary institutions in 60s and 70s
- surge in birth of children from 1947–1965
- changing social norms due to size of boomer population
- shortage of jobs for entry-level workers
- lack of opportunities for career advancement in the 80s and 90s

EXERCISE 22.7
Circle the unsatisfactory point(s) in each group.

1. Why government lotteries
   are harmful
   - they encourage compulsive gambling
   - they are fun to play
   - Lottario, Lotto 6/49
   - they bilk money from people who have little
   - they foster a "something-for-nothing" attitude

2. Some differences between high school and college
   - practical training
   - college students must assume more responsibility for their learning
   - college students are treated like adults
   - college students cannot smoke in the building

3. Some benefits of biofeedback
   - the medical process by which a person learns to control autonomic body processes
   - may relieve asthma and ulcers
   - autonomic responses are involuntary, self-regulating processes
   - may control blood pressure
   - may relieve migraines and anxiety

4. The main points of comparison between football and rugby
   - both games are team ball games
   - football requires helmets
   - both games are rough
   - both games are played on a large field
   - football is more of a spectator sport than rugby

5. Ways to treat the hyperactive child
   - drug therapy
   - intensely active
   - psychiatric counselling
   - cannot concentrate for long
   - change in family routines
   - change in diet

6. How to find a job
- watch employment ads carefully
- prepare a first-class résumé
- send résumés and covering letters to possible employers
- finding a job may take a while
- prepare for interviews
- buy a suit

7. Different kinds of family structure
- nuclear family
- in-laws
- single-parent family
- communal family
- family breakdown
- polygamous family

8. Reasons for legalizing prostitution
- to save taxpayers money
- to control spread of sexually transmitted diseases
- to eliminate juvenile prostitution
- to ensure regular health check-ups for prostitutes
- to decriminalize prostitution

EXERCISE 22.8

Study the main points you chose in exercise 22.5 (p. 230). Cross out any that are not *significant*, *distinct*, or *relevant* to the subject. If necessary, add new main points so that you end up with at least three main points for each subject.

Organizing Your Main Points

Now that you've decided on three or four main points to discuss, you need to decide in what order you wish to present them in your paper. Choose the order that is most appropriate for your particular subject.

> There are four basic ways to arrange main points in an essay: CHRONOLOGICAL, CLIMACTIC, LOGICALLY LINKED, and RANDOM order.

1. **Chronological order** means in order of time sequence, from first to last. Here's an example:

SUBJECT	MAIN POINTS
The process of a relationship	• attraction • meeting • discovery • intimacy • disillusionment

2. **Climactic order** means saving your strongest or most important point for last. Generally, you would present your strongest point last, your second-strongest point first, and the others in between, like this:

SUBJECT	MAIN POINTS
Disadvantages of cigarette smoking	• danger to those around you • disapproval of others • expense • danger to yourself

3. **Logically linked order** means that the main points are connected in such a way that one point must be explained before the next can be understood. Consider this example:

SUBJECT	MAIN POINTS
Main causes of juvenile delinquency	• lack of opportunity for work • lack of recreational facilities • boredom

The logical link here is this: because of unemployment, recreational facilities are needed, and because of both unemployment and inadequate recreational facilities, boredom becomes a problem. The first two points must be explained before the reader can fully understand the third.

4. **Random order** means the points can be explained in any order. A random arrangement of points is possible only if the main points are *equally significant* and *not chronologically or causally linked*, as in this example:

SUBJECT	MAIN POINTS
Reasons for the waste disposal crisis	• disposal sites are hard to find • costs are high • new technologies are not yet fully developed

EXERCISE 22.9

Below we have identified eight subjects, together with several main points that could be used to develop them. For each subject, number the points so that they are arranged in the order suggested.

SUBJECT	ORDER	MAIN POINTS
1. How to start a gas lawnmower	chronological	____ make sure there is enough gas in tank ____ turn switch to start ____ put lawnmower on flat ground ____ when running, adjust to proper speed ____ pull cord ____ mow!
2. Differences between spoken and written language	climactic	____ speech is transitory; writing is permanent ____ speech is direct and personal; writing isn't ____ speech can't be revised; writing can
3. How to write a research paper	chronological	____ read and take notes on selected research sources ____ draft the paper ____ compile a working bibliography of research sources ____ define the subject ____ type and proofread paper ____ prepare footnotes, if needed, and bibliography ____ revise the paper
4. How colleges benefit society	logical	____ they provide the individual with a higher level of general education ____ society benefits from increased productivity and commitment of an educated populace ____ they provide the individual with job skills

SUBJECT	ORDER	MAIN POINTS
5. Some causes of World War II	chronological	____ World Depression in early 1930s ____ Hitler's rise to power in 1933 ____ heavy reparations demanded of Germany at end of World War I ____ German aggression in Europe
6. Effects of malnutrition	logical	____ malnutrition affects the productivity and prosperity of nations as a whole ____ malnutrition impedes the mental and physical development of children ____ undernourished children become sickly adults unable to participate fully in their society
7. Why pornography should be banned	chronological	____ it degrades the people involved in making it ____ it brutalizes society as a whole ____ it desensitizes the people who view it
8. Why pornography should not be banned	climactic	____ organized crime benefits from illegal distribution ____ censorship violates individual civil rights ____ banning pornography would lead to censorship of legitimate art and literature

EXERCISE 22.10

Using your list of subjects and main points from exercise 22.8, arrange the main points for each subject in the most appropriate order. (*Note:* Keep your answer sheet. You will need it in some of the exercises that follow.)

In this chapter, you've learned how to choose a satisfactory subject and how to select and arrange the main points of that subject—the first two steps in the five-step process we outlined at the beginning of the chapter. Now it's time to decide whether you'll develop your paper by the thesis-statement method or by the outline method. We think the former generally works best for short papers and the latter for long papers, but this distinction isn't hard and fast. Your wisest choice is to learn both ways to structure a paper. You will often get the best results if you use them together.

CHAPTER 23

Writing the Thesis Statement

In Chapter 22, you chose a topic and selected some aspects of it to discuss. Now you're ready for the third step in developing a paper. If you're writing a short paper, we recommend that you use the method presented in this chapter. If you're writing a longer paper or if your teacher prefers the outline method, you may prefer to turn now to Chapter 24, "Writing the Outline."

Step 3: Write a Thesis Statement

The key to a clearly organized paper is a **thesis statement**—a statement near the beginning of your paper that announces its subject and scope. The thesis statement is a tremendous help both to you and to your readers. It plans your paper for you, and it tells your readers exactly what they are going to read about. In fiction, letting readers know in advance what they are going to find would never do. But for practical, everyday kinds of writing, advance notice works very well. Term papers, technical reports, research papers, office memoranda, and business letters are no place for suspense or surprises. In these kinds of writing, you're more likely to get and keep your readers' attention if you indicate the subject and scope of your paper at the outset. The thesis statement acts like a table of contents, giving a clear indication of what follows. It's a kind of map of the territory covered in your paper: it keeps your reader (and you) on the right track.

> A thesis statement is a sentence that clearly and concisely indicates the **subject** of your paper, the **main points** you will discuss, and the **order** in which you will discuss them.

To write a thesis statement, you join your **subject** to your **main points,** which you have already arranged in order. To join the two parts of a thesis statement, you use a **link.** Your link can be a word or a phrase such as *are, include, consist of, because, since,* or it can be a colon.[1] Here is the simple formula for constructing a thesis statement:

S	consists of	1, 2, 3 . . . n.
(subject)	*(link)*	*(main points)*

Here's an example:

Three characteristics of a good business letter are conciseness, clarity, and courtesy.

(subject)	*(link)*	*(main points)*

EXERCISE 23.1

In each of the following thesis statements, underline the subject with a wavy line, circle the link and underline the main points with a straight line. Answers are on p. 368.

1. There are three kinds of students whom teachers find difficult to teach: whiners, snoozers, and disrupters.

2. The most prolific producers of unnecessary jargon are politicians, sports writers, advertising-copy writers, and educators.

---

[1] Remember that a colon can be used only after an independent clause. See Chapter 19 if you need a review.

3. Dining in the cafeteria should be avoided if possible, for the food is high in cost, low in nutrition, and unappetizing in taste.

4. Because they lack basic skills, study skills, or motivation, some students run the risk of failure in college.

5. Pay television has faced challenges in Canada because of the relatively small market, the high monthly cost, and the stiff network competition.

6. Political violence has become ingrained in the social fabric of many Latin American countries including Nicaragua, El Salvador, Colombia, and Brazil.

7. The Canadian national character was shaped by early conflicts such as the battle for Quebec, the rebellion of 1837, and the Riel rebellion.

8. Canada is little more than an American satellite, for the United States influences our foreign policy, dominates our culture, and controls our economy.

9. The major improvements Western medical technology has made in impoverished parts of the world consist of widespread immunization, the availability of antibiotics, and improved sanitation.

10. Two cheers for democracy: one because it admits variety and two because it permits criticism. (E.M. Forster)

When you combine your subject with your main points to form a thesis statement, there is an important rule to remember:

> The main points should be **grammatically parallel**.

This rule means that if main point 1 is a word, then main points 2 and 3 and so on must be words, too. If main point 1 is a phrase, then the rest must be phrases. If your first main point is a dependent clause, then the rest must be dependent clauses. Study the model thesis statements you analyzed in exercise 23.1. In every example, the main points are in grammatically parallel form. For each of those thesis statements, decide whether words, phrases, or dependent clauses were used. If you feel your understanding of parallelism is a bit wobbly, review Chapter 9 before doing the following exercises.

EXERCISE 23.2

This exercise will test your grasp of the parallelism principle. In each question below, one main point is not parallel to the others. Circle the faulty main point and rewrite it to make it grammatically parallel.

1. I
   a. came
   b. saw
   c. conquered
   d. pack up and head for Rome

2. I am looking for a husband who is
   a. strength
   b. intelligent
   c. good-looking
   d. well-heeled

3. Her wicked stepsisters were
   a. ill-tempered
   b. ungrateful
   c. ugliness
   d. self-centered

4. Greg completed the requirements
   a. skilfully
   b. with intelligence
   c. correctly
   d. quickly

5. We enjoy travelling
   a. by car
   b. sailing
   c. by air
   d. by train

6. A politician should be
   a.   well-liked by constituents
   b.   respected by colleagues
   c.   esteemed by the party
   d.   even the media trust him

7. We have all been
   a.   watching our diet
   b.   learning to exercise
   c.   not to watch so much television
   d.   thinking of fitness

8. Excessive use of marijuana can
   a.   make you eat more
   b.   diminish ambition
   c.   induce lethargy
   d.   cause psychological dependence

9. Her family has a
   a.   mansion in Westmount
   b.   cottage in the Muskokas
   c.   ski chalet in the Laurentians
   d.   yacht that always seems to be in drydock.

10. To lower the crime rate, we must ensure
    a.   that citizens are involved in their communities
    b.   that jobs and adequate housing are available
    c.   enough fair-minded police visible
    d.   that courts work justly and speedily

EXERCISE 23.3

Put a check mark (√) before the sentences that are grammatically parallel.
Check your answers when you have completed the exercise.

1. _____ His basement apartment was small, damp, cold, and lots of dirt.

2. _____ To be a good marriage counsellor, a person must have insight,

   patient, compassion, and experience.

3. _____ Told to include "Activities and Interests" on his résumé, Elmo de-

   scribed his as chomping potato chips, guzzling beer, and watch-

   ing TV.

4. ____ Too much coffee can give you nervous days, sleepless nights, and your heart may palpitate.

5. ____ We require our employees to be honest, reliable, disciplined, and they have to know something.

6. ____ Roderick is interested in the occult, so he spends his time reading about witches, warlocks, and wizards.

7. ____ We knew we would be suffering from a severe case of jet lag when we got back, so we took a cab home, unpacked our bags, and went right to sleep.

8. ____ Inflation is down, interest rates are up, and many people still don't have jobs.

9. ____ Hobbies are important because they provide recreation, stimulation, and relaxation.

10. ____ Writing acceptable college-level prose involves applying the principles of organization, sentence structure, spelling, and you have to punctuate, too.

EXERCISE 23.4
Now correct the faulty parallelism in the sentences in Exercise 23.3.

EXERCISE 23.5
Correct the faulty parallelism in the following sentences.

1. Do you know the difference among polygamy, bigamy, and marrying only one person at a time?

2. Ahmad has given up not only on the Liberals but also on the Conservatives and the Reform Party.

3. Rudolf decided he'd rather be a plumber than to teach school.

4. A good coach must train and discipline the team, and he must provide motivation.

5. Two features of the semester system are flexibility and it's economical.

6. Going to college is good for broadening one's social life as well as to learn career skills.

7. Compared to those of ten years ago, today's cars are smaller, more efficient, and they cost more.

8. We find it's more interesting to explore the tide pools at the seashore than lying in the sun all day.

9. Children who grow up in the city have a different outlook on life than the country.

10. Do Canadians really care if the United States dominates our economy, political life, and our culture?

EXERCISE 23.6
Correct the faulty parallelism in the following sentences.

1. The four kinds of prose writing are narration, description, exposition, and persuasive.

2. College fraternities and sororities have become less popular in the past twenty years because of expense, they are time-consuming, and they discriminate against some students.

3. Medical scientists are studying the link between weather and such diseases as colds, arthritic ailments, and cancer.

4. If I could have three wishes, I would wish to be gorgeous, absolutely brilliant, and the possessor of fabulous riches.

5. Roots products have won international favour because of their reasonable cost, the designs are fashionable without being faddish, and the quality is unfailingly high.

6. Intramural sports offer three important things to college students: a way to get involved in the school, an opportunity to meet friends, and they can stay fit.

7. Freud's psychoanalytic theories, developed in the early years of this century, not only have affected the course of psychology but also have had profound implications for education, artistic, and literary.

8. Many English words have similar meanings, but they come from very different root languages: for example, *spectre* comes from the Latin *spectrum* (appearance); *phantom* comes from the Greek *phantasm* (image); and *ghost*, Anglo-Saxon *gast*—spirit.

9. Geologists are exploring several phenomena that may lead to an early-warning system for earthquakes: the variation of electrical resistance of rocks under pressure, releasing gas trapped in the crystal lattice of a rock, and the appearance of eerie lights, or luminous flares, in the sky before a quake.

10. It was the best times; it was the worst of times; it was the age of wisdom; it was the age of foolishness; it was the epoch of belief; it was the age of incredulity; it was the season of Light; it was the season of Darkness; it was the spring of hope; and there was a lot of despair that winter, too. (With apologies to Charles Dickens, *A Tale of Two Cities*)

EXERCISE 23.7

This exercise is designed for those who wish to reinforce their understanding of thesis statement construction before proceeding. Turn back to Exercise 23.2. In that exercise, you made all the points grammatically parallel. Now it's time to turn each subject with its list of points into a thesis statement. Before you write each sentence, arrange the main points listed below the subject into an appropriate order: chronological, climactic, logical, or random.

Answers to this exercise may vary. Just be sure you have a good rationale for choosing the order you use in each case. When you've finished the exercise, turn to p. 370, where you will find suggested answers for some of the items.

EXERCISE 23.8

Find the subjects and main points you produced for exercise 22.10 in Chapter 22. Combine each subject with its main points to make a thesis statement. Be sure the main points are expressed in parallel form.

We said at the beginning of this chapter that the thesis statement plans your whole paper for you. Before we turn to the actual writing of the paper, it will be useful for you to have a general idea of what the finished product will look like. In a short paper, each main point can be explained in a single paragraph. The main points of your subject become the **topics** of the paragraphs, as is shown in the model format for a paper that has three main points, below.

Notice the proportions of the paragraphs in the model format. Since the main points are approximately equal in significance, the paragraphs of the body of the paper are approximately equal in length. (If your last main point is more important than the other points, however, the paragraph that explains it may be longer than the other paragraphs.)

Notice, too, that the beginning and ending paragraphs are much shorter than the ones that explain the main points. Your introduction should not ramble on, and your conclusion should not trail off. Get to your main points as quickly as you can, and end with a bang, not a whimper.

_____ Title _____

Paragraph 1:
contains your
introduction
and thesis
statement

_____
_____
_____
_____
S consists of 1, 2, and 3.

Paragraph 2:
explains your
first main
point

Topic sentence introducing main point 1.
_____
_____
_____
_____
_____
_____
_____.

Paragraph 3:
explains your
second main
point

Topic sentence introducing main point 2.
_____
_____
_____
_____
_____.

Paragraph 4:
explains your
third main
point

Topic sentence introducing main point 3.
_____
_____
_____
_____
_____
_____.

Paragraph 5:
conclusion

_____
_____
_____
_____.

EXERCISE 23.9

A good paper that follows the model format exactly is Brian Green's "Writing a Good Business Letter," which appears in Appendix A. Read it and underline the thesis statement and topic sentences. Then turn to Chapter 25.

CHAPTER 24

Writing the Outline

For longer compositions, business and technical reports, research papers, and the like, an outline is often necessary. A good outline maps out your paper from beginning to end. It shows you—before you begin to write— what you have to say about each of your main points. Outlining spares you the agony of discovering too late that you have too much information about one point and little or nothing to say about another.

Step 3: Write an Outline

Once you've chosen a satisfactory subject and main points to discuss, the next step is to expand what you have into an organized plan for your finished paper. To do this, you may need to do some further thinking or reading, to gather additional information and supporting facts. (For ideas about what kinds of information you might use, see "Developing Your Paragraphs," in Chapter 25.) After you've assembled all the information you think you'll need, prepare the outline.

First, write down your main points in the order you've decided is best for your presentation. Leave lots of space under each main point. Using Roman numerals (I, II, III, and so on), number your main points. Now, under each main point, indent and list the examples, facts, ideas, or other supporting information you're going to use to explain it. Again, leave lots of space. Check to be sure these items are arranged in an order that will be clear to your reader.[1] Label your supporting points, *A, B, C,* and so on.

If any of these supporting points need to be explained or developed, indent again and list the second level of supporting points, numbering them, *1, 2, 3,* and so on. Third-level supporting details, if there are any, are indented under the points to which they relate and are labelled, *a, b, c.* Add the introduction and conclusion, and you're done. Your outline might look something like this:

Introduction

    Attention-getter

    Thesis statement/statement of subject

  I. First main point

    A. item that develops first main point

    B. item that develops first main point

        1. supporting material that develops item B

        2. supporting material that develops item B

  II. Second main point

    A. item that develops second main point

    B. item that develops second main point

    C. item that develops second main point

III. Third main point

    A. item that develops third main point

        1. supporting material that develops item A

           a. detail

           b. detail

        2. supporting material that develops item A

    B. item that develops third main point

Conclusion

    Summary

    Memorable statement

You'll probably find that before you can assign a number or a letter to a piece of information, you need to think carefully about where the item belongs in your paper. Questions about how to arrange your information under each main point and how much time to spend on a particular point should be cleared up at the outline stage. If, for example, you find you have

---

[1] The four kinds of order explained in Chapter 22 apply to the arrangement of ideas within a paragraph as well as to the arrangement of main points in a paper.

nine subheadings under main point I and only one under main point II, you need to do some rethinking to balance your paper. Main points should be supported by approximately equal amounts of information.

Preparing a satisfactory outline takes time. Be prepared to spend time adding, deleting, and rearranging your ideas and supporting details until you're completely satisfied with both the arrangement and the proportion of your outline. If you have access to a computer that has a word processing program with an outline feature, be sure to experiment with it. These programs can be very helpful to an inexperienced writer faced with a writing assignment and little knowledge of how to organize it.

EXERCISE 24.1

Below are the main points from a paper that explains, tongue-in-cheek, how to fail. Following the main points are eight statements that might be used to support and develop them. Read through the list and complete the outline by arranging the supporting details logically below the appropriate points. Discard any items that are not relevant to the main points. Turn to p. 370 to check your outline against ours.

I. Antagonize your teacher

   •

   •

   •

II. Disdain your studies

   •

   •

   •

III. Cheat on your work

   •

   •

   •

   • don't buy the text for the course
   • aim an occasional snort or snicker in the teacher's direction
   • copy research assignments out of an appropriate library book
   • wear your Walkman to class and turn up the volume whenever the teacher speaks
   • sit at the back during exams and try to read your classmate's paper
   • never take notes in class
   • stop going to class
   • tattoo your answers on your forearms

With your outline in hand, all you have to do to draft your paper is to make the main points into paragraph divisions, the supporting points into sentences, and add an introduction and conclusion. Chapter 25 explains how.

To show you the relationship between an outline and the final product, we've recreated the outline that was used to write "Writing a Good Business Letter" (reprinted in Appendix A):

Introduction
    Attention-getter: A good business letter is one that gets results.
    Thesis statement: A business letter should be concise, clear, and
                                    courteous.
  I. Concise
      A. The point should be made quickly
          1. assume your reader is busy
          2. assume your reader is not interested in trivia or personal
              messages
      B. Revision is necessary
          1. use precise language
          2. short letters have more impact than long letters
      C. There is still room for style and humour
 II. Clear
      A. Organization is important
          1. know what you want to say
          2. construct the paragraphs to guide the reader through to the
              conclusion
      B. Acceptable letter format should be used
      C. Rereading will aid clarity
          1. take the point of view of your reader
          2. ensure accuracy of facts, figures, explanations
III. Courteous
      A. Tone is important
          1. sarcasm and insults don't work
          2. be polite
      B. Writing and typing must be done with care
          1. correct grammar and spelling are part of courtesy
          2. mistakes will make the reader think less of you
Conclusion
    Summary: The business letter can pay big dividends on the time you
                      invest in giving it a concise message, a clear structure, and
                      a courteous tone.

Once you've mapped out your plan in an outline, the task of writing the essay is much easier. You can see where you're going and how to get there. Remember, the more time you spend on planning, the less time you will spend on writing—and the better your paper will be.

EXERCISE 24.2

Read "Writing a Good Business Letter" in Appendix A. Find the paragraphs that correspond to the various headings and subheadings in the outline (above). Label the paragraphs to show where they fit into the outline: I, A, B, 1, 2, and so on.

EXERCISE 24.3

Read Nell Waldman's "Flunking with Style" in Appendix A and write an outline for it. When you've finished, turn to p. 370 to compare your outline with ours.

EXERCISE 24.4

Turn to the subjects and main points you developed for exercise 22.10 in Chapter 22 and create an outline for a paper on one of those subjects.

CHAPTER 25

Writing the Paragraphs

You are now at step 4 in the writing process. Armed with either your thesis statement or your outline, you are ready to turn your main points into paragraphs. Does that sound like a magician's trick? It isn't. The "sleight-of-pen" involved requires only that you know what a paragraph looks like and how to put one together.

A paragraph looks like this:

Three or more sentences that specifically support or explain the topic go in here.

A sentence that introduces the **topic** (or main idea) of the paragraph goes here.

_____

_____

_____

_____

_____

A sentence that concludes your explanation of the topic goes here.

Sometimes a main point can be explained satisfactorily in a single paragraph. If the main point is complicated and requires lots of support, several paragraphs are needed. Nevertheless, whether it is explaining a main point of a paper or an item supporting a main point, every paragraph contains two things: a topic sentence (usually the first sentence in the paragraph) and several sentences that develop the topic.

Beginning with a sentence that clearly states your main idea is a good way to start a paragraph. The sentences that follow support or expand on the topic. The key to making the paragraph *unified* (an important quality of English paragraphs) is to make sure that each of your supporting sentences relates directly to the main idea introduced in the topic sentence.

EXERCISE 25.1

Turn to Appendix A and read Bertrand Russell's "What I Have Lived For." Study the second, third, and fourth paragraphs and find in each the three basic components of a paragraph: the topic sentence, the supporting sentences, and the conclusion. Compare your answer with ours on p. 371.

Developing Your Paragraphs

How do you put a paragraph together? First, write your **topic sentence,** telling your reader what topic (main point or idea) you're going to discuss in the paragraph. Next, develop your topic. An adequately developed paragraph gives enough supporting information to make the topic completely clear to the reader. An average paragraph runs between 75 and 200 words (except for introductions and conclusions, which are shorter), so you can see you will need lots of supporting information for each point.

Unless you are writing from a very detailed outline and have all the supporting material you need listed in front of you, you need to do some more thinking at this point. Put yourself in your reader's place. What does your reader need to know in order to understand your point clearly? If you ask yourself the six questions listed below, you'll be able to decide what **kinds of development** to use to support a particular topic sentence. The kind of development you use is up to you. Decide on the basis of your topic and what the reader needs to know about it.

1. Is a **definition** necessary?

If you're using a term that may be unfamiliar to your reader, you should define it. Use your own words in the definition. Your reader needs to know what *you* mean by the term—and, besides, quoting from the dictionary is a very boring way to develop a paragraph. Below, Randy Walser defines "cyberspace":

> Cyberspace is a medium that gives people the feeling they have been transported, bodily, from the ordinary physical world to worlds purely of imagination. Although artists can use any medium to evoke imaginary worlds, cyberspace carries the worlds themselves. It has a lot in common with film and stage,

but is unique in the amount of power it yields to its audience. Film yields little power, as it provides no way for its audience to alter film images. Stage grants more power than film, as stage actors can "play off" audience reactions, but still the course of the action is basically determined by a playwright's script. Cyberspace grants ultimate power, as it enables its audience not merely to observe a reality, but to enter it and experience it as if it were real. No one can know what will happen from one moment to the next in a cyberspace, not even the spacemaker. Every moment gives every participant an opportunity to create the next event. Whereas film is used to show a reality to an audience, cyberspace is used to give a virtual body and a role to everyone in the audience. Print and radio tell; stage and film show; cyberspace embodies.

(from Howard Rheingold, *Virtual Reality.* New York: Simon and Schuster, 1991. 26.)

You should include a definition, too, if you're using a familiar term in a specific or unusual way. In the following paragraph, Andrew Nikiforuk defines how he interprets the familiar phrase, "back to the basics":

Let me reiterate what "back to the basics" means. It means teaching subjects that matter—such as English, math, history, geography, and science—because they contain the codes for power in a technological society as well as the only tools for criticizing and analyzing it. It means giving teachers more control over how their classrooms are organized and taught as well as making them more accountable for the results. It means skills in the context of disciplines (that's critical thinking) with the honest realization that not all students will become critical thinkers. It means fair tests and even standardized tests, because product matters in this culture. And finally, it means using the varied cultural backgrounds of students to explore common ground and Canadian realities.

(Andrew Nikiforuk, *School's Out: The Catastrophe in Public Education and What We Can Do About It.* Toronto: MacFarland, 1993.)

EXERCISE 25.2
Write a paragraph in which you define one of the following terms:

respect	friendship	juice (slang)
community	stress	bad apple (slang)
racism	a good job	bird course (slang)

2. Would **examples** help clarify the point?

Listing a number of examples is probably the most common method of developing a topic. Readers become confused, even suspicious, when they read unsupported generalizations or statements of opinion. One of the most effective ways of communicating your idea is by providing clear, relevant examples. In the following paragraph, excerpted from a reading in Appendix A, Sun-Kyung Yi uses examples to explain why her job with a Korean company proved to be a "painful and frustrating experience."

> When the president of the company boasted that he "operated little Korea," he meant it literally. A Canadianized Korean was not tolerated. I looked like a Korean, therefore I had to talk, act, and think like one, too. Being accepted meant a total surrender to ancient codes of behaviour rooted in Confucian thought, while leaving the "Canadian" part of me out in the parking lot with my '86 Buick. In the first few days at work, I was bombarded with inquiries about my marital status. When I told them I was single, they spent the following days trying to match me up with available bachelors in the company and the community. I was expected to accept my inferior position as a woman and had to behave accordingly. It was not a place to practice my feminist views, or be an individual without being condemned. Little Korea is a place for men (who filled all the senior positions) and women don't dare to speak up or disagree with their male counterparts. The president (all employees bow to him and call him Mr. President) asked me to act more like a lady and smile. I was openly scorned by a senior employee because I spoke more fluent English than Korean. The cook in the kitchen shook her head in disbelief upon discovering that my cooking skills were limited to boiling a package of instant noodles. "You want a good husband, learn to cook," she advised me.

Sometimes, one example developed in detail is enough to allow the reader to understand what you mean. In the following paragraph, from "Surviving Your Daughter's Adolescence" (in Appendix A), Janet Read supports her topic "don't argue," with a familiar example: teaching an adolescent to drive.

> Finally we come to the hardest rule for a parent to follow: don't, under any circumstances, argue. Females between the ages of thirteen and eighteen are world-class debaters. They can argue black is white, rain is snow, or bitter is sweet. The most hazardous time is the period when your baby of a few short years ago is learning to drive. She will become, after only two driving lessons, an authority on rules of the road. We have all coped with

back-seat drivers, but nothing will have prepared you for this experience. The teenager feels a learner's permit is a licence to tell her parents how to drive. There are a few useful phrases you can employ to reduce the risk of argument: "Yes, dear." "Is that right?" "How astute of you to notice that!" These simple phrases can forestall an argument that would entertain your entire neighbourhood.

EXERCISE 25.3

Write a six- to ten-sentence paragraph based on the topic sentence below, using examples to develop it.

College is more than just a place to get an education.

3. Is a **series of steps** or **stages** involved?

Sometimes the most effective way to develop the main idea of your paragraph is by explaining how to do it—that is, by relating the process or series of steps involved. Make sure you break the process down into its component parts and explain the steps logically and precisely. Below, Brian Green explains the process of writing a good business letter:

> The business letter must be clear. You should have a firm idea of what you want to say, and you should let the reader know it. Use the structure of the letter—the paragraphs, topic sentences, and transitions—to guide the reader point by point from your introduction, through your reasoning, to your conclusion. Paragraph often, to break up the page and to provide visual cues to the organization of your letter. Use an accepted business-letter format. There are several, and they can be found in any book of business English. Reread what you have written from the point of view of someone who is seeing it for the first time, and revise to be sure that all necessary information is provided (including reference numbers, dates, and other identification) and that all explanations are clear. A clear message, clearly delivered, is the essence of business communication.

EXERCISE 25.4

Write a six- to ten-sentence paragraph developed as a series of steps telling your reader how to make or do something.

4. Would **specific details** be useful?

Providing your reader with concrete, specific, descriptive details can be a very effective way of developing your main point. In some paragraphs, numerical facts or statistics can be used to support your point effectively—just be sure your facts are correct and your statistics up-to-date! In the following paragraph, underline the specific details that help make Denise Chong's description of her grandfather an effective one:

> One Chinese man waiting for the passenger ship to dock at the pier at the foot of Granville Street stood out from the crowd by virtue of his nearly six-foot frame. He had a body that was all limbs, long even in his fingers, which gave his every gesture an elongated emphasis. A fedora graced his head, and he was attired in a custom-tailored three-piece gray suit. His shoes and wire-rimmed glasses were polished and his black hair meticulously combed to expose a high forehead, a physical trait the Chinese consider a sign of intelligence. He owned two suits—one gray, the other brown—and two fedoras. Believing one's appearance mirrored one's inner mind, his appearance today was, as always, immaculate. His manner, like his dress, was sober and serious. At thirty-seven, he was a year younger than the city of Vancouver.

> _____
>
> (from Denise Chong, *The Concubine's Children: Portrait of a Family Divided.* 1994. 11.)

Now consider the following paragraph, excerpted from a reading in Appendix A, in which Nell Waldman appeals to the reader's sense of hearing as well as sight to develop her point:

> [A]ntagonizing your teachers isn't difficult if you keep in mind what it is that teachers like: intelligent, interested, even enthusiastic faces in front row centre. Show that you're bored before the class begins by slouching in a desk at the back of the room. Wear your Walkman, and don't forget to turn up the volume when the teacher starts to talk. Carry on running conversations with your seatmates. Aim an occasional snort or snicker in the teacher's direction when she's putting a complex point on the board. Above all, never volunteer an answer and respond sullenly with an "I dunno" if the teacher has the nerve to ask you a question. Before long, you'll have that teacher bouncing chalk stubs off your head. Once you've earned the loathing of your instructors, you'll be well on your way to a truly memorable failure.

EXERCISE 25.5

Write a six- to ten-sentence paragraph describing one of the following topics. Try to include details that involve several of the physical senses: sight, hearing, touch, smell, and taste. Be sure to begin with a clearly identifiable topic sentence.

> a fast-food restaurant
> a place that makes you feel uncomfortable
> your favourite space
> a younger brother or sister
> the most unusual-looking person you know
> a favourite article of clothing or jewellery

5. Would a **comparison** or **contrast** help clarify your point?

A *comparison* points out similarities between objects, people, or ideas; it shows how two different things are alike. A *contrast* points out dissimilarities between things; it shows how two objects, people, or ideas are different. A *comparison and contrast* identifies both similarities and differences. In the paragraph below, Sun-Kyung Yi contrasts the two sides of her "split personality."

> When I was younger, toying with the idea of entertaining two separate identities was a real treat, like a secret game for which no one knew the rules but me. I was known as Angela to the outside world, and as Sun-Kyung at home. I ate bologna sandwiches in the school lunch room and rice and kimchee for dinner. I chatted about teen idols and giggled with my girlfriends during my classes, and ambitiously practiced piano and studied in the evenings, planning to become a doctor when I grew up. I waved hellos and goodbyes to my teachers, but bowed to my parents' friends visiting our home. I could also look straight in the eyes of my teachers and friends and talk frankly with them instead of staring at my feet with my mouth shut when Koreans talked to me. Going outside the home meant I was able to relax from the constraints of my cultural conditioning, until I walked back in the door and had to return to being an obedient and submissive daughter.

In the following paragraph, Don Gayton begins to develop his subject, how plants grow, by comparing the structure of a leaf to that of a factory:

> At a certain microscopic scale, a leaf begins to lose its biological elegance and starts looking more like a clanking, humming factory. The factory image, in fact, is not far off the mark: a grass leaf is essentially a four-story, double-sided solar-driven manufacturing plant, suspended in space. The roof of this factory is made from thick, transparent cuticle cells. Just below the roof,

on the fourth floor, is a palisade layer, where photosynthesis takes place. The third floor is the spongy mesophyll layer . . . where transpiration occurs. The second and first floors form the underside of the leaf, and they are a rough mirror image of the third and fourth. The stomata on the upper and lower roof vent gases and vapors to and from the mesophyll layer to the outside. Xylem and phloem liquid supply lines come in through the utility space between the second and third floors.

(Don Gayton, *The Wheatgrass Mechanism: Science and Imagination in the Western Canadian Landscape.* Saskatoon: Fifth House Publishers, 1990. 89.)

EXERCISE 25.6

Write a six- to ten-sentence paragraph comparing or contrasting two performers (or instructors or employers). Begin your paragraph with a topic sentence.

6. Would a **quotation** or **paraphrase** be appropriate?

Occasionally, you will find that someone else—an expert in a particular field, a well-known author, or a respected public figure—has said what you want to say better than you could ever hope to say it. In these cases, quotations—as long as they are kept short and not used too frequently—are useful in developing your topic. Notice how Martin Luther King uses a famous quotation to sum up the point of this paragraph.

As long as there is poverty in the world I can never be rich, even if I have a billion dollars. As long as diseases are rampant and millions of people in this world cannot expect to live more than twenty-eight or thirty years, I can never be totally healthy even if I just got a good check-up at Mayo Clinic. I can never be what I ought to be until you are what you ought to be. This is the way our world is made. No individual or nation can stand out boasting of being independent. We are interdependent. So John Donne placed it in graphic terms when he affirmed, "No man is an island entire of itself. Every man is a piece of the continent, a part of the main." Then he goes on to say, "Any man's death diminishes me because I am involved in mankind, and therefore never send to know for whom the bell tolls; it tolls for thee."

(from Martin Luther King, Jr., *The Measure of a Man.* Philadelphia: Christian Education Press, 1959.)

A paraphrase is a summary—in your own words—of someone else's idea. Don't forget to indicate whose idea you are paraphrasing, the way the author of "The Myth of Canadian Diversity" (in Appendix A) does in the following paragraph.

> . . . [O]ur much-discussed ethnic differences are overstated. Although Canada is an immigrant nation and Canadians spring from a variety of backgrounds, a recent study from the C.D. Howe Institute says that the idea of a "Canadian mosaic"—as distinct from the American "melting pot"—is a fallacy. In *The Illusion of Difference,* University of Toronto sociologists Jeffrey Reitz and Raymond Breton show that immigrants to Canada assimilate as quickly into the mainstream society as immigrants to the United States do. In fact, Canadians are less likely than Americans to favour holding on to cultural differences based on ethnic background. If you don't believe Mr. Reitz and Mr. Breton, visit any big-city high school, where the speech and behaviour of immigrant students just a few years in Canada is indistinguishable from that of any fifth-generation classmate.

College writing normally requires that you indicate the source of any material you quote. The easiest way to do this is to give the author's surname and the page reference in parentheses at the end of your quotation— for example: (King 287). At the end of your paper, include a Works Cited page, which is a list, in alphabetical order by authors' surnames, of all the books, articles, and other publications from which you have quoted in your paper. See p. 208 for an example of the format to use. Follow the instructions given in whatever style guide your instructor recommends, or consult Joseph Gibaldi and Walter S. Achtert, *MLA Handbook for Writers of Research Papers,* 4th ed. (New York: Modern Language Association, 1995).

In writing the paragraphs of your essay, remember that you will often need to use more than one method of development to explain your points. The six methods outlined above can be used in any combination you choose.

EXERCISE 25.7

Identify the kinds of development used in the following paragraphs (more than one kind may be present in each). Then turn to p. 371 to check your answers.

1. "Writing a Good Business Letter," paragraph 1

2. "Surviving Your Daughter's Adolescence," paragraph 2

3. "Flunking with Style," paragraph 3

4. "Flunking with Style," paragraph 4

5. "What I Have Lived For," paragraph 2

6. "What I Have Lived For," paragraph 3

7. "The Myth of Canadian Diversity," paragraph 1

8. "The Myth of Canadian Diversity," paragraph 2

9. "An Immigrant's Split Personality," paragraph 4

10. "An Immigrant's Split Personality," paragraph 10

EXERCISE 25.8
Choose one of the following topic sentences or make up one of your own. Write a paragraph of about 100 words, using at least two different methods of paragraph development.

1. Some rock stars lead bizarre personal lives.

2. You are what you wear.

3. I will never forget the moment I ceased being a child.

4. If I had it to do over again, I would _____ .

5. Communicating clearly isn't easy.

Writing Introductions and Conclusions

Two paragraphs in your paper are not developed in the way we've just outlined: the introduction and the conclusion. All too often, these paragraphs are dull or clumsy and detract from a paper's effectiveness. But they needn't. Here's how to write good ones.

The introduction is worth special attention because that's where your reader either sits up and takes notice of your paper or sighs and pitches it into the wastebasket. Occasionally, for a very short paper, you can begin simply with your thesis statement or statement of subject. More usually, though, an **attention-getter** comes before the thesis statement. An attention-getter is a sentence or two designed to get the reader interested in what you have to say.

There are several kinds of attention-getter to choose from:

1. An interesting incident or anecdote related to your subject
2. A statement of opinion you intend to challenge (see "Flunking with Style," paragraph 1)
3. A definition (see "Writing a Good Business Letter," paragraph 1)
4. A quotation or paraphrase
5. A little-known or striking fact (see "An Immigrant's Split Personality," paragraph 1)

Add your thesis statement to the attention-getter and your introduction is complete.

The closing paragraph, too, usually has two parts: a **summary** of the main points of your paper (phrased differently, please—not a word-for-word repetition of your thesis statement or your topic sentences) and a **memorable statement.** Your memorable statement may take several forms:

1. Show the value or significance of your subject (see "Surviving Your Daughter's Adolescence," paragraph 5)
2. Refer back to the content of your opening paragraph (see "Writing a Good Business Letter," paragraph 5; also "What I Have Lived For," paragraph 5)
3. A relevant or thought-provoking quotation, statement, or question (see "The Myth of Canadian Diversity," paragraph 8)
4. A suggestion for change (see "An Immigrant's Split Personality," paragraph 10)
5. A challenge to the reader to get involved (see "Flunking with Style," paragraph 5)

EXERCISE 25.9

Using as many of the different kinds as you can, write an attention-getter and a memorable statement for each of the following topics.

1. I love (*or* hate) baseball (*or* hockey, football, or any other sport).

2. The media pay too much attention to the baby boomers and too little to the rest of us.

3. Movies today are better (*or* worse) than ever before.

4. Honesty is (*or* is not) always the best policy.

5. Cigarette smoking should (*or* should not) be prohibited in the workplace.

6. College students should (*or* should not) be paid to go to school.

7. Surfing the Internet is (*or* is not) great entertainment.

8. Teenagers are (*or* are not) too young to rear children effectively.

9. College professors should (*or* should not) be required to take courses in teaching methodology.

10. It's not easy being a man (*or* a woman).

Keeping Your Reader with You

As you write your paragraphs, keep in mind that you want to make it as easy as possible for your reader to follow you through your paper. Clear **transitions** and an appropriate **tone** can make the difference between a paper that confuses or annoys readers and one that enlightens and pleases them.

Transitions

Transitions are those words or phrases that show the relationship between one point and the next, causing a paragraph or a paper to read smoothly.

Like turn signals on a car, they tell the person following you where you're going. Here are some common transitions you can use to keep your reader on track.

1. *To show a time relation:* first, second, third, next, before, during, after, now, then, finally, last
2. *To add an idea or example:* in addition, also, another, furthermore, similarly, for example, for instance
3. *To show contrast:* although, but, however, instead, nevertheless, on the other hand, in contrast, on the contrary
4. *To show a cause–effect relation:* as a result, consequently, because, since, therefore, thus

Here is a paragraph that has adequate development but no transitions:

> There are several good reasons why you should not smoke. Smoking is harmful to your lungs and heart. It is annoying and dangerous to those around you who do not smoke. Smoking is an unattractive and dirty habit. It is difficult to quit. Most worthwhile things in life are hard to achieve.

Not very easy to read, is it. Readers are jerked abruptly from point to point until, battered and bruised, they reach the end. This kind of writing is unfair to readers. It makes them do too much of the work. The ideas may all be there, but the readers have to figure out for themselves how they fit together. After a couple of paragraphs like this one, even a patient reader can become annoyed.

Now read the same paragraph with the transitions added:

> There are several good reasons why you should not smoke. *Among them, three stand out as the most persuasive. First,* smoking is harmful to your lungs and heart. *Second,* it is *both* annoying and dangerous to those around you who do not smoke. *In addition to these compelling facts,* smoking is an unattractive and dirty habit. *Furthermore, once you begin,* it is difficult to quit; *but then,* most worthwhile things in life are hard to achieve.

In the revised paragraph, readers are gently guided from one point to the next. By the time they reach the conclusion, the readers know not only what ideas the writer had in mind, but also how they fit together. Transitions make the reader's job easier and more rewarding.

Tone

One final point. As you write the paragraphs of your paper, try to be conscious of your **tone.** Tone is simply good manners on paper. The words you use, the examples, quotations, and other supporting materials you choose to help explain your main points—all these contribute to your tone. When you are trying to explain something to someone, particularly if it's something you feel strongly about, you may be tempted to be highly emotional in your discussion. If you allow yourself to get emotional, chances are you won't be convincing. What will be communicated is the strength of your feelings, not the depth of your understanding or the validity of your opinion. To be clear and credible, you need to restrain your enthusiasm or anger and present your points in a calm, reasonable way.

We have two suggestions to help you find and maintain the right tone. First, never insult your reader, even unintentionally. Avoid phrases such as "any idiot can see," "no sane person could believe," and "it is obvious that. . . ." What is obvious to you isn't necessarily obvious to someone who has a limited understanding of your subject or who disagrees with your opinion. Don't talk down to your readers, as though they were children or hopelessly ignorant. Don't use sarcasm. Second, avoid profanity.

And don't apologize for your interpretation of your subject. Have confidence in yourself. You've thought long and hard about your subject, you've found good supporting material to help explain it, and you believe in its significance. Present your subject in a positive manner. If you hang back, using phrases such as "I may be wrong, but . . ." or "I tend to feel that . . . ," your reader won't be inclined to give your points the consideration they deserve. Keep your reader in mind as you write, and your writing will be both clear and convincing.

EXERCISE 25.10

Rewrite the following paragraph, adding transitions where necessary and correcting any lapses in tone. Compare your revision to ours on p. 371.

I'm new to college life. I hardly know anything about it. Don't consider me an expert. There are three ways to achieve academic success. I want to do well. A person doesn't have to go to class, which is nice. Going to class helps you learn more. Teachers don't bug you to do the work. It's easy to miss assignments or notes if they don't. The workload gets heavy all of a sudden in midterm. It sure is tough to keep up. I may be wrong but it seems to me that the keys to academic success are self-discipline and responsibil-

ity for one's studies as a college student.

EXERCISE 25.11
Write a response to the prescription for academic success outlined in exercise 25.10 above. Remember to keep your tone consistent, and don't forget transitions.

EXERCISE 25.12
Do either A or B:

    A. Using one of the thesis statements you prepared in Chapter 23, exercise 23.8, write a paper of approximately 400 words.

    B. Using the outline you prepared in Chapter 24, exercise 24.4, write a paper of approximately 600 words.

CHAPTER 26

Revising Your Paper

No one can write in a single draft an essay that is perfectly organized and developed, let alone one that is free of errors in sentence structure, grammar, spelling, and punctuation. The purpose of the first draft is to get down on paper something you can work with until you're satisfied it will meet your reader's needs and expectations. Planning and drafting should take up about half the time you devote to writing a paper. The rest should be devoted to revision.

Revision is the process of refining your writing until it says what you want it to say in a way that enables your readers to understand your message and to receive it favourably. These two goals, clear understanding and favourable reception, constitute good communication. You can accomplish these goals only if you keep your readers in mind as you revise. Because it reflects the contents of the writer's mind, a first draft often seems all right to the writer. But in order to transfer an idea as clearly as possible from the mind of the writer to the mind of the reader, revision is necessary. The idea needs to be honed and refined until it is as clear to your reader as it is to you. By revising from your reader's point of view, you can avoid misunderstandings before they happen.

What Is Revision?

Revision means "re-seeing." It does *not* mean recopying. The aim of revision is to improve your writing's organization, accuracy, and style. Revising is a three-stage process. Each step requires that you read through your entire essay, painful though this may be. The goal of your first reading is to ensure that your reader's information needs are met. In your second reading, you focus on structure. Your third reading concentrates on correctness. Here are the steps to follow in revising a paper:

1. Improve the whole paper by revising its content and organization.
2. Refine paragraph and sentence structure, and correct any errors in grammar.
3. Edit and proofread to catch errors in word choice, spelling, and punctuation.

Inexperienced writers often skip the first two stages and concentrate on the third, thinking they will save time. This is a mistake. In fact, they waste time—both theirs and their readers'—because the result is writing that doesn't communicate clearly and won't make a positive impression.

The best way to begin revising is to do nothing to the early version of your paper for several days. Let as much time as possible pass between completing your first draft and rereading it. Ten minutes, or even half a day, is not enough. The danger in rereading too soon is that you're likely to "read" what you *think* you've written—what exists only in your head, not on the paper. But if, like many writers, you haven't allowed enough time for this cooling-off period, don't despair. There are two other things you can do to help you get some distance from your draft. If your first draft is handwritten, type it out. Reading your essay in a different form helps you "re-see" its content. Alternatively, read your paper aloud and try to hear it from the point of view of your reader. Listen to how your explanation unfolds, and mark every place you find something unclear, irrelevant, inadequately developed, or out of order.

Step One: Revising Content and Organization

As you read your paper aloud, keep in mind the three possible kinds of changes you can make at this stage:

1. You can *rearrange* information. This is the kind of revision that is most often needed, but least often done. Consider the order in which you've arranged your paragraphs. From your reader's point of view, is this the most effective order in which to present your ideas? If you are not already using a word processing program, now is the time to begin.

With a good word processor, moving blocks of text around is as easy as dealing a deck of cards.

2. You can *add* information. Adding new main ideas or more development is often necessary to make your message interesting and convincing as well as clear. It's a good idea to ask a friend to read your draft and identify what needs to be expanded or clarified. (Be sure to return the favour. You can learn a great deal by critiquing other people's writing.)

3. You can *delete* information. Now is the time to cut out anything that is repetitious, insignificant, or irrelevant to your subject and reader.

Use the checklist that follows to guide you as you review your paper's form and content.

Content and Organization Checklist

ACCURACY

Is everything you have said accurate?

- Is your information consistent with your own experience and observations, or with what you have discovered through research?
- Are all your facts and evidence up-to-date?

COMPLETENESS

Have you included enough main ideas and development to explain your subject and convince your reader? Remember that "enough" means from the reader's point of view, not the writer's.

SUBJECT

Is your subject

- significant? Does it avoid the trivial or the obvious?
- single? Does it avoid double or combined subjects?
- specific? Is it focussed and precise?
- supportable? Have you provided enough evidence to make your meaning clear?

MAIN POINTS

Are your main points

- significant? Have you deleted any unimportant ones?
- distinct? Are they all different from one another, or is there an overlap in content?
- relevant? Do all points relate directly to your subject?
- arranged in the most appropriate order? Again, "appropriate" means from the reader's perspective. Choose chronological, climactic, logical, or random order, depending on which is most likely to help the reader make sense of your information.

INTRODUCTION

Does your introduction

- catch the reader's attention and make him or her want to read on?
- contain a clearly identifiable thesis statement?
- identify the main points that your paper will explain?

CONCLUSION

Does your conclusion

- contain a summary or reinforcement of your main points, rephrased to avoid word-for-word repetition?
- contain a statement that effectively clinches your argument and leaves the reader with something to think about?

TONE

Is your tone consistent, reasonable, courteous, and confident throughout your essay?

When you have carefully considered these questions, it's time to move on to the second stage of the revision process.

Step Two: Revising Paragraphs and Sentences

Here, too, you should allow time—at least a couple of days—between your first revision and your second. Enough time must elapse to allow you to approach your paper as if you were seeing it for the first time. Once again, read your draft aloud, and use this list of questions to help you improve it.

Paragraph and Sentence Checklist

PARAGRAPHS

Does each paragraph

- begin with a clear, identifiable topic sentence?
- develop one—and only one—main idea?
- present one or more kinds of development appropriate to the main idea?
- contain clear and effective transitions to signal the relationship between sentences? Between paragraphs?

SENTENCES

Sentence Structure

- Is each sentence clear and complete?
  1. Are there any fragments or run-ons?
  2. Are there any misplaced or dangling modifiers?
  3. Are all lists (whether words, phrases, or clauses) expressed in parallel form?
- Are your sentences varied in length? Could some be combined to improve the clarity and impact of your message?

Grammar

- Have you used verbs correctly?
  1. Are all verbs in the correct form?
  2. Do all verbs agree with their subjects?
  3. Are all verbs in the correct tense?
  4. Are there any confusing shifts in verb tense within a paragraph?
- Have you used pronouns correctly?
  1. Are all pronouns in the correct form?
  2. Do all pronouns agree with their antecedents?
  3. Have any vague pronoun references been eliminated?

When you're sure you've answered these questions satisfactorily, turn to the third and last stage of the revision process.

Step Three: Editing and Proofreading

By now you're probably so tired of refining your paper that you may be tempted to skip **editing**—correcting errors in word choice, spelling, and punctuation—and **proofreading**—correcting errors in typing or writing that appear in the final draft. But these final tasks are essential if you want your paper to make a positive impression.

Misspellings, faulty punctuation, and messiness don't always create misunderstandings, but they do cause the reader to form a lower opinion of you and your work. Careful editing and proofreading are necessary if you want your writing to be favourably received.

Most word-processing programs now include both a grammar checker and a spelling checker, and it is worthwhile running your writing through these programs at the editing stage. The newer programs have some useful features. For example, they will question—but not correct—your use of apostrophes; they will sometimes catch errors in subject–verb agreement that you may have missed; and they will catch obvious misspellings and typos. But don't make the mistake of assuming the program will do all your editing for you. Many errors slip past a computer's checker; only you (or a knowledgeable and patient friend) can find and correct them.

If spelling is a particular problem for you, it is a good idea to read your paper, word by word, from the end to the beginning. Reading backward forces you to look at each word by itself and helps you spot those that look suspicious. Whenever you're in doubt about the spelling of a word, look it up! If you find this task too tedious to bear, ask a good speller to read over your paper for you and identify any errors.

Here are the questions to ask yourself when you are editing.

Editing Checklist

WORDS

Usage

Have you used words accurately, to communicate meaning rather than to impress?
- Have you eliminated any clichés, jargon terms, and slang expressions?
- Have you cut out any unnecessary words?
- Have you corrected any "abusages"?

Spelling

Are all words spelled correctly?
- Have you double-checked any sound-alikes or look-alikes?
- Have you used capital letters where they are needed?
- Have you used apostrophes correctly for possessives and omitted them from plurals?

PUNCTUATION

Within Sentences

Have you eliminated any unnecessary commas and included commas where needed? (Refer to the four comma rules as you consider this question.)

Have you used colons and semicolons where appropriate?

Are any quotations appropriately marked?

Beginnings and Endings

Does each sentence begin with a capital letter?

Do all questions—and only questions—end with a question mark?

Are all quotation marks correctly placed?

Tips for Effective Proofreading

By the time you have finished editing, you will have gone over your paper so many times you may have practically memorized it. When you are very familiar with a piece of writing, it's hard to spot the small mistakes that may have crept in as you produced your final copy. Here are some tips to help you find those tiny, elusive errors:

1. Read through your essay line by line, using a ruler to guide you.
2. If you've been keeping a list of your most frequent errors in this course, do a scan of your essay looking specifically for the mistakes you know you are most likely to make.
3. Using the Quick Revision Guide on the inside front cover of this book, make a final check of all aspects of your paper.

Your "last" draft may need further revision after your proofreading review. If so, take the time to rewrite the paper so that the version you hand in is clean and easy to read. If a word processor is available to you, use it. Computers make editing and proofreading almost painless, since errors are so easy to correct.

At long last, you're ready to submit your paper. If you've followed the three steps to revision conscientiously, you can hand it in with confidence that it says what you want it to say, both about your subject and about you. One last word of advice:

> DON'T FORGET TO KEEP A COPY FOR YOUR FILES!

EXERCISE 26.1

Revise the following paragraph by applying the questions on the three checklists given in this chapter. Then compare your version with ours, on p. 372.

If the Marlins are ever to win a world series, they must begin immediately to do three things. They must develop a first-class scouting department that will be able to provide advise on the best prospects in the miner leagues, it is crucial to establish a quality miner league or "farm" system that will train and develop young players. The new team must make carefully considered trades for emerging young stars. Everyone knows that a world series Championship is a long-term goal. So there is little point in

trying to sign established stars with huge salaries right away. Start now

and building a solid foundation for the future is the way to go.

EXERCISE 26.2

Using the Quick Revision Guide on the inside front cover, revise the paper
you wrote for exercise 25.12 in Chapter 25.

Beyond the Bare Essentials

Introduction

We have now covered all the essentials for clear, correct, well-organized writing. In this short unit, we will go beyond those essentials to some stylish matters you may encounter when practising what you've learned so far. We'll consider levels of language; how to avoid clichés, jargon, and slang; the problem of wordiness; and what we call *abusages*—misused words and phrases that creep into writing and reveal ignorance of the language.

Many of the errors we discuss in this unit are not grammatical errors, but they do interfere with your ability to communicate effectively. Readers may not understand what you're talking about if you use jargon or slang. They may think poorly of you and your message if your level of language is inappropriate or if you use clichés or abusages. Your message will be communicated only if your writing is clear and correct; that is, if it satisfies the bare essentials. Your message will be more easily understood and more favourably received if your writing is appropriate to your subject and readers—that is, if you care enough to go beyond the bare essentials.

The chapters in this unit contain information that will help you create a positive impression when you write. Now that you're writing longer papers and having less trouble with the essentials, you are ready to master the material presented in this unit as you draft and revise your work. Your reward will be writing that is not only technically correct but also stylistically appropriate.

CHAPTER 27

Levels of Language

All communication involves three factors: a sender, a message, and a receiver. This book is designed to help the sender—the person who has something to say (or who has to say something)—to communicate effectively. What the sender has to say is, of course, the message. Messages should always be adjusted to suit the receiver—the reader. The adjustment is the responsibility of the writer. There is no point in sending a message, whether it's a love letter or a command, in Spanish if the reader understands only English. Similarly, there is little to be gained from sending a message in colloquial English, the sort of language you would use when speaking with close friends, when the receiver is a prospective employer whom you have just met.

Spoken English has several **levels of language.** They range from almost unintelligible mumblings, through colloquial slang and professional jargon, up to the formal English used in the law courts, in the speech from the throne, and on other formal occasions. The same range exists in written English: from graffiti up to the formal report.

The key to finding the appropriate level for your message is to consider not only your subject but also your audience. Sometimes compromises are necessary, such as when you send one message to a wide variety of receivers. In general, you aim at the highest level of receiver and trust that the others will understand. For this reason, wedding invitations, even those sent to the groom's best buddies, are usually stylized and formal.

No one has to tell you what level of language to use when you communicate with your friends or with your family. These levels have been established and practised over many years. In other situations, however, it's not so clear what level is appropriate. At such times, you must consider the expectations of your audience. If your sociology teacher wants you to write papers in a formal, academic style, and you want to get a good grade, you will write at a formal level. Similarly, because employers generally favour formal letters of application over casual ones, to get an interview you will have to write your letter of application using a higher level of language than you might use in a letter to a friend.

The levels of English usage are not clearly distinct from one another. They often overlap. To help you distinguish among them so that you can choose the style most appropriate to your message and to your reader, we have outlined the basic characteristics of informal, general, and formal English in the table that follows.

	INFORMAL	GENERAL	FORMAL
Vocabulary	Casual, everyday; usually concrete; some slang, colloquial expressions, and contractions	The language of educated persons; nonspecialized; balance of abstract and concrete; readily understood	Often abstract, technical, specialized; no contractions or colloquialisms
Sentence and Paragraph Structure	Short, simple sentences; some sentence fragments; short paragraphs	Complete sentences of varying length; paragraphs vary in length, but often short	All sentences complete; sentences usually long, complex; paragraphs fully developed, often at length
Tone	Conversational, casual; sounds like ordinary speech	Varies to suit message and purpose of writer	Impersonal, serious; often instructional
Typical Uses	Personal letters; some fiction; some newspapers; much advertising	Most of what we read: newspapers, magazines, novels, business correspondence	Legal documents; some textbooks; academic writing; scientific reports

No one level is "better" than any other. Each has its place and function, depending on the communication situation. Your message, audience, and purpose in writing are the factors that determine which level of usage is most appropriate.

EXERCISE 27.1

Write three paragraphs explaining why you were late for an important meeting—one for your supervisor or teacher, one for your father or mother, and one for your best friend. Adapt your level of language so that it is appropriate to each situation.

EXERCISE 27.2

In the books, magazines, notes, and any other print material you have with you, find one piece of writing that is clearly informal, one that is general, and one that is formal. Then list briefly the characteristics of the typical person for whom each piece of writing is intended. In your description, include demographic data (age, level of education, socioeconomic status), interests, activities, and anything else that you can speculate on.

CHAPTER 28

Cutting Out Clichés, Jargon, and Slang

A **cliché** is an expression that was created long ago and has been used and overused ever since. Cliché-filled writing is boring and often meaningless. Spoken English is full of clichés. In the rush to express an idea, we often take the easy way and use ready-made expressions to put our thoughts into words. There is less excuse to write in clichés. Writers have time to think through what they want to say. They also have the opportunity to revise and edit what they have said. Consider this example of thoughtless writing:

> Even though I sweated over the notes and worked like a dog on the exercises, quantum theory remained as clear as mud.

"Sweated over the notes," "worked like a dog," and "clear as mud" are clichés. Readers know more or less what these expressions mean, but they have been used so often they no longer communicate vividly. It's almost impossible to get rid of *all* clichés in your writing, but you can be aware of them and try to use them as seldom as possible.

If you are a native speaker of English, it is easy to recognize clichés. When you can read the first word or two of a phrase and fill in the rest automatically, you know the phrase is a cliché. For example: white as a _____ ; stubborn as a _____ ; playing with _____ ; add insult to _____ ; green with _____ . The endings are so predictable that readers can skip over them. And they do. Such phrases give readers the impression that there is nothing new in your writing. It's all been said before.

The solution to a cliché problem involves time and thought. Don't write automatically. Think carefully about what you want to say; then say it in your own words, not everyone else's.

As you read through the following sentences, notice how hard it is to form a mental picture of what the sentences are saying and how hard it is to remember what you've read—even when you've just finished reading it.

EXERCISE 28.1

Rewrite these sentences, expressing the ideas in your own words.

1. For Constanza, work was a rat race, but she hung in until the third time her boss asked her to work overtime. That was the last straw. She hit the street and made tracks, feeling free as a bird and light as a feather.

2. Life in the fast lane agreed with her for a while, but it goes without saying that she soon went broke and, sadder but wiser, began to look for another job.

3. Last but not least, I would like to introduce my better half, the little woman who has stuck by me through thick and thin. It's a crying shame that my pride and joy can't be here as well, but she's safe and sound at home watching her old man accept this award on national television.

4. In an attempt to keep abreast of the times, our college took a quantum leap into the 21st century by hiring a budding American genius to plan its budget. In the long run, I'm sure she'll be worth her weight

in gold, but in her first few days on the job she has seemed totally out of her depth.

5. While variety is the spice of life, too much change can be a pain in the neck. Many of my friends are stressed out because of the day-in, day-out pressure of climbing the ladder of success. I like to take one day at a time and go with the flow. My husband says I'm just bone lazy.

6. Claude tried to break the ice by doing his flamingo imitation; however, Genevieve was not impressed and chewed him out for acting like a fool. The rest of the people at the party were pleased as punch that their relationship seemed to be on the rocks, because no one had a good word to say about Genevieve and most felt that Claude was rotten to the core.

7. After staying out until the wee small hours of the morning, Vince was white as a sheet and sick as a dog when we shook him awake at the crack of dawn. His blushing bride dissolved in tears when she saw his condition, but instead of crying over spilt milk, she took drastic action and by the time they tied the knot, he was bright-eyed and bushy-tailed. Needless to say, they did not live happily ever after.

8. At this point in time, Marie arrived on the scene, dressed to the nines and looking drop-dead gorgeous. Robert was swept off his feet in an instant, making me green with envy since I was head over heels in

love with him. To Robert, Marie was a breath of fresh air, but I thought she was full of hot air.

9. You're taking a big chance when you go out on a limb to buy a new set of wheels from someone you don't know. Listen to these words of wisdom. For peace of mind, you can't go wrong buying from an established dealer who will be there in your hour of need when something goes wrong. The extra money you might pay is a drop in the bucket compared to what the car could cost you in the long run.

10. Although they came out swinging early in the season, the Dinosaurs had to work like animals to keep up with the rest of the league. By midseason, the coach was getting hot under the collar and the team was in the doghouse. Better late than never, they began winning again with only three games left; however, their loss on the last day of the season was the straw that broke the camel's back. The owners bailed out, leaving the team hanging.

Broadcasting is one of the majour sources of clichés. It's a rare newscast that doesn't include the expression "informed sources," "claimed the life," "skyrocketing debt," or "last but not least." Listening carefully for such overworked phrases on radio and television will make you more aware of them in your own writing. When you're aware of them, you can choose not to use them.

EXERCISE 28.2
List ten clichés that you hear frequently from teachers, friends, and parents.

EXERCISE 28.3
List ten clichés that you hear on tonight's news and sports broadcast.

Jargon

Jargon is language that is incomprehensible to the reader. There are two kinds. One kind of jargon is the specialized vocabulary used in the sciences, arts, trades, and professions. Sometimes technical words and phrases ("shop talk") enter the language we use outside our jobs. The sports world, for example, has a highly developed jargon: "third and six," "at the post," "uppercut," "on deck." Many of these expressions have found their way into everyday conversation in contexts that have nothing to do with sports. The jargon of some professions is so highly specialized and technical that it amounts almost to a private language. Those in the profession are familiar with it and use it to communicate. Those not in the profession are "outsiders" to whom it is unintelligible.

The existence of technical jargon is not the problem. The abuse of jargon is the problem. It limits your audience to those who share your professional vocabulary. To the rest of the world, your writing will be difficult to understand or even meaningless. You can't expect to communicate in your English essays with sentences like this: "The interviewer responded with a logical uppercut that caught Senator Sleaze right between the eyes and laid him out for the count." This may be a colourful way to describe an interview with a corrupt politician, but it will be effective only with readers who are boxing fans.

The second kind of jargon is sometimes called **gobbledygook.** This is pompous, pretentious language that *imitates* a specialized vocabulary. It features long, complex sentences and chains of abstract, multisyllable words that are intended to impress the reader. The result is sound without meaning, as the following example, a definition of "available computing," illustrates:

> The use of redundant components in conjunction with appropriate failover and restart mechanisms in both hardware and software to permit event notification of failure conditions coupled with application and/or database checkpointing and rollback/recover algorithms, thus establishing reasonable assurance within predicted norms that a combination of redundancies will allow a confidence factor to exist and that mean time to repair shall be a small enough variable in conjunction with simultaneous mean time between failure of the aforementioned redundant components that the overall system availability will be significantly above normal performance.

Do you know what this means? Do you care? There are three problems with this kind of writing. First, it does not communicate. Second, it leaves readers with the sense that the writer is trying to hide meaning rather than communicate it. Third, it causes readers to lose respect for the writer.

The cure for jargon is simple: be considerate of your readers. If you want your readers to understand and respect you, write in a simple, straightforward style.

EXERCISE 28.4

Write as many examples of technical jargon as you can think of for each of the following occupations. If you do this exercise in a group, you'll quickly see just how many examples there are.

1. film industry: residuals, box office, property . . .

2. fitness: pump iron, pecs, cross train . . .

3. business: bottom line, market share, poison pill . . .

4. computer systems: real-time, GUI, interface . . .

5. advertising: story board, paste-up, rate card . . .

EXERCISE 28.5

In the following sentences, replace the gobbledygook with plain English. As is often the case in jargon-filled writing, the meaning of these sentences is not clear. Figure out what you think the writer means and then state that meaning clearly in your own words.

1. In compliance with the request of the officer of the law, the intoxicated individual exited his vehicle and elevated his upper extremities.

2. It is not at all feasible or even possible to judge accurately and justly the contents of a literary work merely by examining the exterior surface.

3. The actual living through or participating in events is likely in the long run to provide instruction comparable to none.

4. Although solitary under normal prevailing circumstances, raccoons emerging on nocturnal foraging excursions will congregate simultaneously in situations of enhanced nutrient resource availability.

5. The dean advised the faculty that, due to an unforeseen fiscal short-fall adversely affecting the current year's budget, agents of instruction would henceforth and immediately be responsible for delivering designed learning opportunities via alternate methods of delivery rather than shared-location instruction.

Slang

Slang is "street talk": nonstandard language that indicates a close, informal relationship among those who speak it. The innumerable examples of slang range from *A-OK* to *zowie*. Slang changes so rapidly that most dictionaries don't even attempt to keep up with all the terms. Because slang dates so quickly and because it is understood by a limited group of people, you should avoid it in your writing. Unless you are quoting someone who has used slang, use standard written English.

If you're in doubt about a word, check your dictionary. The notation *sl.* or *slang* appears after slang words or after a slang meaning of a word. Some words—e.g., *house*, *neat*, and *bombed*—have both a general meaning and a slang meaning. If the word in the sense in which you want to use it is not in your dictionary, then it may be current slang, too new to have been included. Taking the time to choose words and expressions appropriate to written English increases your chances of communicating clearly and of winning your readers' respect.

EXERCISE 28.6

The following are slang terms in current use. "Translate" them into general-level English words that would be appropriate in writing.

nerd	grind	diss
juice	bad	sick
stoked	wannabe	babe

EXERCISE 28.7

Make a list of the slang expressions you hear during one class period.

CHAPTER 29

Eliminating Wordiness

Wordiness is a problem that may develop if you try too hard to impress your reader. Keep in mind that nobody wants to read "fill" or "padding." Your writing should be as concise as you can make it and still convey your message clearly.

Here's an example of what can happen when, in trying to impress, you lose sight of the need to communicate. Do you recognize any of your writing in this?

> In my opinion, I feel very strongly indeed that the government of this Dominion of Canada is basically in need of an additional amount of meaningful input from its electors, the people of this country, at this point in time, frankly speaking. For too long a period of time, the leaders of this nation in Ottawa have, rightly or wrongly, gone heedlessly off on their own particular course of action without the benefit of consultation or dialogue with the people, who, it stands to reason, are most willing and able to provide, clearly and without doubt, a distinct and clear path to follow into the future world of tomorrow.

By eliminating wordiness, you can make this into a clear statement that might convince your readers rather than irritate them.

The following are some of the worst offenders we have collected from student writing. In some cases, many words are used when one or two would do. In others, the wording is **redundant** (it says the same thing twice).

WORDY	ACCEPTABLE
absolutely complete	complete
absolutely nothing	nothing
actual fact	fact
almost always	usually
at that point in time	then
basic fundamentals	fundamentals
circled around	circled
collect together	collect
completely free	free
continue on	continue
could possibly (*or* may possibly, might possibly)	could (*or* may, might)
dead bodies	corpses
disappear from view	disappear
entirely eliminated	eliminated
equally as good	as good
exactly identical	identical
few and far between	rare
final conclusion	conclusion
having the same thing in common	sharing
I personally feel	I feel
in my opinion, I think	I think
in this day and age	now
new innovation	innovation
personal friend	friend
proceed ahead	proceed
real, genuine leather	leather
red in colour	red
repeat again	repeat
repeat the same	repeat
seven A.M. in the morning	seven A.M.
small in size	small
such as, for example	such as
surround on all sides	surround
take active steps	take steps
totally destroyed	destroyed
true fact	fact
very (*or* most, quite, rather) unique	unique

> To avoid wordiness, eliminate clichés, repetition, redundancy, and unnecessary jargon from your writing.

EXERCISE 29.1

Revise these sentences, making them more concise and understandable. Suggested answers are on p. 372.

1. Basically, I myself prefer the real, genuine article to a phony imitation.

2. There was absolutely nothing they could do except keep on repeating the true facts.

3. In my opinion, I doubt that this particular new innovation will survive to see the light of day.

4. I personally think she is faking her illness and pretending to be sick so she can stay at home and not have to go to work.

5. The final results weren't known until he was completely free to announce himself successfully elected.

6. I will repeat again, for those of you who disappeared from view, that at this point in time we are completely lost.

7. Although his ideas seem to be fairly unique, we must be absolutely and completely positive that we don't repeat our same mistake again.

8. There comes a certain point in time when the last final reckoning is done, and when that time comes, you must reach a final conclusion.

9. They circled around behind the enemy and, at 4:00 A.M. in the morning on July 12, surrounded them on all sides, thus entirely eliminating the threat of an invasion.

10. Although small in size, yellow in colour, and ugly, his brand new car was, in point of fact, exactly identical to his old one.

EXERCISE 29.2

Revise the following paragraph by eliminating repetition, redundancy, clichés, and jargon. Then compare your revision with ours on p. 372.

One of the somewhat unique Christmas customs that I personally enjoy year after year is cutting my very own tree. I don't actually do this to save any actual money; I do it because I find that I can cut a tree equally as good as if not better than one that can be bought at a store, and I can actually have a good time, too, while I'm doing it. It goes without saying that personal friends who have the same idea of fun in common with me are more than welcome to come along and help me make the actual event a truly memorable experience. In this day and age, with things the way they are in the modern world, inexpensive and enjoyable activities are few and far between, and actually tramping off across the fields to a Christmas tree farm to cut one's very own Christmas tree is a very pleasant way to spend an afternoon. I myself almost always select a pine tree that is large in size and dark green in colour. Absolutely nothing conveys the spirit of the season like the clean, pungent, outdoorsy smell of fresh pine. Bringing home the lovely big tree for the Yuletide Christmas season is only part of the joy I experience, however. Just as important to me, personally, is the memory of close friends gathering together in one place to take part in the ceremony of selecting and cutting the year's annual holiday tree.

CHAPTER 30

Avoiding Abusages

Some words and expressions that appear in writing are simply incorrect. We've named these misused, misspelled, or nonstandard expressions **abusages.** Usage mistakes occur when bad speech habits spill over into writing. Using them makes the writer appear ignorant to anyone who knows anything about the English language. Abusages are never good English, even in speech. But we hear them so often in daily conversation that, after a while, they become so familiar they begin to sound right. They aren't, and you need to be aware of the ones that are most likely to trip you up. The list of abusages that follows includes some of the worst offenders. You should add to it the abusages your instructors hate most. Go through the list carefully and mark the expressions that sound all right to you. Then memorize the standard English equivalent beside each one. These are the expressions you will need to look out for when you edit your writing.

alot	There is no such word. Use *many* or *much.*
alright	This is a misspelling of *all right.*
anyways	Also, "anywheres" and "a long ways." There is no *s* on any of these words.
between you and I	A commonly misused expression for *between you and me.*
could of	Also, "would of," "should of," and so on. The helping verb is *have.* Write *could have, would have,* etc.

didn't do nothing	This, along with all other double negatives ("couldn't get nowhere," "wouldn't talk to nobody," and so on), is wrong. Write *didn't do anything* or *did nothing.*
irregardless	There is no such word. Use *regardless.*
irrelevant	This is a misspelling. Spell the word *irrelevant.*
media used as singular word	The word *media* is plural. The singular is *medium.* Write "TV is a mass medium. Print and radio are also examples of mass media."
off of	Use *off* alone: "I fell *off* the wagon."
prejudice used as an adjective	It is wrong to write "She is prejudice against men." Use *prejudiced.*
prejudism	There is no such word. Use *prejudice.* "A judge should show no prejudice to either side."
real used as an adverb	"Real sad," "real good," and "real nice" are wrong. Use *really* or *very.*
reason is because	Use *the reason is that:* "The reason is that I don't use a deodorant."
suppose to	Also, "use to." Use *supposed to* and *used to.*
themself	Also, "theirself," "ourselfs," "yourselfs," and "themselfs." The plural of *self* is *selves: themselves, ourselves,* and so on. Don't use "theirselves," though; there's no such word in standard written English.
youse	There is no such word. *You* is used for both singular and plural. When waiting on tables, don't say "May I help youse?" to a group of English teachers if you want a tip.

EXERCISE 30.1

Correct the following sentences where necessary. Answers are on p. 373.

1. I could of done alot of things, but I chose to become rich and powerful real quickly.

2. Irregardless of what you say, I think the media is generally reliable.

3. The reason Marisa came home was because she couldn't do nothing to
   help at the hospital.

4. They teach us alot of irrelevant things at this school.

5. Debra's father is not prejudiced; he hates all her boyfriends, regardless of their background.

6. Marco was suppose to be in the race, but he fell off of his bike during practice.

7. I should of stayed home, but I went anyways.

8. The reason youse are failing is because you don't do no homework.

9. The police department was accused of prejudism against minority groups.

10. Rudolf didn't do nothing to keep Krystal from doing what she wasn't supposed to do.

EXERCISE 30.2
Eliminate all of the abusages from this dreadful paragraph.

My friend Tim did real good in his last year of high school so his parents gave him a trip to Europe for two months before college. Two friends and him got themselfs on a cheap flight to Amsterdam and rented a car off of a guy who gave them a real good deal. They drove south to the French Riviera where there was suppose to be alot of other young travellers; it rained most of the time they were there. Irregardless of the rain and the cold temperatures, they would of gone swimming anyways, but when they discovered the beach was not sand but rocks, they got real discouraged and decided to go to Paris. There, they should of been more careful because late one night they almost got into a fight even though they didn't do nothing to cause it. The prices were real high as well. Tim thought the Parisians were displaying prejudism against tourists by charging nine dollars for a beer, but anyways they couldn't do nothing about it because they couldn't speak the language too good. They were real glad to get themselfs off of the plane in Vancouver. While they all felt it could of been worse, Europe wasn't nothing like they expected from what their friends had told them. Anyways, they decided it just wasn't like it use to be.

APPENDIXES

Readings

Writing a Good Business Letter

Brian Green

1   A good business letter is one that gets results. The best way to get results is to develop a letter that, in its appearance, style, and content, conveys information efficiently. To perform this function, a business letter should be concise, clear, and courteous.

2   The business letter must be concise. Little introduction or preliminary chat is necessary. Get to the point, make the point, and leave it. It is safe to assume that your letter is being read by a very busy person with all kinds of paper to deal with. Such a person does not want to spend time on a newsy letter about your ski trip or medical problem. Hone and refine your message until the words and sentences you have used are precise. Revision and rereading take time but are a necessary part of writing a good letter. A short business letter that makes its point quickly has much more impact on a reader than a long-winded, rambling exercise in creative writing. This does not mean that there is no place for style or even, on occasion, humour in the business letter. While it conveys a message in its contents, the letter also provides the reader with an impression of you, its author. Your style is part of the message.

3   The business letter must be clear. You should have a firm idea of what you want to say, and you should let the reader know it. Use the structure of the letter—the paragraphs, topic sentences, and transitions—to guide the reader point by point from your introduction, through your reasoning, to your conclusion. Paragraph often, to break up the page and to provide visual cues to the organization of your letter. Use an accepted business-letter format. There are several, and they can be found in any book of business English. Reread what you have written from the point of view of someone who is seeing it for the first time, and revise to be sure that all

necessary information is provided (including reference numbers, dates, and other identification) and that all explanations are clear. A clear message, clearly delivered, is the essence of business communication.

4   The business letter must be courteous. Sarcasm and insults are ineffective and can often work against you. If you are sure you are right, point out the fact as politely as possible, explain why you are right, and outline what you expect the reader to do. Always put yourself in the place of the person to whom you are writing. What sort of letter would you respond to? How effective would sarcasm and threats be in making you fulfill a request? Another form of courtesy is taking care in your writing or typing. Grammatical and spelling errors (even if you call them typing errors) tell a reader that you don't think enough of him or her to be careful. Such mistakes can lower the reader's opinion of you faster than anything you say, no matter how idiotic. There are excuses for ignorance; there are no excuses for sloppiness.

5   The business letter is your custom-made representative. It speaks for you and is a permanent record of your message. It can pay big dividends on the time you invest in giving it a concise message, a clear structure, and a courteous tone.

What I Have Lived For

Bertrand Russell

1   Three passions, simple but overwhelmingly strong, have governed my life: the longing for love, the search for knowledge, and unbearable pity for the suffering of mankind. These passions, like great winds, have blown me hither and thither, in a wayward course, over a deep ocean of anguish, reaching to the very verge of despair.

2   I have sought love, first, because it brings ecstasy—ecstasy so great that I would often have sacrificed all the rest of life for a few hours of this joy. I have sought it, next, because it relieves loneliness—that terrible loneliness in which one shivering consciousness looks over the rim of the world into the cold unfathomable lifeless abyss. I have sought it, finally, because in the union of love I have seen, in a mystic miniature, the prefiguring vision of the heaven that saints and poets have imagined. This is what I sought, and though it might seem too good for human life, this is what—at last—I have found.

3   With equal passion I have sought knowledge. I have wished to understand the hearts of men. I have wished to know why the stars shine. And I have tried to apprehend the Pythagorean power by which number holds sway above the flux. A little of this, but not much, I have achieved.

4   Love and knowledge, so far as they were possible, led upward toward the heavens. But always pity brought me back to earth. Echoes of cries of pain reverberate in my heart. Children in famine, victims tortured by oppressors, helpless old people a hated burden to their sons, and the whole world of loneliness, poverty, and pain make a mockery of what human life should be. I long to alleviate the evil, but I cannot, and I too suffer.

5   This has been my life. I have found it worth living, and would gladly live it again if the chance were offered me.

Flunking with Style

Nell Waldman

1   People often remark that succeeding in school takes plenty of hard work. The remark implies that failure is a product of general idleness and zero motivation. This is an opinion I'd like to challenge. My long and checkered past in numerous educational institutions has taught me that to fail grandly, to fail extravagantly, to go down in truly blazing splendour, requires effort and imagination. To fail your year in the grand style, you must antagonize your teachers, disdain your studies, and cheat on your work. Keep the following guidelines in mind.

2   The first step, antagonizing your teachers, isn't difficult if you keep in mind what it is that teachers like: intelligent, interested, even enthusiastic faces in front row centre. Show that you're bored before the class begins by slouching in a desk at the back of the room. Wear your Walkman, and don't forget to turn up the volume when the teacher starts to talk. Carry on running conversations with your seatmates. Aim an occasional snort or snicker in the teacher's direction when she's putting a complex point on the board. Above all, never volunteer an answer and respond sullenly with an "I dunno" if the teacher has the nerve to ask you a question. Before long, you'll have that teacher bouncing chalk stubs off your head. Once you've earned the loathing of your instructors, you'll be well on your way to a truly memorable failure.

3   The second step, disdaining your studies, is easy to master. They're probably B-O-R-I-N-G anyway. First, don't buy your books until close to midterm and keep them in their original condition; don't open, read, or note anything in them. Better yet, don't buy your texts at all. Second, never attempt to take notes in class. Third, stop going to class completely, but have lots of creative excuses for missed assignments: "My friend's aunt died"; "My gerbil's in a coma"; "My boyfriend was in another car wreck"; "My dog ate the lab report"; "I've got mono." You can bet your teachers will be really amused by these old standbys. By now you are well on your way to disaster.

4   The third step, cheating, will deliver the *coup de grâce* to your academic career. Should an instructor be so sadistic as to assign a research paper, just copy something out of a book that the librarian will be happy to find for you. Your instructor will be astonished at the difference between the book's polished professional prose and your usual halting scrawls; you're guaranteed a zero. During your exams, sit at the back and crane your neck to read your classmate's paper. Roll up your shirtsleeves to reveal the answers you've tattooed all over your forearms. Ask to be excused three or four

From Sarah Norton and Nell Waldman, eds., *Canadian Content* (Toronto: Holt, 1988).

times during the test so you can consult the notes you've stashed in the hall or the washroom. Be bold! Dig out your old wood-burning kit and emblazon cheat notes on the desk. If you want to ensure not just failure but actual expulsion, send in a ringer—a look-alike—to write the exam for you!

5   If you follow these guidelines, you will be guaranteed to flunk your year. Actively courting failure with verve, with flair, and with a sense of drama will not only ensure your status as an academic washout but will also immortalize you in the memories of teachers and classmates alike. The challenge is yours. Become a legend—pick up the torch and fall with it!

Surviving Your Daughter's Adolescence

Janet Read

1   Living with a teenage daughter can cause friction in an otherwise peaceful home. To survive the years of turbulence, you may find it helpful to observe three basic rules: never criticize, never say "No," and never argue. Observing these rules does not mean the teen will always get her own way, but the right words in the right place can turn a potential confrontation into a calm discussion.

2   For a loving mother, the first rule can be extremely difficult. When your beautiful daughter appears at the breakfast table looking as if she were going into combat instead of into class, it will not be easy for you to offer a compliment. Take a deep breath, count to three, and tell her in a convincing tone how much you like her sporty new outfit. A compliment may make her wonder if battle gear is really the look she wants to achieve. After all, if Mom likes it, how can her friends be expected to approve? Don't be surprised if she leaves for school looking almost presentable. In any event, you can be sure that three-quarters of the student population looks just like your child. If all else fails, remember your class picture of 1966.

3   When you are trying to keep peace, the next rule is never to give a negative reply. This simply means that you never say an outright "No." Her request may seem preposterous to you, but not to a fourteen-year-old. During this period in your child's life, peer pressure is the most difficult thing for her to deal with. Often the request—to go to the dance club, for instance—is coming indirectly from her friends. Instead of immediately blurting out the N-word, try to find out her reasons for feeling her life will be over if she can't attend this one event. The strategy may turn your basement into a substitute Palace Pier for an evening, but it will give you peace of mind.

4   Finally we come to the hardest rule for a parent to follow: don't, under any circumstances, argue. Females between the ages of thirteen and eighteen are world-class debaters. They can argue black is white, rain is snow, or bitter is sweet. The most hazardous time is the period when your baby of a few short years ago is learning to drive. She will become, after only two driving lessons, an authority on rules of the road. We have all coped with back-seat drivers, but nothing will have prepared you for this experience. The teenager feels a learner's permit is a licence to tell her parents how to drive. There are a few useful phrases you can employ to reduce the risk of argument: "Yes, dear." "Is that right?" "How astute of you to notice that!" These simple phrases can forestall an argument that would entertain your entire neighbourhood.

5   I am not trying to give the impression that faithful observance of these three rules will mean your daughter's teenage years will be clear sailing all the time. They can, however, make the waters of adolescence a lot calmer.

Student Janet Read wrote this essay in her first term of college.

An Immigrant's Split Personality

Sun-Kyung Yi

1   I am Korean-Canadian. But the hyphen often snaps in two, obliging me to choose to act as either a Korean or a Canadian, depending on where I am and who I'm with.

2   When I was younger, toying with the idea of entertaining two separate identities was a real treat, like a secret game for which no one knew the rules but me. I was known as Angela to the outside world, and as Sun-Kyung at home. I ate bologna sandwiches in the school lunch room and rice and and kimchee for dinner. I chatted about teen idols and giggled with my girlfriends during my classes, and ambitiously practiced piano and studied in the evenings, planning to become a doctor when I grew up. I waved hellos and goodbyes to my teachers, but bowed to my parents' friends visiting our home. I could also look straight in the eyes of my teachers and friends and talk frankly with them instead of staring at my feet with my mouth shut when Koreans talked to me. Going outside the home meant I was able to relax from the constraints of my cultural conditioning, until I walked back in the door and had to return to being an obedient and submissive daughter.

3   The game soon ended when I realized that it had become a way of life, that I couldn't change the rules without disappointing my parents and questioning all the cultural implications and consequences that came with being a hyphenated Canadian.

4   Many have tried to convince me that I am a Canadian, like all other immigrants in the country, but those same people also ask me which country I came from with great curiosity, following with questions about the type of food I ate and the language I spoke. It's difficult to feel a sense of belonging and acceptance when you are regarded as "one of them." "Those Koreans, they work hard. . . . You must be fantastic at math and science." (No.) "Do your parents own a corner store?" (No.)

5   Koreans and Canadians just can't seem to merge into "us" and "we."

6   Some people advised me that I should just take the best of both worlds and disregard the rest. That's ideal, but unrealistic when my old culture demands a complete conformity with very little room to manoeuvre for new and different ideas.

7   After a lifetime of practice, I thought I could change faces and become Korean on demand with grace and perfection. But working with a small Korean company in Toronto proved me wrong. I quickly became estranged from my own people. My parents were ecstatic at the thought of their daughter finally finding her roots and having a working opportunity to speak my native tongue and absorb the culture. For me, it was the most painful and frustrating 2½ months of my life.

8   When the president of the company boasted that he "operated little Korea," he meant it literally. A Canadianized Korean was not tolerated. I

looked like a Korean; therefore, I had to talk, act, and think like one, too. Being accepted meant a total surrender to ancient codes of behaviour rooted in Confucian thought, while leaving the "Canadian" part of me out in the parking lot with my '86 Buick. In the first few days at work, I was bombarded with inquiries about my marital status. When I told them I was single, they spent the following days trying to match me up with available bachelors in the company and the community. I was expected to accept my inferior position as a woman and had to behave accordingly. It was not a place to practice my feminist views, or be an individual without being condemned. Little Korea is a place for men (who filled all the senior positions) and women don't dare speak up or disagree with their male counterparts. The president (all employees bow to him and call him Mr. President) asked me to act more like a lady and smile. I was openly scorned by a senior employee because I spoke more fluent English than Korean. The cook in the kitchen shook her head in disbelief upon discovering that my cooking skills were limited to boiling a package of instant noodles. "You want a good husband, learn to cook," she advised me.

9   In less than a week I became an outsider because I refused to conform and blindly nod my head in agreement to what my elders (which happened to be everybody else in the company) said. A month later, I was demoted because "members of the workplace and the Korean community" had complained that I just wasn't "Korean enough," and I had "too much power for a single woman." My father suggested that "when in Rome do as the Romans." But that's exactly what I was doing. I am in Canada so I was freely acting like a Canadian, and it cost me my job.

10   My father also said, "It doesn't matter how Canadian you think you are, just look in the mirror and it'll tell you who you *really* are." But what he didn't realize is that an immigrant has to embrace the new culture to enjoy and benefit from what it has to offer. Of course, I will always be Korean by virtue of my appearance and early conditioning, but I am also happily Canadian and want to take full advantage of all that such citizenship confers. But for now I remain slightly distant from both cultures, accepted fully by neither. The hyphenated Canadian personifies the ideal of multiculturalism, but unless the host culture and the immigrant cultures can find ways to merge their distinct identities, sharing the best of both, this cultural schizophrenia will continue.

Sun-Kyung Yi, "An Immigrant's Split Personality," as appearing in *The Globe and Mail,* 12 April 1992. Reprinted by permission of Sun-Kyung Yi. Sun-Kyung Yi is a writer broadcaster in Toronto. She is the author of the book *Hidden Korea* (published Fall 1996).

The Myth of Canadian Diversity

1   Canadians cling to three myths about their country. The first is that it is young. In fact, Canada is well advanced into middle age. At 127, it has existed as a unified state for longer than either Italy (unified in 1870) or Germany (1871). Less than a third of the 180-odd nations now belonging to the United Nations existed in 1945, when Canada was already a mature 78. We were 51 when Iraq and Austria—two countries many think of as old—came into being.

2   The second myth is that, in everything but geography, Canada is a small country—small in population, small in economic heft. In fact, our population of 27 million is a fair size by international standards, bigger than that of Austria, Hungary, Sweden, Norway, Finland, Romania, Greece, Algeria, Peru and Venezuela, to name only a few. Our economy, by traditional measures, is the seventh-largest in the world.

3   But the most important myth about Canada—the one that distorts our self-image, warps our politics and may one day tear us apart—is the myth of Canadian diversity. Almost any Canadian will tell you that his Canada is a remarkably varied place. "Canada, with its regional, linguistic and cultural diversity, has never been easy to govern," wrote *The Globe and Mail* when Jean Chrétien became Prime Minister last fall. Provincial politicians routinely parrot this myth to push for greater regional powers; federal politicians repeat it to let people know what a hard job they have.

4   In fact, Canada is one of the most homogeneous countries in the world. A foreign visitor can travel from Vancouver in the West to Kingston in the centre without finding any significant difference in accent, in dress, in cuisine or even, in a broad sense, in values. A highschool student in Winnipeg talks, looks and acts much like his counterpart in Prince George. Where they do exist, our regional differences are no match for those of most other countries.

5   Canada may have a few regional accents in its English-speaking parts—the salty dialect of Newfoundland, the rural tones of the Ottawa Valley—but these are nothing compared with the dozens in the United States or Britain. It may have two official languages, but that is unlikely to impress India, which has 14.

6   To be certain, we have our French–English divide, two "nations" living under one roof. That hardly makes us unique either. Spain has the Catalans and the Basques. Russia has the Tatars, Ukrainians, Belarussians, Chechens, Moldavians, Udmurts, Kazakhs, Avars and Armenians. And, although few would dispute that francophone Quebec is indeed a distinct society, the differences between Quebec and the rest of Canada are diminishing over time.

"The Myth of Canadian Diversity," *The Globe and Mail,* 13 June 1994, A12. Reprinted by permission of the Globe and Mail.

As Lucien Bouchard himself has noted, we share a host of common attitudes—an attachment to the Canadian social system, tolerance of minorities, a respect for government and law.

7   Even our much-discussed ethnic differences are overstated. Although Canada is an immigrant nation and Canadians spring from a variety of backgrounds, a recent study from the C.D. Howe Institute says that the idea of a "Canadian mosaic"—as distinct from the American "melting pot"—is a fallacy. In *The Illusion of Difference,* University of Toronto sociologists Jeffrey Reitz and Raymond Breton show that immigrants to Canada assimilate as quickly into the mainstream society as immigrants to the United States do. In fact, Canadians are less likely than Americans to favour holding on to cultural differences based on ethnic background. If you don't believe Mr. Reitz and Mr. Breton, visit any big-city highschool, where the speech and behaviour of immigrant students just a few years in Canada is indistinguishable from that of any fifth-generation classmate.

8   This is not to say that Canada is a nation of cookie-cutter people. The differences among our regions, and between our two main language groups, are real. But in recent years we have elevated those differences into a cult. For all our disputes about language and ethnicity and regional rifts, our differences shrink beside our similarities, and the things that unite us dwarf those that divide us.

List of Grammatical Terms

adjective   a word that modifies (describes, restricts, relates to, makes more precise) a noun or pronoun. Adjectives answer the questions **What kind? How many? Which?**—e.g., the *competent* student; *five* home runs; my *last* class.

adverb   a word that modifies a verb, adjective, or other adverb. Adverbs answer the questions **When? How? Where? Why? How much?**—e.g., Nino talks *fast* (*fast* modifies the verb *talks*); he is a *very* fast talker (*very* modifies the adjective *fast*); he talks *really* fast (*really* modifies the adverb *fast*). Adverbs often—but not always—end in *-ly*.

antecedent   the word that a pronoun refers to or stands for. Literally, it means "coming before, preceding." The antecedent usually comes before the pronoun that refers to it—e.g., *Karen* believes *she* is possessed. (*Karen* is the antecedent to which the pronoun *she* refers.)

clause   a group of words that contains a subject and a verb. If the group of words can stand by itself and makes complete sense, it is called an **independent clause** (or **principal clause** or **main clause**). If the group of words does not make complete sense on its own but is linked to another clause (depends on the other clause for its meaning), it is called a **dependent** or **subordinate clause**. Here's an example: *The porch collapsed.* This group of words can stand by itself, so it is called an independent clause.

Now consider: ***When Kalim removed the railing with his tractor.*** This group of words has a subject, ***Kalim,*** and a verb, ***removed,*** but it does not make complete sense on its own. It depends for its meaning on ***the porch collapsed;*** therefore, it is a dependent clause.

colloquialism   a word or phrase that we use in casual conversation or in informal writing.

> Steve ***flunked*** his accounting exam.
> ***Did*** you ***get*** what the teacher said about job placement?
> I can't believe that ***guy*** is serious about learning.

comma splice   the error that results when the writer joins two independent clauses with a comma—e.g., ***The comma splice is an error, it is a kind of run-on sentence.*** (See Chapter 7.)

dependent-clause cue   a word or phrase that introduces a dependent clause— e.g., ***when, because, in order that, as soon as.*** See p. 62.

modifier   a word or group of words that adds information about another word (or phrase or clause) in a sentence. See ***adjective, adverb, dependent clause,*** and Chapter 8.

noun   a word that names a person, place, or thing and that has the grammatical capability of being possessive. There are concrete nouns that are **proper** (***Calgary, Beijing, Gaza, January, Sharon***); **common** (***woman, man, city, car, animal***); and **collective** (***group, audience, swarm, jury, committee***). There are also **abstract** nouns (***truth, softness, pride, confidence***). Unlike their concrete cousins, abstract nouns refer to concepts, ideas, characteristics—things we know or experience through our intellect rather than through our senses.

object   the "receiving" part of a sentence. The **direct object** is a noun or noun substitute (pronoun, phrase, or clause) that is the target or receiver of the action expressed by the verb. It answers the question **what?** or **whom?**—e.g., John threw the ***ball.*** (John threw ***what?***)

> He wondered ***where the money went.*** (He wondered ***what?***)
> Munira loves ***Abdul.*** (Munira loves ***whom?***)

The **indirect object** is a noun or pronoun that is the indirect target or receiver of the action expressed by the verb in a sentence. It is *always* placed in front of the direct object. It answers the question **to whom?** or **to what?**

> Doug threw ***me*** the ball. (Doug threw ***to whom?***)
> Lisa forgot to give ***her*** essay a title. (Give ***to what?***)

The **object of a preposition** is a noun or noun substitute (pronoun, phrase, or clause) that follows a preposition—e.g., after the ***storm*** (***storm*** is a noun, object of the preposition ***after***); before ***signing*** the lease (***signing the lease*** is a phrase, object of the preposition ***before***); he thought about ***what he wanted to do*** (***what he wanted to do*** is a clause, object of the preposition ***about***). Notice that what follows a preposition is always its object; that is why the subject of a sentence or clause can never be found in a prepositional phrase.

participle the form of a verb that can be used as an adjective (the *completed* work, the *weeping* willows) or as part of a verb phrase (am *succeeding,* have *rented*).

> The **present participle** of a verb ends in **-ing.**
> The **past participle** of a **regular verb** ends in **-d** or in **-ed.**
> For a list of **irregular verbs,** see pp. 118–19.

person a category of pronouns and verbs. **First person** refers to the person who is speaking (*I, we*). **Second person** refers to the person being spoken to (*you*). **Third person** is the person or thing being spoken about (*he, she, it, they*). Verb forms remain constant except in the present tense third person singular, which ends in *s.*

phrase a group of meaning-related words that acts as a noun, a verb, an adjective, or an adverb within a sentence. Phrases do not make complete sense on their own because they do not contain both a subject and a verb.

> Please order *legal-size manila file folders.* (phrase acting as noun)
> I *must have been sleeping* when you called. (verb phrase)
> *Sightseeing in Ottawa,* we photographed the monuments on *Parliament Hill.* (phrases acting as adjectives)
> Portaging a canoe *in this weather* is no fun. (phrase acting as adverb)

prefix a meaningful letter or group of letters added to the beginning of a word either (1) to change its meaning or (2) to change its word class.

> 1. **a** + moral = amoral
>   **bi** + sexual = bisexual
>   **contra** + indication = contraindication
>   **dys** + functional = dysfunctional
> 2. **a** + board (noun) = aboard (adverb, preposition)
>   **con** + temporary (adjective) = contemporary (noun, adjective)
>   **de** + nude = denude (verb)
>   **in** + put (verb) = input (noun)

Some prefixes require a hyphen, as here:

> **all**-Canadian
> **de**-emphasize
> **mid**-morning

preposition a word that connects a noun, pronoun, or phrase to some other word(s) in a sentence. The noun, pronoun, or phrase is the **object** of the preposition.

> I prepared the minutes *of the union meeting.* (*of* relates *meeting* to *minutes*)
> One *of the parents* checks the children every half hour. (**of** relates *parents* to *One*)

prepositional phrase a group of grammatically related words having the function of a noun, adjective, or adverb and beginning with a preposition. See the list on p. 50.

pronoun a word that is noun-like. Pronouns usually substitute for nouns, but sometimes they substitute for other pronouns.

> *He* will promote *anything that* brings in money.
> *Everyone* must earn *her* badges.

There are several kinds of pronouns:

personal: *I, we; you; he, she, it, they; me, us; him, her, them*
possessive: *my, our; your; his, her, its, their*
demonstrative: *this, these; that, those*
relative: *who, whom, whose; which, that*
interrogative: *who? whose? whom? which? what?*
indefinite: all *-one, -thing, -body* pronouns, such as *everyone, something,* and *anybody; each; neither; either; few; none; several*

subject in a sentence, the person, thing, or concept that the sentence is about—the topic of the sentence (see Chapter 12). In an essay, what the paper is about—the topic of the paper (see Chapter 22).

suffix a letter or group of letters that is added to the end of a word (1) to change its meaning, (2) to change its grammatical function, or (3) to change its word class.

1. king + *dom* = kingdom
   few +*er* = fewer
   tooth + *less* = toothless
2. buy (base form) + *s* = buys (third person singular, present tense)
   eat (base form) + *en* = eaten (past participle)
   instructor + *s* = instructors (plural)
   instructor + *'s* = instructor's (possessive singular)
3. your (adjective) + *s* = yours (pronoun)
   act (verb) + *ive* = active (adjective)
   active (adjective) + *ly* = actively (adverb)
   ventilate (verb) + *tion* = ventilation (noun)

Some words add two or more prefixes and/or suffixes to the base form. Look at *antidisestablishmentarianism,* for example. How many prefixes and suffixes can you identify?

tense The different forms of the verb used to indicate past, present, or future time are called **tenses.** The verb ending (e.g., play*s*, play*ed*) and any helping verbs associated with the main verb (*is* playing, *will* play, *has* played, *had* played, *will have* played) indicate the tense of the verb.

There are simple tenses:
present: *ask, asks*
past: *asked*
future: *will ask*

and perfect tenses:
present: *have (has) asked*
past: *had asked*
future: *will (shall) have asked*

The simple and perfect tenses can also be **progressive:** *am asking, have been asking,* etc.

transition a word or phrase that helps readers to follow the text smoothly from one sentence to the next or from one paragraph to another. See Chapter 25.

verb a word or phrase that says something about a person, place, or thing and whose form may be changed to indicate tense. Verbs may make a statement, ask a question, or give commands. They may express action (physical or mental), occurrence, or condition (state of being).

> Wesley *hit* an inside curve for a home run. (physical action)
> Laurence *believed* the Blue Jays would win. (mental action)
> Father's Day *falls* on the first Sunday of June. (occurrence)
> Reva eventually *became* interested in English. (condition)

Some verbs are called **linking verbs:** they help to make a statement by linking the subject to a word or phrase that describes it.

> William Hubbard *was* Toronto's first Black mayor. (*was* links *William Hubbard* to *mayor*)
> Mohammed *looks* tired. (*looks* links *Mohammed* and *tired*)

In addition to *am, is, are, was, were,* and *been,* some common linking verbs are *appear, become, feel, grow, look, taste, remain, seem, smell, sound.*

Another class of verbs is called **auxiliary** or **helping verbs.** They show the time of a verb as future or past (*will* go, *has* gone), or as a continuing action (*is* reading). They also show the passive voice (*is* completed, *have been* submitted).

voice verbs may be **active** or **passive,** depending on whether the subject of the verb is *acting* (active voice) or *being acted upon* (passive voice).

> In 1995, the Liberal government *introduced* another set of tax reforms. (active)
> Another set of tax reforms *was introduced* in 1995. (passive)

Answers to Exercises

Answers to Chapter 1: Three Suggestions for Quick Improvement (Pages 3 to 13)

Exercise 1.1
1. *blonde*. No, they are not interchangeable. A *blond* is a male; a *blonde* is a female.
2. *humor*. You must use the root *humor* when adding an ending: e.g., *humorous*.
3. The word is spelled *tattoo*, and can be used both as a noun and as a verb.
4. *Ketchup* is the preferred spelling of the word, which can also be spelled *catchup* and *catsup*.
5. *program, theater, center, medieval, judgment*. The preferred spellings are *program, theatre, centre, medieval*, and *judgment*.

Exercise 1.2
1. echoes
2. ratios
3. criteria
4. ghettos
5. personnel
6. crises
7. data (the singular is datum)
8. phenomena
9. nuclei (*or* nucleuses)
10. appendixes (*or* appendices)

Exercise 1.3
1. loneliness
2. copied
3. craziness
4. easily
5. happier
6. replies
7. replied
8. twentieth
9. necessarily
10. trafficking

Exercise 1.4
1. pro-cess
2. man-age-ment
3. ac-com-mo-date
4. dis-tri-bu-tion
5. through (Words of one syllable cannot be divided.)
6. cha-os
7. so-ci-o-path
8. al-go-rithm
9. hi-er-ar-chy
10. Al-gon-qui-an

Exercise 1.6
1. safely
2. arguing
3. sizable
4. accelerating
5. extremely
6. improvement
7. reducing
8. usable
9. immediately
10. requiring

Exercise 1.7
1. sincerely
2. coherence
3. valuable
4. guidance
5. discouraging
6. icy
7. completely
8. purchasing
9. collapsible
10. encouragement

Exercise 1.8
1. boring
2. movement
3. scarcely
4. unusable
5. careful
6. advertisement
7. excusable
8. providing
9. sensible
10. improvement

Exercise 1.9
1. safety
2. ranging
3. reducible
4. balancing
5. entirely
6. insurance
7. definitely
8. careless
9. responsible
10. distancing

Exercise 1.11
1. planning
2. stopping
3. admitted
4. nailing
5. stirred
6. commissioner
7. putting
8. writing
9. mapping
10. interrupted

Exercise 1.12
1. suffering
2. quizzed
3. permitting
4. stripped
5. meeting
6. compelling
7. cropped
8. tipping
9. allotting
10. quartered

Exercise 1.13
1. preferring
2. omitted
3. transferring
4. developing
5. controller
6. occurred
7. equipping
8. forgotten
9. writing
10. preferred

Exercise 1.14
1. overlapped
2. expelling
3. quizzed
4. acquitted
5. focusing

6. excelling
7. developed
8. transferred
9. paralleled
10. rebelling

Exercise 1.15
1. occurrence
2. existence
3. coherence
4. concurring
5. interfering

6. subsistence
7. difference
8. dependence
9. recurrence
10. insistence

Exercise 1.17
1. brief
2. cashier
3. receive
4. pierce
5. relief

6. retrieve
7. ceiling
8. believe
9. deceitful
10. hygiene

Exercise 1.18
1. grieved, vein
2. freight, surveillance
3. receipt, eight

4. relief, conceit
5. achieved, thieves

Exercise 1.19
1. chow mein, stein
2. Neither, Geiger counter
3. neighbour, niece

4. beige, leisure
5. conceivable, either

Answers to Chapter 2: Sound-Alikes, Look-Alikes, and Spoilers (Pages 14 to 27)

Exercise 2.1
1. effect, courses
2. Our, accepted
3. dessert, than
4. you're, losing
5. quiet, hear

6. Your, conscious
7. fourth, than
8. it's, its
9. advise, choose
10. Except, minor

Exercise 2.2
1. You're, conscience
2. fourth, chose
3. quiet, hear
4. principle, principal
5. conscience, your

6. stationary, its
7. lose, too, morale
8. Does, woman
9. lose, it's
10. choose, moral, course

Exercise 2.3
1. peace, quiet
2. many, deserts
3. then, choose, latter
4. Many, lose
5. You're, your, dose

6. affect, morale
7. compliment, than
8. principle, then
9. It's, later
10. counsellor, woman, principle

Exercise 2.4

1. It's, women
2. later, except
3. there, peace, our
4. than, morals
5. Where, we're
6. hear, you're, chose, course
7. whose, advice
8. advice, personal, it's
9. their, moral
10. principal, peace, minor

Exercise 2.5

1. are, conscious
2. affected, personal
3. then, excepted
4. loose, accept
5. it's, principle
6. minors, they're, they're
7. chose, dining
8. than, our
9. too, coarse, to
10. hear, your

Exercise 2.6

Led by my desire to watch more television **than** the six or seven hours a day I normally viewed, I decided to subscribe to satellite TV. The **effect** of this move was **later** to prove detrimental to my health and my wealth. First, I did not know that **there** is a monthly subscription fee in addition to the initial purchase price of almost $1000 for the "unobtrusive pizza-sized **stationary** dish antenna." Second, I was **quite** surprised to find that I was able to get many "pay-per-view" programs in addition to the basic 40 available stations. I was even more surprised to discover how fast I was running up a bill by **choosing** to view these optional programs. To restore my **peace** of mind, not to mention my bank balance, I telephoned the satellite service **personnel** to request that they limit my monthly spending for pay-per-view programs. Seven hockey games, four basketball games, **two** movies, six music specials, and an award ceremony **later**, my TV screen informed me that I had reached my spending limit. I'm afraid I responded with a few **coarse** expressions, since I was all set to see a new fine **dining** show on exotic **desserts** featuring papaya as the **principal** ingredient. Then, my TV screen informed me I could override my limit simply by pressing "star." I did, and went on watching with a clear **conscience** since, after all, I had limited my spending. Besides **its effect** on my budget, satellite service caused me to **lose** what little muscle tone I had left, since the only times I leave the couch are to go **forth** to the kitchen for more food. The **moral** of my sad story is that **you're** probably better off with less choice and poorer quality on **your** TV than in **your** life.

Exercise 2.7

1. Moments after **its** takeoff, the plane banked **too** sharply to the left.
2. I certainly won't **choose** the one **whose** application was late.
3. Please check with the **Personnel** Department before you hire legal **counsel**.
4. If he **does** that again, it will **affect** his chances for promotion.
5. The Canada **Council** will announce its awards **later** this month.
6. When I receive a **compliment**, I feel self-**conscious**.
7. **Whose** turn is it to find the **complement** of the angle?
8. If you could remember these three simple rules, **then your** spelling troubles would be over.
9. **There** are many children who believe the tooth fairy will come if they **lose** a tooth.
10. The **minor** skirmish before the game had the **effect** of making us absolutely determined to win.

Answers for Chapter 3: Capital Letters (Pages 28 to 31)

Exercise 3.1
1. **D**iana always wanted to be a **p**rincess when she grew up.
2. It amazes me that anyone could think *Beavis and Butthead* is funny.
3. Beatrix, queen of **T**he **N**etherlands, visited Canada last **w**inter.
4. The **R**otary **C**lub of Halifax sponsors a scholarship to **D**alhousie **U**niversity.
5. Gina tries hard, but she'll never be as good at **d**ata **p**rocessing as Ravi.
6. *Black Robe* was a Canadian-made film that featured international stars as well as young **C**anadian actors.
7. I should be looking for a sensible **s**edan, but I'm tempted by the **s**ports **m**odels every time I visit the GM, **F**ord, or **H**onda dealer.
8. I wonder how the **c**ollege gets away with requiring us students to take English and mathematics in addition to our **m**ajor subjects.
9. We were late for **P**rofessor Chan's lecture on **t**ime **m**anagement.
10. Stock is running low, so if you need **X**erox paper or toner, you'd better see Carla in **O**ffice **S**upplies right away.

Exercise 3.2
1. My **m**other and **f**ather drive **s**outh each **f**all to look at the leaves.
2. Ali went with his **E**nglish class to the Calgary **S**tampede and then to the West Edmonton **M**all.
3. Alain took a **G**reyhound bus to the **c**oast and then a ferry to Prince Edward Island.
4. Her parents thought they were seeing Gina off to **u**niversity, but in fact she spent the **w**inter in Mexico.
5. I've always wanted to be a **p**ope, but, unfortunately, I am not **I**talian, **C**atholic, or male.
6. Luc went to Paris last **s**ummer to study **F**rench, art history, and gourmet cooking.
7. Although I am generally fairly **c**onservative, I consider myself a **l**iberal on matters such as abortion and gun control.
8. Clement works for **B**ell **C**anada, which has an office on Bayview **A**venue.
9. After the **b**aseball and **h**ockey seasons were cancelled, Sabina became a **b**asketball fan and now is devoted to the **R**aptors.
10. A letter to the **e**ditor in today's *Globe and Mail* says Jean Chrétien's claim to fame is that "he is the only Canadian **p**rime **m**inister to have mastered neither of the country's two **o**fficial **l**anguages."

Exercise 3.3
1. Since you have yet to pass a single **p**hysics or **m**ath course, I suggest you reconsider your decision to be an **e**ngineer.
2. As the official representative of **Q**ueen Elizabeth, Canada's **g**overnor **g**eneral opens each new session of **p**arliament.
3. During the **s**pring break, Saieed drove down to **F**lorida, where he toured **W**alt **D**isney **W**orld, the **E**pcot **C**enter, and Busch **G**ardens.
4. The Quebec **p**remier influences not only the policies of his own **p**rovince, but also those of the rest of Canada.
5. After Clive missed the meeting, the **p**resident told him angrily, "**T**hat, **y**oung **m**an, was what is called a CLM: a career-limiting move."
6. Visitors to Canada are sometimes surprised to find they cannot see the **R**ockies, Niagara **F**alls, Newfoundland, and the arctic **t**undra all in one week.

7. We stopped at **S**afeway for the basics: spaghetti, milk, a box of **K**ellogg's corn-flakes, and a tube of **C**rest.
8. Canada's **I**mmigration **A**ct sets out the policies that govern the conditions for entry into the **c**ountry by immigrants from all over the **w**orld.
9. We went to see Atom Egoyan's film *Exotica*, which was playing at the **C**apitol theatre.
10. Among Canada's great waterways, the St. Lawrence **R**iver, the Mackenzie **R**iver, the Fraser **R**iver, and the **R**ed **R**iver are the most interesting to me because of the role each played in developing our **n**ation.

Answers for Chapter 4: The Apostrophe (Pages 32 to 40)

Exercise 4.1
1. you're
2. we'd
3. they'll
4. can't
5. I'll
6. didn't
7. shouldn't
8. could've
9. who'd
10. everybody's

Exercise 4.2
1. can't
2. she'd
3. didn't
4. let's
5. she'll
6. wouldn't
7. we'd
8. they're
9. won't
10. he'll

Exercise 4.3
1. **We'll** have to postpone the meeting because **they're** still not here.
2. If Krystal finds out **what's** been going on, **she'll** be furious.
3. **It's** been a long time since **we've** had a break, **hasn't** it?
4. **We're** still about 10 km away from where **they'd** planned to meet us.
5. **It's** a tough decision, but **somebody's** got to make it, or **we'll** never get out of here.
6. Hockey is Canada's most popular game, so **I'm** surprised to learn **it's** not our official national sport.
7. **Everyone's** welcome, but if **you're** all coming, **we'd** better buy another keg.
8. **He's** offered to drive all those **who're** going to the game.
9. **Let's** first find out **who's** coming; then **we'll** know if **we've** bought enough to go around.
10. **You'll** have to wait until **he's** sure you **haven't** brought along someone **who's** under age.

Exercise 4.4
1. woman's
2. technicians'
3. the Simpsons'
4. management's
5. workers'
6. someone's
7. Iguassu Falls' (or Iguassu Falls's)
8. memo's
9. babies'
10. Dennis's (or Dennis')

Exercise 4.5
1. **Biff's** favourite pastime is spending his **girlfriend's** money.
2. **Whose** fault is it that the **car's** tank is empty?

3. After about one **second's** hesitation, I accepted a **week's** pay instead of time off.
4. **Bikers'** equipment is on special at **Leather Larry's**.
5. Virtue may be **its** own reward, but I won't refuse **your** offer of cash.
6. Our college aims to meet its **students'** social needs as well as **their** academic goals.
7. To **no one's** surprise, the **children's** scores were higher than ours on every game we tried.
8. The traditional male dominance in medicine and law is disappearing as **women's** acceptance into these programs now exceeds **men's**.
9. The **college's** climate survey revealed that most **students'** opinion of their program is positive.
10. **The United States'** vast wealth makes some Canadians wonder whether it is worth maintaining our **country's** independence.

Exercise 4.6
1. **Mei-ling's** paper got a better grade than **Louis's**.
2. **Gordie Howe's** record may eventually fall, but his **career's** achievements will never be surpassed.
3. Alicia gave one **month's** notice before leaving her position as **children's** wear buyer for **Eaton's**.
4. After the **union's** strike threat, the **owners'** solution was to lock out the players for the rest of the season.
5. One of **Toronto's** landmarks is **Honest Ed's** store at the corner of Bloor and Bathurst.
6. Canadian **authors'** works are increasingly recommended by the **Ministry of Education's** curriculum planners.
7. **Cassandra's** fate was probably more miserable than **anyone's**, including **Achilles'**.
8. Our **group's** presentation was on **Davies'** *Fifth Business,* while **theirs** was on **Yeats's** early poetry.
9. The **survey's** results were not surprising: more than half the voters surveyed were unhappy with **their MP's** performance.
10. **Dorothy Parker's** solution to boredom was to hang a sign on her office door reading "**Men's** Room."

Exercise 4.7
1. **Today's** popular music is returning to the sounds and themes of its roots in the sixties.
2. Our government is not serious about solving its financial problems; in fact, **it's** getting deeper and deeper into debt.
3. **Charles's** feelings about **Diana's** book are well-known, but who knows what **Camilla's** thoughts are?
4. A **patient's** fears can be eased by a sensitive **nurse's** attention.
5. The girls won the **cheater's** money in **Luisa's father's** poker game.
6. The **speaker's** topic was well beyond our **class's** ability to understand.
7. We were told to read Northrop **Frye's** essay, "**Don't** You Think **It's** Time to Start Thinking?" for **tomorrow's** class.
8. In the paper today, **there's** a short article entitled, "**It's** Clear the **Apostrophe's** Days are Numbered, **Isn't** It?"
9. At her **wits'** end, the angry mother turned to her daughter and shouted, "**Who're** you to tell me what **you'll** do and **won't** do?"

10. **The Crash Test Dummies'** first major hit was the off-beat "**Superman's** Song"; in contrast, their award-winning *God Shuffled His Feet* features Brad **Roberts'** songs, which are rich in symbolism and insight.

Exercise 4.8
1. The **men's** changing room is easy to find; **it's** across the hall and around the corner from the **women's** gym.
2. A good grasp of grammar and spelling **doesn't** guarantee success in **your** chosen career, but it helps.
3. **Tennis's** appeal is probably due to the fact that **it's** a game that can be played by people of all **ages**.
4. An **actor's** talent can ensure a **play's** success, even when the **critics'** reviews are negative.
5. Our instructor recommended we buy either *Roget's Thesaurus* or *Soule's Dictionary of Synonyms,* **didn't** she?
6. Professor **Green's** patience quickly evaporated when he discovered the class had not done **their** assignment on the use and abuse of **apostrophes**.
7. T-shirt **ads** are a bonus for a **product's** manufacturer, who **doesn't** have to pay for the **wearer's** (*or* **wearers'**) time or effort in promoting the product.
8. **It's** clear their idea of a good time is not the same as **ours**, since **they've** invited us to an **opera's** opening performance and a formal reception afterward.
9. Dwight struggled to get into his **brother's** tuxedo, but **its** sleeves were about 8 cm too short for his arms.
10. **Children's** wear and **women's** shoes are on the first floor, next to the **odds-and-ends** department.

Exercise 4.9

Jess decided that she should buy a dog for **its** ability to protect her and her apartment. Several of her **neighbours'** houses had been broken into recently, and Jess felt that the **dog's** bark might discourage intruders. So Jess went to the library and began to research various **breeds'** characteristics and **breeders'** reputations. A **day's** work in the stacks convinced her that she **couldn't** possibly learn everything there was to know about every breed of dog, so she focussed her research on three **whose** temperament seemed suitable for her purposes: the Doberman, the Bouvier, and the German Shepherd. The **Doberman's** reputation for fierceness was impressive, but the **Bouvier's** loyalty and the **Shepherd's** intelligence were also appealing. Finally, Jess concluded that **it's** a gamble no matter how you choose a dog, and one **animal's** individual characteristics might well outweigh the **breed's** general traits. In the end, **Jess's** decision was to go to the Humane Society and choose a mutt **whose** big, brown eyes and cheerful disposition she found irresistible. As she paid her money and collected her dog, together with the **veterinarian's** certificate of the **animal's** fitness, Jess consoled herself with the thought that even if she couldn't train it to protect it's owner, at least **she'd** have a cuddly companion.

Answers for Chapter 5: Cracking the Sentence Code (Pages 43 to 56)

Exercise 5.1
1. <u>Algy</u> <u>met</u>
2. <u>bear</u> <u>met</u>
3. <u>bear</u> <u>was</u>
4. <u>bulge</u> <u>was</u>
5. <u>Grizzlies</u> <u>are</u>
6. <u>Meeting</u> . . . <u>is</u>
7. <u>bears</u> . . . <u>run</u>
8. <u>(You)</u> <u>take</u> it from me. <u>They</u> <u>do</u>.
9. <u>Females</u> . . . <u>are known</u>
10. <u>Defending</u> . . . <u>presents</u>

Exercise 5.2
1. <u>Change</u> <u>is</u> the only constant in life.
2. <u>Information</u> <u>doubles</u> every 18 months.
3. Our <u>survival</u> <u>depends</u> on our ability to adapt to change.
4. Today, effective <u>planning</u> <u>means</u> training for change.
5. Otherwise, <u>we</u> <u>risk</u> becoming roadkill on the highway of life.
6. <u>Learning</u> to adapt to change <u>is</u>, therefore, everyone's challenge.
7. <u>Silicon</u>, a form of sand, <u>is</u> a computer chip's main component.
8. To get ahead in the 90s, <u>people</u> <u>need</u> knowledge from many fields.
9. Soon, a single <u>crystal</u> <u>will hold</u> the entire Library of Congress.
10. Ironically, high <u>technology</u> <u>is</u> now our forests' best friend.

Exercise 5.3
1. <u>Canada</u> <u>is</u>
2. <u>word</u> . . . <u>means</u>
3. <u>Newfoundland</u> <u>is</u>
4. <u>Are</u> <u>you</u>
5. <u>is</u> . . . <u>CN Tower</u>
6. <u>Money</u> . . . <u>does</u>
7. <u>are</u> . . . <u>steps</u>
8. <u>Flin Flon</u> <u>is named</u>
9. <u>idea</u> <u>was</u>
10. <u>(You)</u> <u>drive</u>

Exercise 5.4
1. <u>Doing</u> . . . <u>is</u>
2. <u>Were</u> <u>they</u>
3. <u>were</u> . . . <u>children</u>
4. <u>Are</u> <u>you</u>
5. <u>Stampede</u> <u>is held</u>
6. <u>(You)</u> . . . <u>stop</u>
7. <u>address</u> <u>is</u>
8. <u>Have</u> <u>you</u> <u>finished</u>
9. <u>lives</u> . . . <u>family</u>
10. <u>lived</u> . . . <u>tribe</u>

Exercise 5.5
1. <u>Dwight</u> <u>is sleeping</u>
2. <u>You</u> <u>should have been paying</u>
3. <u>Should</u> <u>we</u> <u>conclude</u>
4. <u>fall</u> <u>arrives</u>
5. <u>did</u> <u>you</u> <u>get</u>
6. <u>We</u> <u>do</u> . . . <u>want</u>
7. <u>are</u> <u>we</u> <u>meeting</u>
8. <u>old</u> <u>will</u> . . . <u>think</u>
9. <u>coach</u> <u>has</u> . . . <u>begun</u>
10. <u>swam</u> . . . <u>shark</u>

Exercise 5.6
1. <u>country</u> <u>is covered</u>
2. <u>would</u> <u>anyone</u> <u>want</u>
3. <u>Canadians</u> <u>should be</u>
4. <u>will</u> I <u>agree</u>
5. <u>person</u> <u>may forgive</u>
6. <u>have been</u> . . . <u>players</u>
7. <u>You</u> <u>can become</u>
8. <u>did</u> . . . <u>you</u> <u>stay</u>
9. <u>Have</u> <u>you</u> . . . <u>been</u>
10. <u>has</u> . . . <u>coach</u> <u>become interested</u>

Exercise 5.7
1. <u>gasoline</u> . . . <u>will be</u>
2. <u>network</u> <u>will have been completed</u>
3. <u>are</u> . . . <u>records</u> <u>called</u>
4. <u>provinces</u> <u>were</u> . . . <u>railroaded</u>
5. <u>I</u> <u>am</u> . . . <u>studying</u>
6. <u>Could</u> . . . <u>government</u> <u>have managed</u>
7. <u>Have</u> . . . <u>you</u> <u>been caught</u>
8. <u>little</u> <u>is known</u>
9. <u>do</u> . . . <u>we</u> . . . <u>agree</u>
10. <u>Are</u> . . . <u>you</u>

Exercise 5.8
1. A <u>bird</u> ~~in the hand~~ <u>is</u> worth two ~~in the bush~~.
2. Only a <u>few</u> ~~of us~~ <u>have done</u> our homework.
3. <u>Most</u> ~~of your answers~~ <u>are</u> entertaining but wrong.
4. More than a dozen <u>brands</u> ~~of video recorders~~ <u>are</u> now ~~on the market~~.
5. <u>(You)</u> <u>meet</u> me ~~at six~~ <u>at the corner</u> ~~of Robson and Granville~~.

6. A <u>couple</u> ~~of hamburgers~~ <u>should be</u> enough ~~for each of us~~.
7. <u>Do</u> <u>you</u> <u>know</u> anything ~~about the latest rumours~~ ~~in the government~~?
8. There <u>is</u> a <u>show</u> ~~about laser technology~~ ~~on television~~ tonight.
9. ~~After eight hours~~ ~~of classes~~, the <u>thought</u> ~~of collapsing~~ ~~in front~~ ~~of the TV set~~ <u>is</u> very appealing.
10. One <u>episode</u> ~~of *Geraldo*~~ <u>was</u> more than enough for me.

Exercise 5.9
1. The <u>verb</u> ~~in this sentence~~ <u>is</u> "is."
2. ~~For many students~~, <u>lack</u> ~~of money~~ <u>is</u> probably the most serious problem.
3. ~~In the middle~~ ~~of May,~~ ~~after the end~~ ~~of term~~, the <u>Intercollegiate Arm-Wrestling Championships</u> <u>will be held</u>.
4. One <u>strand</u> ~~of fibre optics~~ <u>can carry</u> both telephone and television signals.
5. ~~During the second week~~ ~~of term~~, the <u>class</u> <u>will be taken</u> ~~on a tour~~ ~~of the resource centre~~.
6. ~~Contrary to your expectations~~, and ~~despite the rumours~~, your <u>instructor</u> <u>does</u> not <u>bite</u>.
7. ~~On Callisto~~, one ~~of Jupiter's thirteen moons~~, <u>snow</u> <u>"falls"</u> up, not down.
8. ~~On the eastern shore~~ ~~of Vancouver Island~~, <u>you</u> <u>can find</u> both oysters and clams.
9. <u>One</u> ~~of the most entertaining comedies~~ ~~of the 1990s~~ <u>was</u> *Wayne's World*.
10. ~~In similar circumstances~~, <u>most</u> ~~of us~~ <u>would</u> probably <u>have taken</u> the money.

Exercise 5.10
1. ~~By this time~~, <u>you</u> <u>must be</u> tired ~~of the pointless game shows~~ ~~on TV~~.
2. The <u>happiness</u> ~~of every country~~ <u>depends</u> ~~on the character~~ ~~of its people~~.
3. ~~Above my desk~~ <u>hangs</u> someone else's <u>diploma</u>.
4. ~~During the course~~ ~~of the discussion~~, <u>several</u> ~~of us~~ <u>lost</u> our tempers.
5. ~~In law~~, a <u>sentence</u> <u>is</u> a decision ~~by a judge~~ ~~on the punishment~~ ~~of a criminal~~.
6. The <u>"short side"</u> ~~of a goalie~~ <u>is</u> the side closer to the post.
7. New <u>steps</u> <u>should be taken</u> to encourage the flow ~~of capital into small businesses~~.
8. ~~After waiting~~ ~~for more than an hour~~, <u>we</u> finally <u>left</u> ~~without you~~.
9. So far only <u>two</u> ~~of your answers~~ ~~to the questions~~ <u>have been</u> incorrect.
10. <u>One</u> ~~of the country's most distinguished reporters~~ <u>will speak</u> ~~on the responsibilities~~ ~~of the press~~.

Exercise 5.11
1. The average <u>height</u> ~~of Canadian women~~, excluding those ~~in Quebec~~, <u>is</u> 165 cm.
2. ~~By waiting~~ ~~on tables,~~ ~~(by) babysitting~~, and ~~(by) doing other jobs~~, <u>I</u> <u>manage</u> to make ends meet.
3. The <u>pile</u> ~~of books and papers~~ ~~on your desk~~ <u>is</u> about as neat as a tossed salad.
4. Only a <u>few</u> ~~of the news reporters~~ ~~on television~~ <u>are</u> responsible ~~for researching and writing~~ ~~in addition~~ ~~to reading the news~~.
5. ~~Except for Biff~~, <u>everyone</u> <u>understands</u> prepositions.
6. No <u>book</u> ~~of Canadian humour~~ <u>would be</u> complete ~~without a couple~~ ~~of "Newfie" jokes~~.
7. Our teacher's <u>uncertainty</u> ~~about the date~~ ~~of the War of 1812~~ <u>made</u> us less than confident ~~about his knowledge~~ ~~of Canadian history~~.
8. A daily <u>intake</u> ~~of more than 600 mg~~ ~~of caffeine~~ <u>can result</u> ~~in headaches,~~ ~~(in) insomnia~~, and ~~(in) heart palpitations~~.
9. Six to ten <u>cups</u> ~~of coffee~~ <u>will contain</u> 600 mg ~~of caffeine~~.
10. ~~Despite its strong taste~~, <u>espresso</u> <u>contains</u> no more caffeine than regular coffee.

Exercise 5.12
1. The current trend ~~in electronics~~ is to put telephones ~~in our pockets~~ and televisions ~~in our telephones~~.
2. ~~Like many other Canadian expressions~~, the term *bluenose*, meaning a Nova Scotian, ~~is of uncertain origin~~.
3. ~~Within a week~~, please give me your report ~~on the pyrazine anion project~~. (The subject is you.)
4. ~~In the spring~~, parked ~~in front of his TV set~~, Barry trains ~~for the Stanley Cup playoffs~~.
5. Government programs ~~to encourage training in basic skills~~ have been cut back steadily ~~over the past few years~~.
6. ~~In the Arctic wastes~~ of Ungava, there is a mysterious stone structure ~~in the shape of a giant hammer~~ standing ~~on end~~.
7. There is no obvious explanation ~~for its presence in this isolated place~~.
8. ~~According to archeologist Thomas E. Lee~~, it may be a monument left ~~by Vikings~~ in their ~~travels west~~ from Greenland.
9. Here, ~~on an island~~ called Pamiok, are the ruins ~~of what may have been a Viking longhouse~~.
10. If so, then centuries ~~before Columbus's "discovery" of America~~, the Vikings were ~~in what is now northern Quebec~~.

Exercise 5.14
1. Maple sugar, wild rice are
2. Kim, Avi will go
3. Professor Singh handed, wished
4. I tried, tried, did (not) succeed
5. canoeists, dog were missing
6. Point, Click . . . are sleeping
7. Point, Click . . . killed, slaughtered
8. Timothy Findley farms, writes, lectures
9. (you) wait, call
10. Shooting, scoring are

Exercise 5.15
1. Misspellings can create, (can) cause
2. *Durham County Review* printed
3. soldier was praised, was described
4. soldier called, demanded
5. writer, editor soothed, promised
6. paper apologized, explained
7. (you) drive, see; (you) drive, see
8. drivers obey, lose
9. (you) drink, you want, (you) drive, you do
10. Come-by-Chance, Blow-Me-Down, Run-by-Guess, Jerry's Nose are

Exercise 5.16
I have news for all you short people out there. Being tall is not an enviable condition. First of all, tall people are the butt of constant jokes: "How' [i]s the weather up there?" "What great kneecaps you have!" The humour is pretty lame. Next, there is the risk of serious head injury. I have been bashed by cupboard doors, concussed by sign boards, and even, on one memorable occasion, knocked senseless by a chandelier. Clothes present another problem. Finding anything to fit is a challenge. Finding anything remotely fashionable is next to impossible.

Clerks in men's clothing departments <u>are</u> apparently <u>hired</u> for their ability to humiliate outsized men. <u>They</u> <u>seem</u> genuinely surprised at one's reluctance to appear in public wearing pants at the mid-calf. And finally, there <u>is</u> <u>basketball</u>. Like many tall people, I <u>detest</u> the game. Contrary to popular belief, not all <u>persons</u> more than 2 m tall <u>have been blessed</u> with the natural ability to dribble, jump-shoot, and slam-dunk. <u>Many</u> of us <u>would</u> rather <u>join</u> a chain gang than a basketball team. To be honest, though, for the most part, <u>I do like</u> being tall. But <u>I wouldn't mind</u> fewer jokes, more sympathy, and less basketball.

Answers, Chapter 6: Solving Sentence-Fragment Problems (Pages 57 to 69)

We have made the sentence fragments into complete sentences for the first set, to give you an idea of how the sentences might be formed. Many different sentences can be made out of the fragments given; just be sure each of your sentences has a subject and a verb.

Exercise 6.1
1. F   This <u>chapter</u> <u>is</u> about sentence fragments.
2. F   <u>We</u> <u>have</u> to go to the wall.
3. F   <u>I'll</u> <u>be</u> glad to do it for you.
4. F   <u>She</u> <u>keeps falling asleep</u> in class, after working all night.
5. F   The Doom <u>players</u> <u>are meeting</u> in the upper lounge.
6. S
7. F   <u>Watching</u> television <u>is</u> a cheap form of entertainment.
8. F   <u>I am hoping</u> to hear from you soon.
9. F   <u>We</u> <u>were</u> saved by the bell.
10. S

Exercise 6.2
1. F   6. F
2. F   7. S
3. F   8. F
4. F   9. F
5. F   10. S

Exercise 6.3 (suggested answers)
__F__ Professional athletes <u>make</u> millions of dollars a year. __F__ At the same time, owners of sports franchises <u>grow</u> fantastically rich from the efforts of their employees, the players. __F__ The fans <u>are</u> the forgotten people in the struggle for control over major league sports. __F__ <u>They</u> <u>are</u> the people paying the money that makes both owners and players rich. __S__ I have an idea that would protect everyone's interests. __S__ Cap the owners' profits. __S__ Cap the players' salaries. __F__ And most important, (<u>you</u>) <u>cap</u> the ticket prices. __F__ This <u>plan</u> <u>would ensure</u> a fair deal for everyone. __S__ Fans should be able to see their teams play for the price of a movie ticket, not the price of a television set.

Exercise 6.4 (suggested answers)
__S__ Procrastination is my most serious fault. __F__ It <u>is</u> worse even than my addiction to Saturday morning cartoons. __S__ I will do almost anything to avoid doing what I'm supposed to be doing at any given time. __S__ Sometimes the things I do in order to avoid my real task are more difficult or more distasteful than the task itself. __F__ I <u>know</u> this makes no sense. __F__ For example, I <u>will</u>

waste time phoning old friends, or new acquaintances, or co-workers, or, when really desperate, even relatives. __S__ Other examples of my time-wasting activities include cooking, cleaning the apartment, doing laundry, rearranging my books or my CD collection, or walking the neighbours' dog. __F__ Finally, I am confronted with the inescapable: deadline day. __F__ Only then do I kick into overdrive, work day and night until the job is finished, and collapse from exhaustion. __S__ It's an exciting, if not very sensible, way to live.

Exercise 6.5 (suggested answers)
__F__ The fact is that I have to hold down at least one part-time job to go to school. __F__ The cost of tuition, books, rent, food, and other living expenses, not to mention clothing and a little money for entertainment is too high. __S__ I can't survive without working. __F__ I don't mind getting the minimum wage for work that is heavy, dirty, or boring. __F__ I have held jobs such as dishwasher, stock clerk, warehouser, cleaner, and short-order cook throughout my college years. __F__ There is one thing [t]hat I do find upsetting, though. __F__ Some teachers do not understand that I work out of necessity, not out of choice. __S__ I wish I did have the luxury of concentrating on nothing but school work. __F__ Instead, I must deal with problems such as class schedules that conflict with my work schedule [F] or assignments that are due with less than a week's notice. __F__ The inescapable fact, however, is that I can't attend all my classes and hand in all my assignments on time because I'm too busy working to pay for the education I'm not getting!

Exercise 6.6
1. F   After
2. F   Whatever
3. F   Even if
4. F   As long as
5. F   When

6. F   Unless
7. F   who
8. S
9. F   When
10. F   although

Exercise 6.7
1. F   So that
2. F   Though
3. F   Since
4. F   If
5. F   Provided that

6. F   Even if
7. S
8. F   Whenever
9. S
10. F   so that

Exercise 6.8
1. F   who
2. F   that
3. S
4. S
5. F   Where

6. F   when
7. F   Whether
8. F   whichever
9. F   until
10. F   that

Exercise 6.9
1. S
2. F   Though, who
3. F   that
4. S
5. S

6. S
7. F   If
8. F   Because
9. F   Until, as long as, whichever
10. F   When, where, that

Exercise 6.11

Although spring is my favourite season, and I look forward eagerly to its arrival after the long winter, there are some things about the season **that** I could do without. **When** the warm weather begins, I am always tempted to buy new, fashionable shoes **which** are ruined in the wet muck **that** is everywhere. **Unless** I act quickly, my dog also becomes a problem in the spring. She delights in tracking mud from the backyard into the house. **After** she creates a mess that Mr. Clean would need steroids to tackle, she will go back outside and find something sticky and smelly to roll in. **Until** the warm weather dries up the mud and my dog loses the annual urge to coat herself with disgusting substances, my joy at the arrival of spring is always a little restrained.

Exercise 6.12

Since my marks at the end of high school were anything but impressive, I thought the chances of my acceptance at college or university were not very good. Secretly, however, I wasn't at all sure that college or university was where I wanted to go. I had also applied to the Armed Forces program that pays for your education **if** you agree to serve for four years after graduation, **provided that** you meet certain conditions. On the same day **that** the official transcript of my dismal marks appeared in the mail, two schools I had applied to sent their rejections, **as** did the Armed Forces, calling me "an academic risk." **Until** the next day, **when** a fourth letter arrived, I hid the marks and the rejection letters from my parents and suffered **as** I have never suffered before or since. Fortunately, **since** the fourth letter was an acceptance from an unusually enlightened (or desperate) school, I was able to enjoy the summer. Eventually, I graduated with a respectable average and became a writer. Last year, I got my revenge on the Armed Forces for their lack of faith in my academic potential **when** they bought three thousand copies of my text book—to teach their recruits how to write.

Exercise 6.13

My parents own a diesel car, a car that they claim was a wonderful buy because it gets good mileage and seldom needs a tune-up. Apparently, they are not concerned about the smell or the noise. If I borrow it to go anywhere with my friends, I have to put up with their laughing at the awful noise and complaining about the disgusting smell. My parents are not keen on lending me their car, anyway, probably because I have had an unfortunate history of bad luck with cars. Due to no fault of mine, I totalled two cars in three years, so my parents consider the fact that I am embarrassed by their car as yet another advantage of diesel ownership. Why, I wonder, can't my parents be like other people's parents? Why can't they drive a nice big Buick, or a comfortable Volvo, or even a compact that runs on normal gasoline and doesn't sound as if it's about to explode every time you turn the key in the ignition? And, most important, why can't they drive a car that doesn't smell like the exhaust system of an 18-wheel transport truck? My parents are so inconsiderate. They never think of others, only of themselves.

Exercise 6.14

Although I had been well-trained by my parents in the arts of dishwashing and kitchen clean-up, when I moved away from home to go to college and began to keep house for myself, my roommate and I somehow let things slide in this department. Every dish we used found its way into the sink or onto the kitchen counter, without being washed or even rinsed. Naturally, as the days and weeks went by, the food hardened and eventually bonded to the surface of the dishes. The prospect of cleaning up became less and less appealing. We made trips to junk shops and lawn sales, where we added to our collection of chipped and mis-matched dinnerware. We would do anything to avoid tackling the piles of food-encrusted plates that filled our kitchen. Then, one day, my roommate looked out of the window of our apartment just in time to see my parents drive up to surprise us with one of their rare visits. After a moment of paralyzing panic and indecision, my roommate began piling dirty dishes in a closet, while I opted for stashing them under the bed and in the oven. In a frenzy of activity, while my parents were in-nocently parking their car and unloading the care packages of home-baked good-ies they always brought us, we managed to dispose of most of the evidence of our laziness. After taking us out for dinner and before heading back home, my mother even commented on how tidy our apartment seemed to be. This nerve-shattering experience taught us a lesson, however. My roommate and I resolved to wash dishes at least once a week. But first we had to get them out of the closet, out from under the bed, and out of the oven.

Answers for Chapter 7: Solving Run-On Sentence Problems (Pages 70 to 82)

Exercise 7.1
1. I hate computers; they're always making mistakes.
2. correct
3. Stop me if you've heard this one. **T**here was this cab driver on her first day at work.
4. Rudolf is bone lazy; Dwight isn't much better.
5. Chocolate is Ninik's weakness; she cannot resist a Toblerone bar.
6. I'll probably be going out tonight, **since** Gretta offered to take me to a movie.
7. Efficiency is what most consumers look for in a new car. **H**igh performance isn't as important as it used to be.
8. I have a 3000-word assignment due tomorrow; if it weren't for that, I'd love to teach you to play solitaire.
9. It bothers me to see Krystal and Sparkle playing cards all the time; they could easily fail the term.
10. Anand was transformed. **O**vernight he had changed from a normal-looking student into a fashion plate.

Exercise 7.2
1. A fine mess this is; I'll never forgive you for getting me into this situation.
2. Let's take the shortcut. **W**e need to get there as quickly as possible.
3. No one in the department supports her, **because** she's both arrogant and indolent.
4. I want to play the banjo; the only thing stopping me is a complete lack of mu-sical talent.
5. Of course, it would also help if I owned a banjo.
6. I'd rather be lucky than good; on the other hand, I'd rather be good than unlucky.
7. Many environmentally aware people are heating their homes with woodstoves nowadays; the result is "ecologists' smog."
8. The snow is turning into freezing rain. **W**e'll be lucky to get home before dawn if these conditions persist.
9. When you are looking for a new car, there are many factors to consider, **but** the most important is probably price.
10. Many good films are made in both Canada and the United States. **I** wish I could tell which ones they were before paying my admission to a movie theatre.

Exercise 7.3

1. The largest dog in the world is the Irish Wolfhound; the strongest dog in the world is the Newfoundland; the stupidest dog in the world is my Afghan.
2. Please go to the door and see who's there. **I**'m on the phone.
3. Early Canadian settlers saw the Americans as a constant menace. **E**ven Ottawa—miles from anywhere and hardly a threat to anyone—was not considered safe.
4. They can crawl on their knees and beg. **T**hat's the only way they'll ever get any more money from me!
5. Think carefully before you answer; a great deal depends on what you decide.
6. Cooking is my favourite pastime, **but** I don't enjoy it nearly so much when I have to do it as when I choose to do it.
7. correct
8. My chiropractor has given me a sheet of exercises that he says will make my back stronger, **and** he has convinced me that if I do these exercises daily, my pain will disappear.
9. Karin was given the choice of joining her father's firm as a driver or continuing her education at college. **K**nowing Karin, I think she's sure to take the job.
10. There are two students in this class named Xan; one is from China, the other from Russia. **T**he latter's name is a nickname. **I**t is a short form of Alexandra.

Exercise 7.4

1. When our team travels to Moncton, we always stay at the same motel. **I**t's not expensive, but it is centrally located and well-maintained.
2. I don't know whose boots those are; they were left here after our party. **P**robably they belong to one of your friends.
3. With his huge, brown, adoring eyes and his obedient disposition, my dog is the most important creature in my life. I know I'll never find a man so good-natured and well-trained.
4. Cats are wonderful creatures; they are often more sensitive than humans, as any true cat lover will tell you.
5. correct
6. Backing the car off the shoulder and onto the highway, Krystal neglected to check her rearview mirror; as a result, she produced a significant alteration to the front end of a Honda.
7. correct
8. Appraising Rudolf's progress is difficult. **W**hen you realize that he has submitted none of the assignments, written none of the tests, and attended only about a third of the classes, you can see why I despair.
9. Fast food is generally less nutritious than home-cooked meals; although I know of some home cooking that rates below cardboard in nutritional value, I still prefer it as a rule.
10. correct

Exercise 7.5

Last year, an exchange student from the south of France came to live with us. **H**er name was Simone and she came to Canada to practise her English and to experience something of our culture. Simone was amazed by our fondness for fast food; she found it inedible. Another cultural difference she observed was the emphasis many Canadian women place on their appearance. **T**hey often applied fresh makeup between classes, **and** they dressed as if they were going out to a fashionable restaurant instead of school. As everyone exposed to the international media knows, no women in the world are better groomed, dressed, and coiffed than the French, **and** Simone was no exception. She loved to dress up; she delighted in showing off the designs, both subtle and dramatic, that the French are famous for. **S**he wore them only on special occasions, however. The emphasis on multiculturalism in Canada, the relative newness of our towns and cities, and the vast size of our country all impressed her during her stay with us. **T**he huge expanses of untouched wilderness she found a little intimidating. Though she was homesick, especially in the first few weeks, Simone enjoyed her year with us. **W**hen she was packing up to return to her home in Provence, she was already planning her next visit to Canada—a camping holiday in Banff.

Exercise 7.6

An acquaintance of mine recently became a Canadian citizen. **W**hen she told me about her citizenship hearing, however, I couldn't bring myself to offer her the congratulations she was obviously expecting. In preparation for the hearing, she had been told to study a small book containing basic facts about Canada, its government, history, and people. **S**he was told the judge who interviewed her would ask questions based on the information in this book, **but** she neglected to study, or even to read the book. At the hearing, the judge asked her to identify the name of the current governor general, to explain some of the advantages of being a Canadian citizen, and to tell him whether health care was a federal or a provincial responsibility. Unable to answer any of these questions, my friend just giggled and shrugged; then she listened while the judge gave her the answers. She expected to be told to come back when she had learned more about her adopted country, **so** she was astonished when the judge congratulated her for successfully completing the interview and set a date to confirm her citizenship. I find the judge's decision appalling for three reasons. **F**irst, my friend's failure even to open the book she was given suggests she doesn't have much respect for Canadian citizenship. **S**econd, her low opinion of our citizenship process was reinforced when the judge passed her. **T**hird, I can't help but feel that she was passed because she is an attractive blonde woman, a university professor, and speaks with a polished, upper-class English accent. If she had been a man or woman of colour, or spoken little or no English, or had a less impressive job, I cannot help but think she would have been rejected, **as** she deserved to be.

Exercise 7.7

1. Special effects have been the focus of sci-fi movies since Stanley Kubrick made a computer and a space ship the stars of *2001: A Space Odyssey.* George Lucas continued the trend with the *Star Wars* trilogy, and movie makers ever since have been employing increasingly powerful computers to generate increasingly spectacular effects.
2. A great many films have been made about Count Dracula. **F**rom *Buffy the Vampire Slayer* to *Nosferatu,* Dracula has been portrayed as a depraved monster, a legendary warrior, and even a misunderstood social outcast. **S**o many versions of his story have been told that fact and fiction are now inseparable.
3. For more than thirty years, Clint Eastwood has held the Hollywood record for successful films. **W**hile others have had longer careers, no one has equalled his record in producing box-office winners. **F**urthermore, he is internationally acclaimed as a director as well as an actor.
4. An annual poll is taken among film critics to determine the best movies ever made. **E**very year one film ranks first, and this movie didn't even win the Academy Award as best picture for its year. Shot in black and white, it is the story of a newspaperman who is driven to succeed. **M**ade in 1941, this film is *Citizen Kane.*

5. Some of the worst movies ever made have become big money-makers, thanks to the industry's practice of describing all movies as "the best," "the biggest," and "not-to-be-missed," no matter how mediocre or even downright bad they may be. **A** good example is the work of Edward D. Wood, Jr., the man known as the world's worst director. **I**f you want to see a couple of sensationally dreadful films, check your local video store for Wood's *Bride of the Monster* and *Plan 9 from Outer Space.*

6. Animated features have always had a special place in the hearts of their audiences. **E**ven though most of them were designed for children, this doesn't mean that adults don't find cartoon characters just as affecting as live actors. Indeed, William Goldman, the well-known writer of *Butch Cassidy and the Sundance Kid* and *The Princess Bride,* claims that the most traumatic moment in any movie, animated or live, produced before 1960, is the death of Bambi's mother.

7. One of Hollywood's favourite subjects is sports. **W**e have baseball films, such as *Bull Durham, Field of Dreams,* and *A League of Their Own,* glorifying both the game and the men and women who play it. **T**hen we have films such as *The Longest Yard* and *Knute Rockne, All American* celebrating the heroism of the football field. **E**ven hockey has attracted the attention of a few filmmakers, though films like *Slapshot* and *The Mighty Ducks* have not done much to enhance the image of Canada's favourite game.

8. Some of the most successful television series started life as movies. **A**mong them is one of television's longest running shows, *M*A*S*H,* which began as a huge hit on the big screen in 1970. **M**ore recently, the movie *The Last of the Mohicans* was reworked into a weekly TV show called *Chingachook.* **B**oth these examples began their popular life as best-selling books.

9. Horror films have been with us since the beginning of cinema, but they have undergone drastic changes since 1931 when *Frankenstein* first lumbered across the screen. **I**n the 50s, Alfred Hitchcock, the master of psychological suspense, turned a generation of people off showers with his masterpiece, *Psycho.* **I**n the 80s, horror films became "butcher films." **T**oday's directors seem to be competing to see who can show the most blood spilled by deranged maniacs wielding a mind-boggling array of weapons.

10. Documentaries, though less popular and certainly less lucrative than feature films, are often more interesting thematically and technically because they explore the thoughts and actions of real people. **D**ocumentaries require a different technique from fiction features. **B**ecause the story is factual, the director has limited control over the actions of the people in the film. **O**nly in the editing room can the director shape the movie, deciding what to use and what to discard, and how to sequence scenes to achieve a particular effect. Canadians are recognized as being among the best documentary filmmakers in the world. **I**n this field, as in so many others, we give ourselves too little credit.

Exercise 7.8

Having decided to spend two weeks canoeing in La Verendrye Park, northeast of Ottawa, Chantal and Yoko began to make plans. It didn't take them long to realize that they had some problems to overcome because, while Chantal was an experienced canoe tripper and even owned her own kevlar canoe, Yoko had only been in a canoe once before. **S**he could not imagine what two people would eat for two whole weeks in the wilderness with no local convenience store to supply such necessities as potato chips and soft drinks. Chantal took charge of the planning, and she drew up a list of supplies and equipment that they would have to buy or borrow. **T**ogether they worked out a menu that would be nutritious, tasty, and easy to pack and prepare. Planning and preparing for the trip brought them closer together and made both a little more confident that the trip might prove to be a lot of fun. Nevertheless, when they arrived at the park and registered with the park officials before loading up the canoe, each still had some doubts. Yoko was worried about whether they would run out of food, and Chantal was still uncertain about her friend's canoeing ability.

Despite a constant drizzle and a 500-metre portage that got them soaked up to the knees and dampened their spirits as well as their clothes, they managed to survive the first day. Their camp that night was a huge success because Yoko turned out to have a real talent for fishing. They ate fresh-caught trout; the weather cleared; and they sat around the campfire watching the moon come up. Eventually, the mosquitoes became a nuisance, forcing them into the protection of their tent. The two weeks flew by, and back home, when they reflected on the trip, they agreed that their fears had been needless. Yoko had gained 2 k, and Chantal confessed that she had never canoed with a better bow paddler. In fact, they had had such a good time they decided to make it an annual event.

Exercise 7.9

American gun laws are a mystery to most Canadians. We look at the annual death toll south of the border and compare it to our own more modest statistics, and it seems obvious that our restrictive regulations are responsible for our relatively few gun incidents. We wonder at the blind prejudice of Americans that they cannot see that open access to firearms leads to more deaths. One statistic clearly supports our point of view. For every intruder killed by a privately owned handgun in the United States, two hundred innocent people are killed in domestic disputes and accidents. This figure does not take into account those killed in incidents related to drugs or organized crime.

In using these figures to question the wisdom of our southern neighbours, we overlook the reason for their insistence on free access to firearms. Their country was born out of a revolution against a despotic king. What made their revolution successful was that every household had at least one gun and at least one person who knew how to use it. Armed civilians were responsible for the founding of America, a fact that led directly to the provision in their Constitution that every citizen has the right to bear arms. (I know a couple of people who assume this means that every American has the constitutional right to wear short-sleeved shirts.) To argue against the right to bear arms is to be un-American in the minds of many U. S. citizens. It makes no difference to them that the right to own a gun to protect the United States of America is an almost comically archaic concept in the age of nuclear missiles.

Answers for Chapter 8: Solving Modifier Problems (Pages 83 to 93)

Exercise 8.1
1. Fernando has insulted almost everyone he's gone out with.
2. On Friday, the boss told me I was being let go.
3. They decided to pay me nearly $350 a week.
4. correct
5. My sister could only pray to win the lottery.
6. I hate parties where the food is served on tiny paper plates to the guests who are all standing around.
7. Elmo bought a cigarette lighter costing $29.95 for his girlfriend.
8. In a rage, the angry hippo chased me toward the exit.

9. Most pet owners don't bother having their dogs professionally groomed unless they are poodles or terriers.
10. I appreciate a car with an air bag and soft seat designed for the safety and comfort of the driver.

Exercise 8.2
1. In Minoan Crete, there are wall paintings of boys with no clothes on jumping over bulls.
2. Only two suitable jobs were advertised.
3. This course can be completed in six weeks by anyone who has learned English grammar.
4. For a small fee, the obituary column lists the names of people who have died recently.
5. Walking through Wonderland, Alice discovered a mushroom.
6. She ate only one bite and found herself growing larger.
7. They told me to come back every week and check the notice board.
   Or: They told me to come back and check the notice board every week.
8. For their own satisfaction, parents want to know what their children are doing in school.
9. The cause of the accident was a little guy with a big mouth driving a small car.
10. Once I bought the VCR, the salesperson told me I would need an instruction manual to learn how to operate it.

Exercise 8.3
1. People who shoplift get caught frequently.
2. Stan watched television almost all night.
3. Dolly enthusiastically tried to convince the members of her fan club to wear two or three sets of false eyelashes.
4. In a saucepan, stir the sifted flour into the melted butter.
5. correct
6. No one except petrochemical company executives is allowed to dump any pollutants into the river.
7. With an old black-powder rifle, he took a stand against a tree while waiting for the bear.
8. Walking to school, Rosa passed the security guard and two workmen.
9. Here in Petawawa, I am pleased to meet with student representatives from all of our colleges.
10. Perhaps you're on your own in Vancouver, with a sparkling city to explore and a couple of tickets in your pocket to an event at the covered stadium.

Exercise 8.4
1. As a college English teacher, I am annoyed by dangling modifiers.
2. When writing, you will find that your best friend is your dictionary.
3. Driving recklessly, Sula was stopped at a roadblock by the police.
4. Our neighbours love their Cornish Rex cats because they don't shed their hair.
5. Before applying the varnish, sand the surface smooth.
6. Upon entering, I saw the store was empty.
7. Attempting to hotwire a '95 Mercedes 318, a suspect was arrested by the police.
8. Having rotted in storage, the grain could not be sold for the profit the farmers were counting on.
9. In very cold weather, you should warm up the engine thoroughly before attempting to drive.
10. Driving through the desert, we found that our mouths became drier and drier.

Exercise 8.5
1. After changing the tire, you should release the jack.
2. Having decided on pizza, we should decide next whether to order beer or wine.
3. After waiting for you for an hour, I knew the evening was ruined.
4. Jogging through Stanley Park, I saw a cluster of totem poles.
5. After spending nine dollars on them, I have lost most of the spare keys.
6. Having set the microwave on automatic, I quickly cooked the turkey to perfection.
7. Having completed the beginning, we will turn to the ending, the second most important part of the essay.
8. Convicted of aggravated assault, she was sentenced to two years in Kingston.
9. After scoring the goal in overtime, the team led a huge victory parade through the city.
10. It was a great moment: after making the speech of a lifetime, he was elected to the leader's office.

Exercise 8.6
1. Since I am a college English teacher, dangling modifiers annoy me.
2. When you are writing, you will find that your best friend is your dictionary.
3. Because she was driving recklessly, the police stopped Sula at a roadblock.
4. Because Cornish Rex cats don't shed their hair, our neighbours love them.
5. The surface must be sanded smooth before you apply the varnish.
6. When I entered, the store was empty.
7. While he attempted to hotwire a '95 Mercedes 318, a suspect was arrested by the police.
8. Because the grain had rotted in storage, the farmers could not sell it for the profit they were counting on.
9. In very cold weather, the engine should be thoroughly warmed up before you attempt to drive.
10. As we drove through the desert, our mouths became drier and drier.

Exercise 8.7
1. After you change the tire, release the jack.
2. The next question is whether to order beer or wine, now that we have decided on the pizza.
3. After I had waited for you for an hour, the evening was ruined.
4. As I jogged through Stanley Park, a cluster of totem poles came into view.
5. Most of the spare keys, after I spent nine dollars on them, have been lost.
6. After I set the microwave on automatic, the turkey quickly cooked to perfection.
7. After you have completed the beginning, the ending is the second most important part of the essay.
8. After she was convicted of aggravated assault, the judge sentenced her to two years in Kingston.
9. After the team scored the goal in overtime, a huge victory parade wound through the city.
10. It was a great moment: after he had made the speech of a lifetime, the election put him in the leader's office.

Exercise 8.8
1. Because the glasses are made of very thin crystal, the dishwasher breaks them as fast as I can buy them.

2. As we were driving through Yellowstone, a buffalo blocked the road.
3. As a college student constantly faced with stress, I find the pressure intolerable.
4. If you're looking for both style and economy, a Geo is the car to get.
5. My guests loved the coq au vin, which had been stewed in wine.
6. We were impressed as she rode by in a bikini on a horse.
7. After deciding whether the wine should be blended, add the sugar.
8. The sign in the restaurant window read, "Just Like Mother, Our Establishment Serves Tea in a Bag."
9. As I peered out of the office window, the Goodyear Blimp sailed past.
10. They took the seagull, which had broken its wing, to the SPCA.

Exercise 8.9
1. Although he lives more than 50 km away, he manages to come to nearly every class.
2. The sign said that only students are admitted to the pub.
3. The lion was recaptured by the trainer before anyone was mauled or bitten.
4. While asleep, the child kicked the blankets off the bed.
5. Through a plate-glass window, I saw the Queen and her entourage arrive.
6. Having ruled out the other two Japanese imports, we chose the Mazda.
7. Swimming isn't a good idea if the water is polluted.
8. The man wore a hideous hat on his head.
9. In last week's letter, I learned about Joan's having a baby.
10. The counsellor who recently admitted he was not familiar with the college's harassment policy has alienated the students.

Exercise 8.10
1. Joe found his dog gnawing on a bone.
2. He said we would have a test on Tuesday. *Or:* On Tuesday, he said we would have a test.
3. Our guests didn't find the food, which was left over from last week's party, very appetizing.
4. Employees who are frequently late are dismissed without notice. *Or:* Employees who are late are frequently dismissed without notice.
5. Since Jim forgot twice this week to pick me up, I'm quitting his car pool.
6. Maria turned the badly bruised avocados into great guacamole.
7. Before going to bed, you should set the alarm for 6:00 A.M.
8. Though they drink it daily, many people don't trust Lake Ontario water.
9. It is a tradition to pay one's respects in a funeral parlour to friends and relatives after they have died.
10. After completing the study of staffing requirements, the personnel manager will hire an assistant.

Answers for Chapter 9: The Parallelism Principle (Pages 94 to 104)

Exercise 9.1
1. The three main kinds of speech are demonstrative, informative, and persuasive.
2. . . . Two of the most difficult are supporting her household and being sole parent to her child.
3. She advised me to take two aspirins and call her in the morning.
4. Books provide us with information, education, and entertainment.
5. To make your court appearance as painless as possible, prepare your case thoroughly and maintain a pleasant, positive attitude.
6. The apostrophe is used for two purposes: contraction and possession.

7. Swiftly and skilfully the woman gutted and scaled the fish.
8. I am overworked and underpaid.
9. You need to develop skill, strategy, and agility to be a good tennis player.
10. The two main responsibilities of a corrections officer are security and control of the inmates.

Exercise 9.2
1. A part-time job can develop your decision-making skills, your sense of responsibility, your self-confidence, and your independence.
2. The three keys to improving your marks are study, hard work, and bribery.
3. I couldn't decide whether I should become a chef or a data processor.
4. . . . the widespread lack of strong religious beliefs and the absence of strict moral codes.
5. A course in logical reasoning will help us evaluate what we read and make sound decisions.
6. My supervisor told me that my performance was generally satisfactory but that my writing must improve.
7. Ms. Hencz assigns two hours of homework every night and an essay each week.
8. The two most important characteristics of a personal work space are how neat and well organized it looks and how private it is.
9. Playing with small construction toys is beneficial to young children because it develops their fine motor skills, encourages concentration and patience, and stimulates their creative imagination.
10. When you're buying a new car, you should look at more than just the size, style, and cost. The warranty, operating cost, and trade-in value should also be taken into consideration.

Exercise 9.3
1. The role of the health instructor is to teach preventive medicine, care of the sick, and rehabilitation of the injured.
2. The most common causes of snowmobile accidents are mechanical failure, poor weather conditions, and driver carelessness.
3. The portable classrooms are ill-equipped, poorly lighted, and inadequately heated.
4. The advantages of a thesis statement are that it limits your topic, clarifies the contents of your paper, and shows how your paper will be organized.
5. Unemployment deprives the individual of purchasing power and reduces the country's national output.
6. A good nurse is energetic, tolerant, sympathetic, and reliable.
7. The money spent on space exploration should be used to provide aid to under-developed countries and funding for medical research.
8. The best house cats are quiet, clean, affectionate, and elsewhere.
9. . . . : a new appreciation for the beauty of nature and a new admiration for members of the opposite sex.
10. You can conclude a paper with a summary of main points, a question, or a quotation.

Exercise 9.4
1. Our winter has not been very pleasant; we've had vicious ice storms, heavy snowfalls, and dangerous freezing rain.
2. Baseball is a game that requires a high level of skill and a large measure of natural talent.

3. Many foreigners see Canadians as conservative, patriotic, and orderly.
4. Patience and dexterity will make you a good piano player, meat cutter, or Lego builder.
5. Being a dutiful son, a loyal husband, and an affectionate father made Jason so stressed that he took up boxing as an outlet for his aggression.
6. There are some parents who think that rock music is dangerous and addictive.
7. Selena has three passions in her life: dancing with her boyfriend, listening to Charlie Major's music, and driving fast cars.
8. After this year at school, I intend to go into nursing or teaching.
9. After nine years of making up faulty sentences for students to fix, Brian can no longer write properly or express himself correctly.
10. Both managers and workers must make compromises if this joint committee is to succeed.

Exercise 9.5
1. I'm looking for a sitter who is patient, intelligent, and kind.
2. Be sure your report is comprehensive, clear, readable, and accurate.
3. Health care workers must be objective, sympathetic, and understanding.
4. We were told to study the report carefully and (to) make our recommendations in writing.
5. Dwight's chances for a lasting relationship with Krystal aren't good, considering their differences in goals, temperament, and religion.
6. Her small build, quick temper, and criminal record will disqualify her from becoming a corrections officer.
7. Anand is everything a girl could want: handsome, intelligent, successful, and considerate to his mother.
8. The designer kitchen, fully equipped spa, and burglar-proof security system were what sold us on our condominium.
9. Its location, design, and staff make the UBC hospital a more pleasant place to stay than most.
10. Darla explained that, through constant repetition and quiet firmness, she had trained her gerbil to be obedient and affectionate.

Exercise 9.6

1. mechanically	manually	
2. being a nurse	being a pilot	
3. achieve her goals	find true happiness	
4. humorous	wealthy	intelligent
5. daily exercise	wholesome food	regular checkups
6. a good cigar	a glass of brandy	conversation with friends
7. speed	comfort	manoeuverability
8. look for bargains	choose quality	shop for value
9. security	value	safety
10. tanned golden brown	clothed in a skimpy bathing suit	accompanied by a big boyfriend

Exercise 9.8
When they buy a car, most people consider a number of factors such as safety, style, **speed, reliability, and cost.** For some buyers, the most important consideration is the impression their new car will make on their relatives and **friends.** Unfortunately, these would-be buyers often make an unfavourable impression on their loans officer or **bank manager** by choosing a vehicle that is beyond their

means. Another kind of car buyer will settle for nothing less than the loudest, flashiest, **most powerful** vehicle available. As I plug along in my aged, **rusty**, underpowered Ford, I console myself with the thought that people who drive flashy, **overpowered** sports cars are trying to make up for other inadequacies.

Answers for Chapter 10: Refining by Combining (Pages 105 to 114)

Exercise 10.1
1. The picketers left the streets when the police arrived.
2. The angry bystanders knocked down the assassin, tearing him limb from limb.
3. Maria is forty-one years old, but she looks about twenty.
4. He always quits just when you need him.
5. Roy Rogers, who was known as Leonard Sly, made much money in cowboy movies.
6. Even though football is violent, North Americans love it.
7. Politicians charge that newspapers distort facts.
8. Many people are not aware that television manipulates feelings.
9. Although Vesna hates zucchini, she planted some anyway to please her husband.
10. Whereas scientists in the ancient world looked to the stars for guidance, modern scientists may travel to the stars.

Exercise 10.2
1. If I don't get there by noon, come looking for me because I may be in trouble.
2. When the moon was full, we sat huddled in our warm, down-filled sleeping bags for a long time before it was time to turn in for the night.
3. Begging for mercy, the student who had been caught plagiarizing threw herself at her instructor's feet.
4. Lonely, disillusioned, and bitter, Jamie stumbled into the rest room, her shoulders bowed and her school books heavy in her hand.
5. Sensing danger, the moose lifted its head, ears stiff and straight, body tense, ready to explode into action at the slightest sound.
6. The old train station, which was once the hub of the city, is now the dilapidated refuge of rats.
   Or: The old train station, which is now the dilapidated refuge of rats, was once the hub of the city.
7. Key glanced at first base, went into his windup, and then threw a hanging curve up in the strike zone that Murray, anticipating, unloaded over the right field wall.
8. Gasping for air, Matthew stumbled down the stairs and was horrified by the sight of Sadik wrestling in the living room with two of his friends.
9. The rich, dark, unbelievably sweet chocolate sauce covered my Death by Chocolate dessert like a thick blanket.
10. Thinking it is a tough course, few students register for philosophy, but Philosophy 101 is Monika's favourite course.

Exercise 10.3
1. The City of Toronto boasts about its CN Tower which, at 555 metres high, holds the record as the world's tallest freestanding structure.
2. Nursing is a discipline concerned with promoting the well-being of the individual in society. A good nurse respects the dignity, autonomy, and individuality of each human being.
3. Lawyers, doctors, and businesspeople are professionals who constitute fewer than 10 percent of the Canadian work force, but they occupy almost three-

quarters of the seats in the House of Commons and two-thirds of the offices in local party organizations.

4. Blue-collar workers comprise nearly 50 percent of the population, but they hold fewer than 10 percent of the positions in local parties and Parliament. Moreover, women, native people, and minorities are underrepresented in Canada's political and economic institutions, a fact that calls into question our nation's commitment to democracy.

5. For most people, citizenship is an abstract term meaning loyalty, obedience, and conformity. It is often used as a passive term meaning to play one's part in the existing scheme of things, no questions asked. For a few people, citizenship means thinking for themselves, acting independently, and taking control of their own lives.

6. The new Exclusiva, priced for the successful executive, is the ultimate in luxury automobiles. Engineered for safety, built for comfort, and powered by a state-of-the art, 24-valve, 6-cylinder engine, the Exclusiva has a sleek, sophisticated, eye-catching design.

7. On May 13, 1989, in Beijing, China, 3000 students began a hunger strike in Tiananmen Square. During this largely peaceful demonstration, which lasted four weeks, the students erected a homemade, 10-metre replica of the Statue of Liberty, calling it the "Goddess of Democracy." Then thousands of armed troops descended on the square, first firing off tracer bullets and tear gas. After using loudspeakers to urge the students to leave, the soldiers opened fire directly on the crowds and charged them with bayonets. They killed and wounded hundreds of demonstrators. By Sunday morning, June 4, 1989, there had been a massacre.

8. All across Canada, we find unusual place names that sound strange to outsiders. Saskatchewan and Newfoundland, in particular, are rich in peculiar place names. In Saskatchewan, we find Cut Knife, Moose Jaw, Cudworth, and, perhaps the most famous of all, Climax. Newfoundland offers Jerry's Nose, Fogo, Bumble Bee Bight, and Come-by-Chance. Names such as these are often amusing to people who don't live there.

9. Computer help-line personnel get some very strange calls from new computer owners who, confused about their new purchase, call to get assistance with their problems. One woman, for example, who had bought a new laptop computer, called to ask how to install the battery. When the technician told her the directions were on page one of her manual, she retorted that she had just spent $2000 on a computer, and she wasn't about to read a book to tell her how to use it. Another caller complained that he couldn't get his computer to turn on. The technician checked to be sure the customer had plugged in the computer and pressed the power switch. The customer said he kept pressing on the foot pedal but nothing happened. "What foot pedal?" asked the puzzled technician. The "foot pedal" turned out to be the mouse.

10. Culture shock can occur anywhere, in one's own country, even in one's own city. Rudi was an advertising executive who wanted to find out more about multimedia, an interactive combination of computers and television, which he thought his company should be exploring. So Rudi put on his best blue suit, a dark conservative tie, and his black wing-tip shoes, and went to a conference on multimedia programming. Everyone there was under 30. The men, all of whom had earrings, wore their hair long or in a ponytail; the women had very short hair and wore heavy black boots. These men and women were Canada's best, most creative, multimedia programmers. As he watched and listened to their presentations, Rudi experienced culture shock.

**Answers for Chapter 11: Choosing the Correct Verb Form
(Pages 117 to 126)**

Exercise 11.1

1. bore, borne
2. ridden, rode
3. tore, torn
4. lay, lain
5. shaken, shook

6. froze, frozen
7. laid, lay
8. lent, lent
9. rose, risen
10. swum, dived, swam, dived (*or* dove)

Exercise 11.2

1. When I **raised** the issue of a salary increase, my supervisor **rose** from her desk without a word and pointed to the door.
2. After Kareem became tired of **lying** in the sun, he **swam** thirty lengths of the pool.
3. I was happy that my bike, which had been **stolen**, was found, but I wasn't happy to find that it had been **broken**.
4. After we **paid** our admission, we were **given** free popcorn and soft drinks, probably to keep us from demanding our money back after we'd seen the dreadful movie.
5. A feather **lying** on the carpet and a fat cat **lying** contentedly on the windowsill were the only clues in the case of the missing canary.
6. Only hours after I had **bought** my new lawn ornaments, they were **stolen** from my yard.
7. My roommate insists on listening to a nauseating call-in show that is **broadcast** every day at noon, just as I am **sitting** down for lunch.
8. Frank had **brought** some European beer to the party for everyone to taste, but before anyone could try it, Frank had **drunk** it all himself.
9. I was so **shaken** by the incident that I took off my jacket and **hung** it in the refrigerator, then poured myself a tall, refreshing glass of floor wax from the cupboard.
10. After the judge had sentenced my uncle to be **hanged**, my father removed his brother's portrait from our living room, where it had **hung** for years.

Exercise 11.3

1. After Mildred had **written** one final letter to the editor, she retired from public life, confident that she had **done** her duty to the community.
2. We **saw** what we had **come** to see and **did** what we had **come** to do.
3. Lori should have **known** better than to challenge me at pogs because I have never been **beaten**.
4. The final scene in the play has **shaken** the audience so badly that they have all **gone** to a bar to argue over the meaning of the ending.
5. I don't mind so much that they have **stolen** my honour and wounded my pride, but they should never have **taken** my coffee mug.
6. After **lying** around all day watching TV, Kim had no time to write her essay so I **lent** her mine.
7. Harvey thought that he had **written** a masterpiece, but he **began** to realize that perhaps it wasn't all that great when his mother **threw** it in the garbage.
8. The tornado had **torn** a path right through the centre of town, but luckily it hadn't **struck** the hospital or hit any schools as it **sped** by.
9. We have **forgiven** Sparkle for ruining our project, but none of us was unhappy to learn that she was **chosen** "least likely to succeed" by her Poise and Personality class.

10. "Strike three!" yelled the umpire as soon as I **swung** the bat, but I **ran** around the bases anyway.

Exercise 11.4
1. If Tanya had read the weather report and **known** it was going to rain, she would have **worn** a raincoat and a hat.
2. We **lay** in the grass for over an hour, completely **hidden** from the other players.
3. Revenue Canada has not **forgiven** my uncle who claimed for three years that he had no income; meanwhile he had **taken** frequent trips to the Caribbean and had **bought** a sports car.
4. Dwight's jacket is **woven** from camel hair and would be very attractive if it weren't for the hump that has **arisen** in the back.
5. As soon as I opened my mouth, I wished I had **sung** a song I was familiar with instead of having **chosen** "Mon Futon" from the list of karaoke tunes.
6. The rookie **slid** into first base, despite the fact that the coach had told him again and again that he should run right across the base to avoid being **thrown** out.
7. I have **spoken** on the phone to the sales manager, **written** to the personnel director, and **seen** the president in person, but none of them will agree to consider my application because they say I am illiterate.
8. The elbows on my old sweater are just about **worn** through and it is **torn** at the shoulder, but it is still my favourite because it was **given** to me by my first love.
9. We **saw** that the goldfish **lay** on the bottom of the pond once it had **frozen**, so they would survive the winter.
10. After the students had got the assignment from Ms. Critelli, several claimed that they had not been **given** a due date, so Ms. Critelli **sent** all students an e-mail message to remind them of the date she had set at the beginning of term.

Chapter 12: Mastering Subject–Verb Agreement (Pages 127 to 141)

Exercise 12.1
1. *Thriller*
2. numbers
3. invoices
4. you
5. Respect
6. Superman
7. reasons
8. anyone
9. Reports
10. pressures

Exercise 12.2
1. Those policy **changes affect** our entire program.
2. They **like** to work with children, so **they are** looking for jobs in a child care centre.
3. Those **women are** here in Canada because their **husbands** wanted to emigrate from Poland.
4. He **does** his best work when **he is** unsupervised.
5. She **insists** on doing things **her** way.
6. Men who **worry** about baldness should consider having a hair transplant.
7. Our flights **have** been delayed because of the storm.
8. Both of Cinderella's sisters **were** horrid in **their** own way.
9. He often **spends** the weekend at **his** cabin up north.
10. Civil servants with **indexed pensions stand** to gain from future inflation.

Exercise 12.3
1. Clothes **are** what Vinh spends most of his money on.
2. The only junk food Tim eats **is** Hostess Twinkies.
3. My least favourite meal **is** brown rice and tofu.
4. Strong leadership and more jobs **are** what Canada needs now.
5. Too many absences from class **were** the reason for Eugene's failure.
6. Computer games, especially *Doom* and *Myst,* **are** Vince's favourite pastime.
7. The cause of strikes **is** often disputes over wages and benefits.
8. The differences between the Chinese and the Canadian attitudes toward the elderly **are** what I find fascinating.
9. Political discussions **are** something Tanh always enjoys.
10. The only known protection against a vampire attack **is** garlic, a cross, and a stake through the heart.

Exercise 12.4
1. seems
2. is
3. is
4. are
5. are
6. is
7. were
8. cause
9. remain
10. know

Exercise 12.5
1. is
2. writes
3. is
4. is
5. remains
6. wants
7. is
8. is
9. expects
10. has

Exercise 12.6
1. was
2. was
3. believes
4. is
5. seems
6. is
7. is
8. dares
9. has
10. looks

Exercise 12.7
1. works
2. is
3. interests
4. hopes
5. is
6. is
7. was
8. has
9. answers
10. has

Exercise 12.8
1. is
2. seems
3. prides
4. fight
5. Has
6. was
7. gives
8. find
9. is
10. sits

Exercise 12.9
1. seems
2. seems
3. seems
4. is
5. is
6. was
7. is
8. is
9. goes
10. takes

Exercise 12.10
1. A group of unbiased students and faculty **is** . . .
2. Anybody who really **wants** to . . .
3. correct
4. Every one of the contestants **thinks** . . .
5. You'll find that not only ragweed but also cat hairs **make** . . .
6. If there **are** . . .
7. Neither Amelash nor I **am** . . .
8. The lack of things to write about **causes** . . .
9. Michael Jackson, along with his handlers, pets, and bodyguards, **has** . . .
10. The amount of money generated by rock stars on concert tours **is** . . .

Exercise 12.11
The joys of being a disk jockey at a dance club **are** sometimes hard to explain. At times the DJ's job, like other public performances, **results** in embarrassment and stress. When someone who doesn't like your selections **starts** to complain loudly, for example, or when the audience you are trying so hard to please **doesn't** respond, you wish you were a waiter or even a dishwasher. However, there **are** many positive things about the job, as well. When you hit the combination of songs that **gets** the crowd up and dancing for number after number, you feel a real sense of satisfaction. Either your instincts or your knowledge of the dance tunes **has** given these people a great deal of enjoyment and **has** contributed to making their evening a success. Your co-workers, not to mention your boss—the bar owner—**are** also happy, because when everybody out on the dance floor **is** having a good time, more money gets spent. Another reward is people's gratitude. When someone who has enjoyed the evening because of the music—and maybe your introductions and comments—**comes** up to you and **compliments** your work, that praise makes it all worthwhile. The experience you gain from dealing with people and performing in front of an audience **is** also a plus, as **is** the salary you make. Not everyone would want to be a DJ at a dance bar or night club, but it can be a rewarding and interesting part-time job.

Exercise 12.12
There **are** many good reasons for staying fit. The diminished strength, flexibility, and endurance that **result** from lack of exercise are very compelling factors, but everyone who joins the many health clubs in this city **has** individual reasons as well. The people I talked with **say** appearance or weight loss **is** their main motivation for working out. No one among the two hundred patrons of a local health club **was** there for the social life, according to my poll. Either weightlifting or daily aerobics was what they wanted from their club, and the intensity of the workouts **was** clear evidence that they were serious. The manager of the club, along with all the members of the staff, **was** careful to point out that supervised exercise is essential for best results, but neither she nor her staff **were** in favour of fad diets or sweat programs.

Exercise 12.13
1. singular	6. singular
2. singular	7. singular
3. plural	8. plural
4. singular	9. singular
5. singular	10. singular

Exercise 12.14
1. could be singular or plural
2. singular
3. singular
4. plural
5. singular
6. singular
7. singular
8. plural
9. singular
10. singular

Exercise 12.16

The rewards of obtaining a good summer or part-time job **go** well beyond the money you earn from your labour. Contacts that may be valuable in the future and experience in the working world **are** an important part of school-time employment. Even if the jobs you get while attending school **have** nothing to do with your future ambitions, they **offer** many benefits. For example, when scanning your résumé, an employer always likes to see that you know what working for other people **requires**: arriving at the work site on time, getting along with fellow workers, following directions. Neither instinct nor instruction **takes** the place of experience in teaching these basic facts of working life. These long-term considerations, in addition to the money that is the immediate reward, **are** what make part-time work so valuable. Everyone who **has** gone to school and worked part-time or during vacations **is** able to confirm these observations.

Chapter 13: Keeping Your Tenses Consistent (Pages 142 to 147)

Exercise 13.1
1. Allan went home and **told** Guljan what happened.
2. Kristi was so tired that, about ten minutes after class started, she **went** right to sleep.
3. The umpire stands there, rubbing his eyes, unable to believe what he **is** seeing.
4. correct
5. When I answered the phone, there **was** yet another person on the line soliciting a contribution to some worthy cause.
6. First, gently fry the onion, garlic, and seasonings; then **brown** the meat.
7. correct
8. My deadline is next Thursday, by which time I **have** to have an outline and a rough draft ready for my prof's inspection.
9. I drank a half-litre of milk, then I **ate** two protein- and veggie-stuffed sandwiches, and I **was** ready for anything.
10. When Roch Voisine came on stage, the crowd **went** crazy.

Exercise 13.2
1. First, backcomb your hair into spikes, then **coat** your head with glue.
2. The guard walked over and **punched** me in the stomach.
3. The Peter Principle states that every employee **rises** to his or her level of incompetence.
4. Amin and Mia go on their first date and it is a disaster; however, they **decide** to try again.
5. The couple living in the next apartment had a boa constrictor that **kept** getting loose.
7. Prejudice is learned and **is** hard to outgrow.
8. As usual, Professor Campbell began by asking a rhetorical question that he **proceeded** to answer without waiting for anyone in the class to attempt to respond.
9. Are you going to this week's game? **It's** sure to be the best one of the series.

10. Just as time runs out, Emir **launches** a shot at the basket from the centre line. It **misses** the rim by about two metres.

Exercise 13.3

As a boy, Ralph had a remarkable knack for making accurate predictions about the future. When he was 7, he **announced** to anyone who would listen that he would be a millionaire by the time he **was** old enough to vote. When he was 11, he **predicted** that he would star in a major motion picture by the time he **reached** the legal driving age. At the age of 14, he **prophesied** that he would be elected mayor before his twenty-third birthday. Incredibly, his predictions **came** to pass, one after the other. At 16, he **became** the youngest person ever to play James Bond in a movie, and this role **led** to other projects and a salary well into six figures. Good financial advice and careful investing **made** him a millionaire in two years. With all that money behind him, there **was** no stopping Ralph's campaign to **become**, at 22, the youngest mayor in Red Deer's history. However, his amazing early successes **were** not sustainable, and Ralph **became** a has-been by the time he **turned** 25.

Exercise 13.4

The sea squirt is a tiny marine creature that **is** shaped like a bottle. It is a mollusc, so when it **reaches** its juvenile stage, it **wanders** through the sea searching for a suitable rock or shell or hunk of coral to cling to. When it **finds** just the right solid object, it **makes** this object its home for life. To complete its biologically determined task, the sea squirt **is** equipped with a rudimentary nervous system; however, once it **finds** the perfect spot and **establishes** its roots, it no longer **has** any use for its brain. So it **eats** it. As Professor D. Dennett **observes** in his book, *Consciousness Explained,* the process the sea squirt **goes** through is much like the process of getting tenure in an academic institution.

Answers for Chapter 14: Choosing the Correct Pronoun Form (Pages 148 to 155)

Exercise 14.1
1. Those video tapes belong to Patrick and **me**.
2. I can't believe that the committee would choose Bennie along with **us**.
3. Neither **they** nor **we** deserve to be treated like this.
4. Danny and **he** think no one knows they smoke in the stairwell.
5. Just between you and **me**, the engagement between Yolande and **him** is off.
6. If I have to choose between **him** and you, I'm afraid it is **he** who will be going to the lake with me.
7. As devoted television watchers, **we** love it when **we** and the program producers share similar tastes.
8. It would be preferable for **them** to come here rather than for **us** to go there.
9. I can't believe Chandra would break up with me after **she** and **I** got matching tattoos and navel rings.
10. It is likely that **we** musicians would get more favourable reviews from the critics if we and **they** met socially more often.

Exercise 14.2
1. **She** and **I** have completely different tastes in music, though we agree on practically everything else.
2. There aren't many vegetarians besides Ettore and **me** who are so strict that they will not wear leather or wool.

3. It is not for you or **me** to decide whether they go to the game or stay home.
4. Iain and **she** are the best curlers on our team; if it weren't for **them**, we would be in last place.
5. **She** and Marie took the magazines before either Tom or **I** had had a chance to read them.
6. **We** and **they** were exhausted from studying all night, so we can't be blamed for the explosion.
7. Fate has put **us** two together and no matter what **she** or your father says, it is **we** who will live happily ever after at the end of the story.
8. Have you and **he** finally finished your project, or must **we** seniors do your work for you again?
9. It is up to you and **him** to piece together the clues and come up with the solution to the crime so that **we** innocent victims can be set free.
10. I don't need to see my doctor because I know that my chiropractor and **she** agree that I should not play in the championship game tonight, and they are both fans of **us** "Fighting Treefrogs."

Exercise 14.3
1. Nobody hates English more than **I**.
2. She is more frightened of being alone than **he** [is].
3. Everyone wanted to go to the movies except Yvon and **me**.
4. More than **I**, Yuxiang uses the computer to draft and revise his papers.
5. Only a few Mexican food fanatics can eat jalapeno peppers as well as **he** [can].
6. At last I have met someone who enjoys barbecued eel as much as **I** [do].
7. After our instructor handed out the papers, Rudolf and **I** got into a fight.
8. Since he had copied his essay from me, he shouldn't have got a better grade than **I** [did].
9. Rudolf's thinking is that since he is better looking than **I**, he deserves the higher mark.
10. I have a real problem with a teacher who gives good marks to **those** who are blessed with a winning smile and great hair.

Exercise 14.4
You and **I** can both learn a lesson from a story that happened to our village priest and his curate. **They** and their congregation were plagued by a colony of bats that had moved into the church. Whenever the priest began his sermon, the bats and **he** had to compete for the attention of **us** in the congregation. Unfortunately for the priest, the bats always won because they were more interesting than **he** [was]. Then the curate had an idea. He suggested that every night for a week, **he** and the priest would go into the church and fire a blank shotgun shell. This strategy didn't bother the bats at all, but the congregation was most alarmed and asked the priest and curate if it was **they** who had been causing mysterious explosions in the church at night. Sheepishly, they had to admit that it had been **they**. The priest's next move was to ring the church bells while the curate played the organ at top volume, hoping that the racket would drive the bats away. Instead, the awful noise almost drove **us**, the parishioners, to another church. The bats, who have more patience than **we** [do]—or perhaps they're tone-deaf—didn't seem to mind at all.

Finally, the priest, the curate, and **we** had a long meeting to resolve the problem. One member of the congregation had an idea: she suggested that the priest hold a special service, to be attended by all of **us** parishioners, during which the bats would be baptized. The priest duly performed this service, and neither **he**, nor the curate, nor **we** ever saw bats in the church again.

**Chapter 15: Mastering Pronoun–Antecedent Agreement
(Pages 156 to 170)**

Exercise 15.1
1. Clive is the only one **who** wants his picture hung in the board room.
2. Everyone **who** went to the party had a good time, though a few had more punch than was good for them.
3. Is this the dog **that** bit the mail carrier **who** carries a squirt gun?
4. The path led me past the home of a hermit **who** lives all alone in the forest **that** surrounds our town.
5. A filmmaker **who** stays within budget on every production will always have work, no matter how mediocre his movies might be.
6. The open-office concept is one **that** makes sense to anyone **who** has worked in a stuffy little cubicle all day.
7. One advantage of the open office is that it lets you see who is working hard and who is taking it easy. It also allows you to spot people **(whom)** you'd like to meet.
8. The four tests **that** we wrote today would have defeated anyone **who** wasn't prepared for them.
9. Sales clerks **who** want to make good commissions must have good people skills as well as knowledge of the products **(that)** they are selling.
10. The winning goal, **which** was made with only two seconds left in the game, was scored by a player **(whom)** I used to know in high school.

Exercise 15.2
1. herself
2. a
3. the
4. his or her
5. a
6. the
7. his or her
8. itself
9. his, their
10. who, his

Exercise 15.3
1. Every child is a product **of environment** as well as **heredity**. (*Or:* **Children are products** of their environment as well as their heredity.)
2. Anyone who would write a sentence like that last one should give up **the** computer.
3. The team agreed that everyone would have to show up for **the** practices.
4. Everybody must get in **place** for the game to begin. (*Or:* **All players** must get in their places for the game to begin.)
5. Anybody without a partner will have to try to find one approximately **the same** height.
6. Golf is a game that is good for anyone who wants to enjoy outdoor exercise without **getting sweaty or hurt**.
7. We have asked **all students with complaints to see their instructors**. (*Or:* We have asked every student with a complaint to see **his or her** instructor.)
8. Do you know whether anyone in your neighbourhood wants **a house-painter** or **a grass-cutter** this summer? (*Or:* Do you know whether **your neighbours** want their houses painted or their grass cut this summer?)
9. Few people I know **enjoy themselves** on a squash court, but they like to play tennis whenever they can.
10. We're looking for someone **with outstanding intelligence and creativity, who** can work unsupervised.

Exercise 15.4 (suggested answers)
 1. Max is **good at skating,** which he practises daily. (*Or:* Max is a good skater, **and** he practises daily.)
 2. He didn't hear her cry for help **because he was** wearing earplugs.
 3. That **she** would be Betty's teacher never occurred to **Miss Grundy**. (*Or:* That Miss Grundy would be **her** teacher never occurred to **Betty**.)
 4. Every time David looked at the dog, **it** barked.
 5. **Biff cracked his ghetto blaster when he threw it on the floor** in a rage.
 6. **"You're sure to get a job soon,"** Carla told her mother.
 7. Whenever Rudolf and Biff met, **Rudolf** acted in a relaxed, friendly fashion so that no one would suspect he hated **Biff**.
 8. Krystal told Sparkle **that Sparkle** was losing her looks.
 9. At our college, the administration introduced a "no smoking" policy three years ago. (*Or:* Our college introduced a no-smoking policy three years ago.)
 10. I am writing this letter in response to your ad for a waiter and bartender, male or female. **I have experience both waiting tables and tending bar,** so I wish to apply for the position.

Exercise 15.5 (suggested answers)
 1. Did anyone **who** submitted **a late** essay get a passing grade?
 2. George is the only person I know who can whistle while **he eats** crackers.
 3. Quilting is something Becky has a real passion for, but she hasn't had time to complete **a quilt** in months.
 4. **Are** there any **people** in the world so confident of success that they never contemplate an excuse for failure, just in case?
 5. Each of the three cars I could afford had **its** drawbacks, but the '89 Honda had the best maintenance-cost record.
 6. correct
 7. How can anyone, after twelve years of schooling, still misplace modifiers?
 8. I know that smoking is bad for me, but I just can't manage to give up **cigarettes**.
 9. She'll put her **baby** to bed now because **the infant** is so overtired she can't stop crying.
 10. **Eugene** said **Biff** wasn't trying hard enough, and that anyone who said he was would get a punch on **the** nose.

Exercise 15.6 (suggested answers)
 1. Neither the jacket nor the pants fit the way **they** should.
 2. There's nobody around to help you since **the other performers** left hours ago to get their **costumes** fitted.
 3. Bernice would love to meet someone **who** is tall, dark, handsome, and rich; in fact, **he doesn't** even have to be tall, dark, or handsome.
 4. **The motel owners** said they would try to find accommodation for the tourists, even though they didn't really know what **the tourists** wanted.
 5. I remember the old days when **those who** used computers wore thick glasses, solved calculus problems for fun, and didn't know whether their shoes were tied.
 6. This is a beaten team; the players don't care anymore whether **they perform** well or poorly.
 7. Denise told Mara that **Mara** had an excellent chance of making the team if she just did everything **Denise** told her to do when she spoke to the coach.
 8. Omar sat down next to Barry in the cafeteria and ate **Barry's** lunch.
 9. Every twelve-step program is based on the belief that nobody can rise above dependency or addiction without faith in a higher power and the help of friends.

10. Someone who has many friends is truly rich; friends will help when all else fails.

Exercise 15.7 (suggested answers)
1. Each car in the rally must have **its** own mechanic and navigator.
2. Lisa and Nasreen plan to share an apartment next year, providing **Lisa** gets the student loan she applied for.
3. Every time that Rudolf sat next to Dwight during an exam, **Dwight** tried to copy his answers.
4. The colour television with which we are familiar will become obsolete as **it is** replaced by HDTV, the high resolution broadcast standard that is common in Europe.
5. Isn't anyone going to try to beat the house at blackjack?
6. Medical researchers have found that some forms of **cancer** may be linked to the consumption of red meat.
7. Brandi's dream is to meet just one man **who** will live up to her expectations of **him**.
8. Akil wrote to tell Mikail that, because of the political unrest in **Akil's** country, it probably wasn't safe for **Mikail** to visit him this summer.
9. Can there be any Canadian culture buffs so out of touch with significant cultural events that they don't know about my recent victory in the national clog dancing championships?
10. I've been told repeatedly that postsecondary education is essential to my chances of future employment, but I don't bother to go **to school** anymore, now that I've found a full-time job loading trucks.

Exercise 15.8 (suggested answers)
1. **All students** graduating from high school should be careful to choose a college or university program designed to prepare them for the career they are interested in.
2. Before **she buys** vitamins, drugs, or any over-the-counter medication, a woman should get a pharmacist's advice.
3. Fishing is a sport I have enjoyed for many years, but I have never caught one **fish** of record size.
4. My mother's constant nagging would make anyone lose **his or her** mind.
5. Rick and Clement agreed that they could go camping on the weekend, so long as they left early enough to be sure **Clement** got back in time to get to work.
6. Everybody I know is going, even though **everyone has** to rent a tux.
7. **Those who have** finished all their homework so quickly can't possibly have done **it** properly.
8. In this company, **all employees are** encouraged to find their own path to success, according to their own definition of success.
9. I have never advocated banning fighting in hockey because I think a good **fight** now and then releases tensions **that** might otherwise result in much worse violence, among the fans as well as the players.
10. Professor Chan, obviously annoyed, told Kathy and Tamara that she had thought **Tamara** would have known better than to copy her friend's homework assignment.

Exercise 15.9
Anyone **who** has competed in a triathlon (a three-part race consisting of swimming, cycling, and running) knows that proper training is an absolute necessity, not only to success, but also to survival. Swimming is one of the toughest contests, because it demands cardiovascular fitness as well as strength, and it

makes demands on the whole body. While each of the three segments has **its** own challenges, the cycling part of the triathlon is the event **that** separates serious athletes from part-time fitness buffs. Here, **the latter** will find **they** can't summon enough energy after **their** swim to stay close to **their opponents** if **their opponents have** trained harder [**than they**]. **Serious athletes** will begin to assert their dominance now, and by the end of the bike ride, **those who** have achieved a high level of physical efficiency through their training will still have a chance of a high placing. For the competitor in a triathlon, survival is often the primary goal. The body's reserves are called on, and only the dedicated, well-trained athlete will be able to **survive**. For most, reaching the finish line is a personal test, and the only competition is against one's previous finish times. **Those who** still have winning in mind after the swim, the cycle race, and the run **have** physical and mental reserves beyond the ordinary.

Answers for Chapter 16: Maintaining Person Agreement (Pages 171 to 179)

Exercise 16.1
1. you want
2. she
3. you
4. you
5. we
6. you
7. You
8. we, we, our
9. you don't, your, you are
10. you know, you, you know

Exercise 16.2 (suggested answers)
1. A great worry is lifted from **your** mind when you learn your application has been accepted.
2. If only **I** had read the instructions carefully, I wouldn't have messed up the answer on the test.
3. If any of you are planning to go to the class party, **you** can pick up **your** tickets now.
4. Men who don't think women are their equals may have to get used to living on **their** own.
5. It has taken most Canadians far too long to recognize the seriousness of **their** debt and deficit problems.
6. If **you are** convicted on that charge, a fine is the least of your worries.
7. After we had driven about 400 km, the lack of sleep made it hard to keep **our** eyes open.
8. If you can't cope with the pressure, **you** must expect to be replaced by someone who can.
9. The penalties for plagiarism are severe, but one doesn't usually think about penalties until after **he or she is** caught. (*Or:* . . . **you don't** usually think about penalties until after you are caught.)
10. It's very difficult for **14-year-olds** to control **their** temper when **they** feel frustrated or angry.

Exercise 16.3 (suggested answers)
1. When **you have** completed all the sentences in an exercise, don't forget to check your answers in the back of the book.
2. In this country, **one receives** more acclaim, not to mention more money, as a hockey player than one does as a symphony conductor.
3. Can you really blame me for getting so tired of picking up after **my** messy children all day long?

4. **Those who ride** a motorcycle and **do** not wear a helmet should be aware of the risk **they're** taking.
5. When we left the comfort of the air-conditioned hotel, the heat was enough to knock **us** over.
6. I wonder why people always long for what they don't have, even when **they** have more than **they** need?
7. I enjoy living in the country, because there **I don't** have to deal with traffic or pollution, and **I** can always get to the city if **I** want to.
8. Ken collects art because, if **you know** something about it, you can always get your money back on **your** investment, and **you** can sometimes make a killing.
9. An expert wine taster will find this a very acceptable vintage, and even **those who know** little about wine will enjoy **themselves** with a bottle or two.
10. Canadian history may seem dull if **one doesn't** know much about it, but to someone who is fascinated by the unusual and the eccentric, it is a goldmine of wonderful stories. (*Or:* Canadian history may seem dull if you don't know much about it, but if **you are** fascinated by the unusual and the eccentric, it is a goldmine of wonderful stories.)

Exercise 16.4

How can **you** fight the common cold? If **you** had the energy to research the subject, **you** would find books, television programs, and thousands of articles in newspapers and magazines advising **you** how to cope with a cold. A cold cannot be prevented or cured since it is not known what organism actually causes it. However, **your** research will not be wasted: **you** will find no shortage of folk remedies and "personally guaranteed" cures, most of which do nothing more than make **you** feel better while **you wait** for the cold to go away. Advertisements for pharmaceutical companies promise their pills, syrups, lozenges, and capsules will relieve **your** symptoms, but no one claims to offer a cure. There is something strangely comforting in this fact. Since the only thing **you** can do for a cold is wait for it to go away, **you** need not spend any [of **your**] energy or effort visiting a doctor or seeking a miraculous remedy. **You** might as well relax, spend a day or two indulging **yourself** snuggled up in bed, and enjoy whatever restorative **you find** most to **your** liking. **You** might discover, for example, that chicken soup is **your** treatment of choice. Or **you** might prefer a large hot rum, with brown sugar and lemon. (Most medical practitioners agree that, when suffering from a cold, **you need** additional Vitamin C.) Whatever **your** preferred treatment, **you** should indulge and enjoy **yourself**! This is one of the few times in **your** life when **you** can pamper **yourself** not just without guilt, but in the knowledge that self-indulgence is good for **you**.

Exercise 16.5

How can **people** fight the common cold? If **they** had the energy to research the subject, **they** would find books, television programs, and thousands of articles in newspapers and magazines advising **them** how to cope with a cold. A cold cannot be prevented or cured since it is not known what organism actually causes it. However, **their** research will not be wasted: **readers** will find no shortage of folk remedies and "personally guaranteed" cures, most of which do nothing more than make **sufferers** feel better while **they wait** for the cold to go away. Pharmaceutical companies promise their pills, syrups, lozenges, and capsules will relieve **the** symptoms **of a cold**, but no one claims to offer a cure. There is something strangely comforting in this fact. Since the only thing **sufferers** can do is wait for **the cold** to go away, **they** need not spend any energy or effort visiting a doctor or seeking a miraculous remedy. **They** might as well relax, spend a day or two indulging **themselves** snuggled up in bed, and enjoy whatever restorative **they find** most to **their** liking. **Some** might discover, for example, that chicken soup is **their** treatment of choice. **Others** might prefer a large hot rum, with brown sugar and lemon. (Most medical practitioners agree that, when suffering from a cold, **our bodies need** additional Vitamin C.) Whatever **their** preferred treatment, **cold sufferers should** indulge and enjoy **themselves**! This is one of the few times in life when **people** can pamper **themselves** not just without guilt, but in the knowledge that self-indulgence is good for **them**.

Exercise 16.6
   People who get married while **they're** still in college may have an especially hard time completing **their** studies. If both spouses are in school, **they** may not have enough money for an apartment, and they may have to live with **their** parents for a while. Students whose spouses work may find **themselves** studying on weekends while **their** spouses rest or socialize. The wife who supports a student husband, along with the husband who supports a student wife, may find that the responsibility weighs heavily on **her**. People in such situations are likely to feel at the end of **their** wits sometimes, so students whose marriages are shaky may find that **they are** having a very hard time of it and that **their** schoolwork is suffering. On the other hand, these various demands may strengthen a marriage, and a student who marries may find that **his or her** motivation to succeed at school has increased. Some married students may even find **themselves** studying more, spending on schoolwork the time **they** would otherwise have spent dating.

Exercise 16.7
   A woman who enjoys baseball may have difficulty explaining **her** passion to those who find the game a bore. Each February, the die-hard fan begins to sharpen **her** listening and watching skills by tuning in to spring training games. If you have ever seen one of these fanatics watch a baseball game, **you** can't help but notice the alertness and intensity with which **she** follows the play. It is this single-minded dedication that the non-fan finds **himself** unable to comprehend. How can one be so interested in something that **one** must watch for three hours to see almost nothing take place? How can **one** get excited by a no-hitter, which, by definition, means that nothing has happened during the game? Baseball fans maintain that the game to which **they are** addicted has many more pleasures than mere action. They cite fielding plays and the strategy of pitcher-versus-hitter matchups in defence of the game that **they** would rather watch than any other. Those for **whom** these pleasures hold little appeal might enjoy watching golf or lawn bowling.

Answers to Chapter 17: The Comma (Pages 183 to 192)

Exercise 17.1
1. Does anyone remember John, Paul, George, and Ringo?
2. correct
3. Krystal thinks she wants to get married, but she can't decide whether Dwight, Rudolf, or Eugene should be the lucky man.
4. Fans of rock, folk**(,)** and ska all enjoyed the Days of You concert.
5. MacDonald, Laurier, Borden**(,)** and Pearson are four dissimilar men who have one thing in common.
6. Arnold is an all-round athlete; he enjoys skating, skiing, cycling, tobogganing**(,)** and showering.
7. Marieke has strong ambition, a cool head, good health**(,)** and an inquiring mind; everyone hates her.

8. Careful investment of time and money can lead to a luxurious lifestyle, international fame**(,)** and early retirement.
9. Mowing the lawn, shopping for groceries**(,)** and doing my teenagers' homework are my least favourite activities.
10. Most of the world sees Canada as a land where French is spoken, ice and snow are year-round hazards**(,)** and violent hockey is the natives' favourite pastime.

Exercise 17.2
1. My mother's favourite singer is Gordon Lightfoot, the former Elvis imitator from Orillia.
2. The winner of the 1994 Yorkton Film Festival Jury Award was Janis Lundman's documentary, *Lawn and Order.*
3. The underlying message of the film is that, whether you like it or not, your lawn says a lot about who you are.
4. correct
5. Despite her reputation as an air head, Leticia is, we have discovered, fairly bright.
6. To no one's surprise, Professor Lam, a popular mathematics instructor, won the distinguished teacher award again this year.
7. correct
8. In a radical departure from tradition, the bride wore a bright red gown and matching veil.
9. One of the wedding guests remarked, rather cattily I thought, that the bride looked like a Tomato Festival Queen.
10. Not surprisingly, a recent study of driver stress shows that aggressive behaviour, such as flashing high beams at other drivers, increases during high-congestion traffic.

Exercise 17.3
1. He and I are good friends, yet we often disagree.
2. We have a choice: we could try bribery, or we could resort to force.
3. We can't win this game, nor can we afford to lose it.
4. correct
5. Mona tried and tried to pass her driver's test, and her persistence finally paid off.
6. My wife and I would like to buy a house, but we don't have enough money for a down payment.
7. I'm bored and underpaid at work, so I'm going back to school next fall.
8. Ravi and Denis are travelling to Whitehorse this summer, and Sandy is going to St. John.
9. This is Bambi's last semester, so she's concentrating on school for a change.
10. Please pay close attention, for the instructions are a little complicated.

Exercise 17.4
1. In the end, quality is what counts.
2. Second, our department is required to cut costs by fifteen percent.
3. If there were any justice in this world, I'd have been rewarded for my performance.
4. Moved beyond words, the victorious candidate was able only to gesture his thanks to his supporters.
5. Carefully placing one foot in front of the other, she managed to walk along the white line for several metres.

6. Where a huge hardwood forest had once stood, only acres of tree stumps remained.
7. Finally, it is clear that we must make our decision today.
8. While Rudolf may be short on brain, he's long on brawn.
9. As her fortieth birthday approached, Drusilla met the challenge by trading in her sedan for a sports car and her husband for a boyfriend ten years her junior.
10. When the first robin heralds the return of spring, I begin to dream of lazy summer days lying beside the pool with a cool drink in my hand and a ball game on the radio.

Exercise 17.5
1. Despite some excellent action sequences, the movie was a failure because of the terrible script.
2. Your fall order, which we received last week, has been shipped.
3. These cold, wet(,) grey days are not good for the crops.
4. If starvation and lack of recognition made great artists, Canada would be a land of Picassos.
5. What you hear, what you read(,) and what you experience all help to form your cultural background.
6. A few days after we sailed, the boat sprang a leak.
7. Inside, the band was playing at full blast.
8. The letter of application is one of the most important documents you will ever write, yet you have spent only an hour composing it.
9. Despite some early problems, Ottawa's National Gallery has become the home of one of the most interesting collections in North America.
10. correct

Exercise 17.6
1. There is something wrong with this proposal, but I haven't yet figured out what it is.
2. Our hope, of course, is that the terrorists will be caught and punished.
3. George Washington, the first president of the United States, was an officer in the British army before he was engaged in the American Revolution.
4. Charlottetown, Quebec(,) and Kingston were the sites of the conferences that eventually led to Confederation in 1867.
5. If you can cope with overloaded logging trucks passing you at high speeds on narrow mountain roads, you'll enjoy the spectacularly scenic drive from Hope to Princeton.
6. correct
7. A good dictionary, consulted frequently, is probably the most important resource for any student who wishes to develop a mature vocabulary.
8. While I respect your opinion and your right to express it, that doesn't mean that I necessarily agree with you.
9. After our guests had gone home, we discovered that they had drunk all the beer but had left most of the food, so we'd be dining on leftovers for the next two weeks.
10. If there were any point in protesting the president's decision, I would have complained long ago, but I don't think anything will change her disastrous course of action.

Exercise 17.7
1. My world includes gorgeous men, fast cars, loud music, expensive clothes(,) and other dreams.

2. After carefully wrapping the watch in a handkerchief, the magician produced a hammer and smashed the expensive timepiece to smithereens, or so it appeared.
3. The retirement of Bobby Orr from hockey was the end of an era for the game, but those who saw him play will never forget it.
4. A 25 m heated pool is available for those who like to swim, and, for those who play golf, there is a beautiful eighteen-hole course.
5. Ever since, I have been a regular theatre-goer.
6. correct
7. When you enter the store, go to the counter on your immediate left, ask for Ms. Seth(,) and tell her you would like to see samples of the new shipment.
8. Flattery, the old saying goes, will get you nowhere, but this has not been my experience.
9. The head of our physics department, Professor Vector, despite his vast theoretical knowledge of his subject, couldn't change a light bulb if his life depended on it.
10. Before he was asked to leave, Rudolf managed to offend the host, insult the hostess(,) and humiliate the guest of honour.

Exercise 17.8

One of the psychologists in our department, a mild-mannered man under most circumstances, burst into my office one day last spring and spent twenty minutes pouring out his frustration. It seemed that just as he was about to enter his classroom to teach a lesson on stress management, he had been confronted by a student who asked whether he was going to do anything important in class that day. This is a question teachers are often asked, and every teacher I know finds it infuriating. Most, however, are able to control themselves and respond politely. But our psychologist obviously had been asked this question once too often. He ranted, raved(,) and roared despite my best efforts to reason with him and calm him down. Finally, he ran out of steam and collapsed into a quivering blob. When I could see that he was more or less under control, I suggested he try some of the time-honoured defence mechanisms teachers have developed in response to students' insensitivity. For example, one response to The Question, the one that happens to be my personal favourite, is to ask why today's class should be any different from any other class in the term. Some students take this as sarcasm, but others assume that I'm giving them permission to skip. The beleaguered psychologist found my recommendation helpful, I think, because he was smiling as he left my office on his way to teach another class on stress management.

Exercise 17.9

Over the past couple of decades, young people have adopted a number of strange, novel(,) and inexplicable fads. How can one explain the popularity among adolescents of "Docs," footwear which was originally designed by a Dr. Marten for therapeutic use? Why wear a baseball cap with the visor, which is supposed to protect one's eyes from the sun, facing backward? Why on earth, given the initial pain and the continuing risk of infection, would young people choose to pierce sensitive parts of their anatomy for the purpose of inserting rings and studs? These contemporary fashion statements, however, are no more peculiar than some of the fads of the 60s and 70s, such as bouffant hairdos, bell-bottomed pants(,) or platform shoes, which, unfortunately, seem to be making a comeback. All these design horrors make me shudder, but my mother's experiment with permanent false eyelashes probably wins the prize for fashion idiocy. Long, thick, curled lashes were *de rigueur* for the chic 50s matron. While most of my mother's contemporaries were content to glue their false eyelashes to their lids each day, my mother was not. A fashion slave from her four-inch spike heels to her beehive hairdo, my mother decided to make her "eyelash enhancement" permanent. So off she went to her local beauty salon, an establishment in which she spent hours each week, and submitted to the torture of having individual hairs inserted, one by one, into her eyelids. Triumphant, though in considerable pain, she emerged with thick, luxuriant, black eyelashes that Elizabeth Taylor would die for. Unfortunately, my mother's beauty transformation did not have a happy ending. A few weeks after her "enhancement," she gave a dinner party. Moments before her guests were to arrive, she opened the oven to check on her roast, and her eyelashes melted into black blobs, bonding themselves to her eyelids. The salon had not thought to warn her that her "permanent" lashes were made of nylon and could not, therefore, be exposed to extreme heat. The surgery my mother had to endure to have her "permanent" lashes removed is another story.

Exercise 17.10 (new commas in bold type)

The Canadian appetite for sports entertainment seems insatiable. In the past, three sports dominated the year for the sports fan, but now, thanks to specialty television, some very unusual and exotic competitions are finding fans in this country. Australian-rules football, a game that belies its name by seeming to have no rules, is gaining in popularity, though purely as a spectator sport. Triathlons, biathlons, marathons, mini-marathons, and a host of similar endurance events are now avidly watched by the armchair athlete and enthusiastically entered by the physically fit. Sumo wrestling, while not accessible to most of us as a participatory activity, seems to have a devoted following, and even darts and lawn bowling have their supporters. And then there is golf. To some, watching golf on television is as exciting as watching paint dry, but during inclement weather, when golf addicts can't be on the course themselves, they follow their heroes' every televised step and agonize with them over every shot for hours. The challenge for Canadian jocks of both sexes and all ages is to tear themselves away from these various spectator entertainments in order to play their favourite sports.

Answers to Chapter 18: The Semicolon (Pages 193 to 200)

Exercise 18.1

1. correct	6. incorrect
2. incorrect	7. incorrect
3. correct	8. correct
4. incorrect	9. correct
5. incorrect	10. correct

Exercise 18.2

1. correct	6. correct
2. incorrect	7. incorrect
3. correct	8. correct
4. correct	9. incorrect
5. incorrect	10. incorrect

Exercise 18.3

2. He sat down near a refreshing stream, for he was very tired.
4. It's a beautiful day, just right for a long walk.
5. Six of the Indian nations joined together in a loose union; they were called Iroquois.

6. The lawn, a little ragged, needs to be cut; the hedge, shrubs, and ivy need to be trimmed; the flowers need to be watered; and, most important, the gardener needs to be paid.
7. I'd like to help; however, I'm supposed to rest all day.

Exercise 18.4
2. There are only a few who could catch him, and I'm sure she isn't one of them.
5. We'll have to go soon, for it's getting late.
7. If ever there were a time to act, it is now.
9. She disobeyed the rules, so she will have to be punished.
10. Krystal is always late; however, she's worth waiting for.

Exercise 18.5
1. There seems to be no end to the work that must be done; furthermore, there isn't enough time in which to do it.
2. There must be a way, or we're finished before we've even begun.
3. I can't afford a Porsche; therefore, I drive a Neon.
4. Jana is one of my favourite people; she can always cheer me up.
5. There will be ample opportunity to finish your homework, but right now I need your help.
6. The floor was knotty pine; the furniture and walls were designed and finished to complement it.
7. Brock was killed early in the morning, but the Americans were driven from Queenston Heights by nightfall.
8. Canada's history is not a very violent one; however, we've had several rebellions of note.
9. Jon has gone away to become a teacher; Marta now has twin baby girls; Kevin is unemployed; Julie is a lawyer or stockbroker (I forget which); and Pavel is, as usual, drifting from job to job.
10. When the rain started, they were trapped in the open; nevertheless, they stayed where they were until it let up and then made their way to the nearest shelter.

Exercise 18.6
1. The entire town is in an uproar; it seems Rudolf has been missing since Tuesday.
2. Of course, everyone knows Rudolf is a bit wacky; he's been very strange since his close encounter of the fourth kind.
3. Rudolf's story is that a hamburger-shaped, chrome-coloured, smoke-belching UFO pinned him under its wheels; its inhabitants, he claims, kept him prisoner for several hours.
4. The creatures spoke to him through little slits; however, Rudolf says he got a good look at them.
5. correct
6. These creatures told Rudolf many secrets; for example, they told him they had searched the universe for a perfect specimen like him.
7. Rudolf considered this overture a friendly gesture; he immediately felt more kindly toward the aliens.
8. In fact, as Rudolf later confessed, he is under the aliens' control; perhaps this explains why he talks like Donald Duck.
9. But now people are beginning to worry; there's an unexplained burned spot in Rudolf's backyard, and he's been gone since Tuesday.
10. correct

Exercise 18.7
1. Alicia and Eddie are both very shy; therefore, they dread being called upon to speak in class.
2. We wondered what Ninik was scribbling so furiously; it turned out to be a letter to the dean.
3. I think you need to put the matter in perspective; therefore, I suggest you consider carefully what it is you want to accomplish.
4. Nancy wants to be helpful; in fact, she is always the first to volunteer.
5. Banish the thought of defeat from your mind; concentrate, instead, on victory.
6. If I could push defeat out of my mind, there would be only a vast emptiness left; victory is impossible when you play on this team.
7. Buying a house involves enormous responsibilities, not to mention enormous debt; consequently, I plan to live with my parents until I'm 40 or so.
8. For reasons I do not understand, my parents are not as enthusiastic about my plan as I am; in fact, they're downright hostile.
9. Turn left when you come to the fork in the road; otherwise, you'll end up at the nuclear waste-disposal site and come out all aglow.
10. I'm sure you understand that I would like nothing better than for you to pass this course; however, there may be a small fee involved.

Exercise 18.8
1. Please leave dinner in the oven for a little while; I'll eat when I've finished this exercise.
2. Taking the corner at 90 kph, the police car swerved into the oncoming lane; fortunately, no one was coming.
3. The chair called the meeting to order; however, it quickly became apparent that none of us had done the background reading.
4. One of the products of the computer age is increased leisure; this, in turn, has led to increased opportunities for physical fitness.
5. A glance at the calendar will reveal that there are on 212 shopping days left until my birthday; that's just enough time for you to find the present I deserve.
6. Computers are marvellous tools; they are fast, efficient, and accurate, but they can't think. They remind me of a secretary I used to know; she's now my boss.
7. The Four Horsemen of the Apocalypse are Conquest, Slaughter, Famine(,) and Death.
8. Some Biblical figures are familiar to people from many different cultures; for example, the stories of Samson and Delilah and of David and Goliath are widely known.
9. We're unhappy about our instructor's evaluation procedures; in fact, we think they are irrational, arbitrary(,) and often unfair.
10. Every year at tax time, I am faced with the same problem: assembling my bills and receipts; figuring out my gas mileage; trying to recall which expenses were business-related and which were personal; finding my T4s, T5s, and other T forms; and organizing this mess so my accountant can attempt to keep me out of jail for another year.

Exercise 18.9
1. I played squash, went jogging, and even tried weight-lifting this weekend; in addition, I signed up for a six-month, satisfaction-guaranteed fitness program.
2. I have mixed memories of my tour of Europe; for example, while I think fondly of gorgeous little towns like Gordes and Orvieto, I think less fondly of Venice, where I was robbed.

3. As I was buying a gelato at a little stand across from our hotel, a man slipped his hand into my purse, grabbed my passport**(,)** and was promptly seized by two plainclothes detectives who had been keeping an eye on him.

4. I was required to fill out a complaint, which took hours, since it had to be translated from English to Italian and back to English; consequently, the only view of Venice's famous canals that I got was from a police boat.

5. For my birthday last year, my husband gave me a dozen roses. This year he gave me a shovel; as a result, I'm wondering if the romance has gone from our relationship.

6. For years, students complained that the English teachers couldn't calculate grades accurately; finally, the Math Department offered to give a seminar to introduce the English Department to the mysteries of addition and subtraction.

7. Louis Riel led a Métis rebellion in Manitoba in 1885, but he was defeated, tried**(,)** and executed the same year; his death caused a deep rift between English and French Canada.

8. The Canadian political scene has become much less interesting since the departure of men like Pierre Trudeau and Brian Mulroney; whether you liked them or not, they both provoked a lot of public debate over political issues.

9. In preparation for the final exam, please bring your text and any notes you may have taken in class; at least two pens; a scientific calculator; lots of scrap paper on which to work out the problems; and a drafting set.

10. Reading spy novels is, I admit, a waste of time, but it beats sitting in front of the tube being bombarded with ads for products I don't need; learning intimate, even embarrassing details about the lives of people I don't know, will never meet, and would never want to know; and being subjected to the so-called humour that is characteristic of the average American sitcom.

Answers to Chapter 19: The Colon (Pages 201 to 204)

Exercise 19.1

1. correct		6. incorrect
2. incorrect		7. correct
3. correct		8. incorrect
4. incorrect		9. incorrect
5. correct		10. incorrect

Exercise 19.2

1. incorrect		6. incorrect
2. incorrect		7. correct
3. incorrect		8. incorrect
4. correct		9. correct
5. correct		10. correct

Exercise 19.3
1. correct
2. They finally realized there was only one course open to them: obedience.
3. Gary had trouble with his canoe: it tipped and sank.
4. There is someone who can save us, though: Captain Canuck!
5. He tossed and turned all night and found the same images recurring in his dreams: a river and a wolf.
6. Her body was beyond the point of exhaustion, but she tried to force herself on by thinking of one thing: victory.
7. correct

8. I have a large garden, but it grows only two things: weeds and worms.
9. Two issues remained to be settled: wages and benefits.
10. She has one goal that she is determined to achieve: the world record.

Exercise 19.4
  2. Only one thing was missing: the boat.
  4. On the list, we must include chips, mix, ice, and peanuts.
  6. Three qualities of a good quarterback are leadership, intelligence, and physical strength.
  8. The lake is deep and cold.
  9. Dogs have many qualities that make them superior to cats: loyalty, intelligence, working ability, and friendliness.
10. Let me give you an example: Louis Riel.

Exercise 19.5
  1. I'd like to help, but I can't.
  2. I'll take the following volunteers: Marie, Susan, Ngoc, and Lewis.
  3. We'll have to go back to get tent poles, matches, and paddles.
  6. No one wants to go with him, for two very good reasons: money and time.
  8. My boss is so mean she must be bitter or crazy.

Answers to Chapter 20: Quotation Marks (Pages 205 to 211)

Exercise 20.1
  1. "Three thousand is a bargain for that coat," said Drusilla, eyeing the floor-length mink.
  2. correct
  3. "Put that gun down," shouted the officer, "or I'll shoot!"
  4. "The time has come," the Walrus said, "to talk of many things."
  5. Canada's national anthem, "O Canada," was written by Calixa Lavallée.
  6. My father likes to remind me of John F. Kennedy's words: "Too often we enjoy the comfort of opinion without the discomfort of thought."
  7. In his novel, *Generation X* (Generation X), Douglas Coupland warns, "Less is a possibility."
  8. Two singles from Sheryl Crow's first album, *Tuesday Night Music Club* (Tuesday Night Music Club), became hits: "All I Wanna Do" and "Strong Enough."
  9. *The Guinness Book of Records* (The Guinness Book of Records) claims that the world's most-married man is former Baptist minister Scotty Wolfe, who got married 27 times.
10. When asked how many children were born of these marriages, Mr. Wolfe replied, "I think I had 41."

Exercise 20.2
  1. correct
  2. After his best player suffered another injury, the coach pleaded with him, "Please, Marcel, wear a face mask!"
  3. correct
  4. Brian inquired, "When are we going to eat?"
  5. "When you cook dinner," Val replied.
  6. Marshall McLuhan's insight, "The medium is the message," appears in his most famous book, *Understanding Media* (Understanding Media).
  7. The headline in today's *Winnipeg Free Press* (Winnipeg Free Press) is "Canada's dollar sinks to new low."

8. We've decided to rent a video this evening, but we can't decide between *The Lion King* (<u>The Lion King</u>) and *Priscilla, Queen of the Desert* (<u>Priscilla, Queen of the Desert</u>).
9. "This is the second time you've been thrown out of class," the dean told Biff. "I'm inclined to suspend you for a week."
10. "Say you love me," he pleaded. "OK," she replied, "You love me."

Exercise 20.3

1. Rust Hills wrote a very funny essay with a very boring title, "How to Wash and Wax Your Car," which appears in his recent book, *How to Do Things Right* (<u>How to Do Things Right</u>).
2. Pierre Elliott Trudeau made many memorable statements during his years in office, but he is probably best known for two: "The state has no business in the nation's bedrooms," and "Fuddle-duddle."
3. "Television is a vast wasteland," complained Newton Minnow, "and is largely responsible for the fact that people today can't read."
4. For tomorrow's class, we are supposed to read the chapter called "Hunger March to Edmonton" in Myrna Kostash's book, *All of Baba's Children* (<u>All of Baba's Children</u>).
5. According to Robertson Davies, "The world is burdened with young fogeys."
6. "I suggest that the victim then tried to defend himself with this feather," cried the prosecuting attorney dramatically.
7. There was an uproar in the courtroom. "How could he defend himself with a feather?" was the question on everyone's lips.
8. "Well," suggested the prosecutor, "since he couldn't reach the banana in time, the feather was the best he could do."
9. At this, the defendant leaped to his feet and admitted that he was, indeed, guilty. "How did you know about the banana?" he muttered as he was led away.
10. "Elementary, my dear Winston," laughed the prosecutor, misquoting the great Sherlock Holmes.

Exercise 20.4

1. "Lights! Camera! Action!" These three words, so often used by Hollywood directors, have entered the language as a synonym for an exciting beginning.
2. Quietly and deliberately, A.J. turned to his tormentor and spoke. "I don't want to play this game anymore."
3. If I had to choose one song from The Tragically Hip's *Fully Completely* (<u>Fully Completely</u>), I'd pick "Hundredth Meridian."
4. One of my favourite Canadian actors is Saul Rubinek who, after a shaky beginning in *The Littlest Hobo* (<u>The Littlest Hobo</u>), moved on to guest spots on *The Equalizer* (<u>The Equalizer</u>) and then to major roles in mega-hits such as *Unforgiven* (<u>Unforgiven</u>), *True Romance* (<u>True Romance</u>), and *Wall Street* (<u>Wall Street</u>).
5. City employees recently received guidelines for dealing with phoned-in bomb threats. "Be calm," the instructions advise the lucky call-taker. "Be courteous, listen carefully, and do not interrupt."
6. correct
7. "We are all immigrants to this place," wrote Margaret Atwood, "even if we were born here."
8. In his poem, "Keine Lazarovitch," Irving Layton sums up the experience of aging as "the inescapable lousiness of growing old."

9. Political correctness has moved abroad: the headmistress of an English secondary school refused to allow her students to attend a performance of Romeo and Juliet because, she said, "The play is blatantly heterosexual."

10. In another part of England, Beatrix Potter's children's classics *Benjamin Bunny* (<u>Benjamin Bunny</u>) and *The Tale of Peter Rabbit* (<u>The Tale of Peter Rabbit</u>) were banned from use in public schools. "These stories," explained the Curriculum Council, "portray only middle-class rabbits."

Answers to Chapter 21: Question Marks, Exclamation Marks, and Punctuation Review (Pages 212 to 220)

Exercise 21.1
1. What more could I possibly do to help?
2. Val asked Biff if he was absolutely positive he had paid the bill.
3. Why is there always a cop around when I'm speeding but never when I need help?
4. Have you checked the weather forecast to see when the weather is expected to clear?
5. I will always wonder if Rhonda handed in my essay.
6. Is it true that voters will act rationally only when all other possibilities have been exhausted?
7. Did the committee consider all the options carefully before making this decision?
8. I don't understand why sociology is so important in a business program.
9. Eugene is still asking the math teacher to raise his mark to at least a pass.
10. The question isn't whether or not there is intelligent life on Mars, it's whether there's intelligent life on earth.

Exercise 21.2
1. I'm not sure whether there is a game tonight or not.
2. Is there life after long days of boring classes, followed by long nights of homework?
3. If we can't complete the project on time, will we be penalized?
4. Our question was what to do after the boss had burst into tears and gone home.
5. What good will it do if I continue to be pleasant to people who take such delight in making me look foolish?
6. How can anyone just stand by while some innocent person is being attacked?
7. Whoever would have thought that the Canadian dollar would fall below the U.S. seventy-cents mark?
8. I am surprised and hurt that you would question my motives in asking you for help with my studying.
9. Please take a look at these tests and tell me whether you think these two students were cheating.
10. Why can't the sports fans who yell so loudly at players' mistakes try to put themselves in the same position as those they criticize and be a little more forgiving?

Exercise 21.3
1. Take that, you monster!
2. Ready, aim, fire!
3. I can't believe it! We've got the winning number!

4. That's the last straw. (*or* !) I quit!
5. There's a fly in my soup!
6. Run! It's right behind you!
7. "Slide!" The whole team was screaming in unison.
8. I can't believe it! The thing actually flies!
9. Turn the heat up. (*or* !) I'm freezing!
10. The girls descended on the mall waving their plastic and crying, "Charge!"

Exercise 21.4
1. The question was whether we would spend the night in Abbotsford or push on to Vancouver.
2. Just think! We have two glorious weeks free of English class! (*or* .)
3. Bruce thought he looked absolutely irresistible in his new leather pants.
4. If you think you're confused, just imagine how I must feel.
5. correct
6. Katy asked Ramon if he'd like to stay over.
7. correct
8. Today we read a poem by Irving Layton, who was born in Rumania, I think.
9. After seeing your test results, I wonder if you even bought the text, let alone read it.
10. Congratulations! You've just mastered end punctuation marks.

Exercise 21.5

When Ricky Henderson, the lead-off hitter, came to the plate, I was ready. My first pitch, a slow curve, caught the outside corner. "Strike one!" howled the umpire. Why was I pitching to Ricky? What was an English teacher doing on the mound in the Baseball All-Star game? Who was that rag-tag collection of players surrounding me? The answers make one of the strangest chapters in baseball history. Undefeated in our recreational league, we had challenged the semi-pro team in our community, defeated it, and gone on to beat three other professional teams from nearby cities. Then *Sports Illustrated* printed a story about our exploits. It was inevitable that major league teams would want to take advantage of the publicity we were getting, so they invited us to play at the All-Star break before the regular National League versus American League game. They even paid our transportation to New York. (*or* !)

I struck out Henderson with my slider, took care of Ruben Sierra on three pitches, and got Ken Griffey, Jr. with an overpowering fast ball. Hey! This was easy. The second and third innings were repeats of the first. All nine batters struck out. (*or* !) My teammates were getting restless, so in the fourth and fifth, I allowed a couple of easy ground balls and gave the outfielders their turn with a couple of easy fly balls in the sixth. Then I went back to work and struck out the side in the seventh, eighth, and ninth. Meanwhile, I had driven in the only run with a hard-hit double down the first-base line. The crowd went berserk. "Sarah!" they chanted over and over. After the game, the Yankees, Dodgers, Blue Jays, and Marlins began a bidding war for my services as a free agent, but when they reached twelve million for a single season, I smiled and said, "Thanks, but grammar is my game."

Punctuation Review

Exercise 21.7
1. "Enjoy the view," we called out as they left for the mountaintop; we had wisely decided to wait for them in a meadow halfway up.

2. To be a millionaire by the time you are thirty, you will have to take large risks, be lucky, and have creative ideas.
3. High School was, indeed, the best time of my life, because I met the friends there that I would continue to see for many years, and I learned the principles that were to guide me through later, more difficult years.
4. The question of whether evolution is a fact or a myth doesn't worry most of the people in my class; they're more concerned about whether there's a dance on Friday night.
5. "Why won't he listen?" Marsha whispered tearfully.
6. With the crowd chanting, "Out! Out!" the referee had a hard time justifying his decision: a ten-minute misconduct.
7. Typing as though his life depended on the completion of the assignment, Ted managed to get through the first chapter before supper. This left him with Chapter Two, "The Next Day," to complete before bedtime.
8. The rain looked as though it would never let up, so Gary and the two girls packed up to go home, their vacation plans ruined.
9. "Don't go," Angela fell to her knees and begged her friend to stay. "Why must you leave now," she asked, "just when we're about to succeed?"
10. You'll find he has just one fault, my friend: he snores.

Exercise 21.8
1. "Jump! It's the only way out!" she cried.
2. Since there is so much time left, why don't you go for a swim or have a sauna?
3. If you keep this behaviour up, you'll certainly go a long way: all the way to jail!
4. Within minutes of the blast, pushing past the horrified onlookers, the police officers entered the building and encountered chaos.
5. The Montreal Expos, like the Toronto Blue Jays before them, are winning friends among baseball fans in the United States.
6. "Don't go near the water," warned the twins' mother; however, they were far too busy playing with the alligators to hear her.
7. My computer is a big improvement on the old typewriter I used to use; it still makes the same number of spelling errors, though.
8. "You'll never make it, Stella! We've got the whole building surrounded," the detective yelled through his bullhorn. "You might as well come out with your hands up!"
9. Her lips curling into a sneer, she replied, "You'll have to come in and get me, copper!"
10. The director, his patience at an end, screamed, "Cut! That scene is too long, too boring, and too bad. We'll have to take it again."

Exercise 21.9
For having saved the leprechaun's life, Devin was granted three wishes. The first he squandered on a mere one hundred dollars, because he didn't believe the little man when he told Devin that his wishes would come true. After more careful consideration, Devin wished again.

"I want a bank account in a Swiss bank," he shouted, "and enough money so that I will never run out."

The leprechaun frowned and looked very disappointed in Devin's wish, but he screwed up his face, went very red for a minute, and then announced, "It's done," but under his breath he muttered, "Greedy young cub; he needs a lesson."

Devin was all ready with his next wish; it was his greatest desire. He stared sternly at the leprechaun and in a loud voice said, "My last wish is the most important. I want to live for one thousand years."

The tiny old man grinned, then he screwed up his face and went very, very red for a minute. Finally, he relaxed, sighed a deep satisfied sigh, and, very pleased with himself, walked twice around the young redwood tree that had just sprouted in front of him.

Exercise 21.10
All too often, it seems that the Canadian national pastime is complaining about the weather. Our summers are criticized because they're too hot, while our springs are too wet, our autumns too cool, and our winters too long. If the climate is so bad here, why does anyone live north of the U.S. border? Perhaps the problem is not that Canadians don't like living in Canada, but that they love to complain.

Two of the most popular sports teams in Canada were at one time those with the worst records: the Argonauts and the Maple Leafs. Could this popularity be due to the ample opportunity and scope they gave to their fans for complaint? Not only do we bemoan the record of such teams when they lose, but, when they win, we dwell with glee on the possibilities of disaster for next year.

The same syndrome can be seen in our attitude toward Canadian heroes. It has often been said that we are a nation without heroes, but I suspect that we have plenty of candidates. It's just that we enjoy complaining so much, we try to find fault wherever we can and prefer to focus on clay feet rather than great works. One cannot help but wonder how Canadians fare in heaven, where everything is perfect. I suspect they must be desperately unhappy!

Answers for Chapter 22: Finding Something to Write About (Pages 223 to 237)

Exercise 22.1
1. Not specific. It's too large a topic.
2. Not specific, nor is it supportable without a great deal of research.
3. Not significant. Every child knows what they are.
4. Not significant.
5. Not single. Choose one.
6. Not single or specific.
7. Not supportable. How can we know?
8. Not significant.
9. Not specific. Whole books have been written on this topic.
10. Not single.

Exercise 22.2
1. Not significant. It's a commonplace fact.
2. Not specific or significant. Again, it's a simple fact.
3. Not single or specific.
4. Not specific. Nor is it supportable, for most of us, without substantial research.
5. Not specific.
6. Not significant.
7. Not supportable.
8. Not specific.
9. Not significant.
10. Not specific.

Exercise 22.6
1. Alcohol (not a reason)
2. Large bakeries; saving money (these "points" are not part of the process)

3. Improved looks (overlaps with "improved appearance"); improved social life (not *directly* related to S)
4. White shark; hammerhead shark (these are species, not characteristics of sharks)
5. Make travel plans (overlaps with "plan a client's itinerary"); get a passport (client's responsibility)
6. May be dangerous; weight is often gained back (these points are not related to S: they are not fad diets)
7. Largely female audience (unrelated); quiz shows (overlaps with "game shows")
8. Surge in birth of children from 1947–1965 (unrelated: it's a definition of the postwar baby boom, not an effect)

Exercise 22.7
1. They are fun to play; Lottario, Lotto 6/49 (unrelated to S)
2. Practical training (offered in both); college students cannot smoke in the building (unrelated to S—students cannot smoke in high school either—and not significant)
3. The medical process by which a person learns to control autonomic body processes; autonomic responses are involuntary, self-regulating processes (these are definitions, not benefits)
4. Football requires helmets; football is more of a spectator sport (unrelated to S; these are contrasts, not comparisons)
5. Intensely active; cannot concentrate for long (unrelated to S; these are characteristics, not treatments)
6. Finding a job may take a while (unrelated to S); buy a suit (not significant)
7. In-laws; family breakdown (unrelated to S; these are not structures)
8. To ensure regular health checkups for prostitutes (overlaps with "to control spread of sexually transmitted diseases"); to decriminalize prostitution (not related; it means exactly the same thing as S)

Exercise 22.9

SUBJECT	ORDER	MAIN POINTS	
1. How to start a gas lawnmower	chronological	2	make sure there is enough gas in tank
		3	turn switch to start
		1	put lawnmower on flat ground
		5	when running, adjust to proper speed
		4	pull cord
		6	mow!
2. Differences between spoken and written language	climactic	3	speech is transitory; writing is permanent
		2	speech is direct and personal; writing isn't
		1	speech can't be revised; writing can

SUBJECT	ORDER	MAIN POINTS
3. How to write a research paper	chronological	<u>3</u> read and take notes on selected research sources <u>4</u> draft the paper <u>2</u> compile a working bibliography of research sources <u>1</u> define the subject <u>7</u> type and proofread paper <u>6</u> prepare footnotes, if needed, and bibliography <u>5</u> revise the paper
4. How colleges benefit society	logical	<u>2</u> they provide the individual with a higher level of general education <u>3</u> society benefits from increased productivity and commitment of an educated populace <u>1</u> they provide the individual with job skills
5. Some causes of World War II	chronological	<u>2</u> World Depression in early 1930s <u>3</u> Hitler's rise to power in 1933 <u>1</u> heavy reparations demanded of Germany at end of World War I <u>4</u> German aggression in Europe
6. Effects of malnutrition	logical	<u>3</u> malnutrition affects the productivity and prosperity of nations as a whole <u>1</u> malnutrition impedes the mental and physical development of children <u>2</u> undernourished children become sickly adults unable to participate fully in their society
7. Why pornography should be banned	chronological	<u>1</u> it degrades the people involved in making it <u>3</u> it brutalizes society as a whole <u>2</u> it desensitizes the people who view it

8. Decide on your own climactic arrangement for this question. Be sure you can explain your choice.

Answers for Chapter 23: Writing the Thesis Statement
(Pages 238 to 247)

Exercise 23.1

1. There are three kinds of students whom teachers find difficult to teach: whiners, snoozers, and disrupters.
2. The most prolific producers of unnecessary jargon are politicians, sports writers, advertising-copy writers, and educators.
3. Dining in the cafeteria should be avoided if possible, for the food is high in cost, low in nutrition, and unappetizing in taste.
4. Because they lack basic skills, study skills, or motivation, some students run the risk of failure in college.
5. Pay television has faced challenges in Canada because of the relatively small market, the high monthly cost, and the stiff network competition.
6. Political violence has become ingrained in the social fabric of many Latin American countries including Nicaragua, El Salvador, Colombia, and Brazil.
7. The Canadian national character was shaped by early conflicts such as the battle for Quebec, the rebellions of 1837, and the Riel rebellion.
8. Canada is little more than an American satellite, for the United States influences our foreign policy, dominates our culture, and controls our economy.
9. The major improvements Western medical technology has made in impoverished parts of the world consist of widespread immunization, the availability of antibiotics, and improved sanitation.
10. Two cheers for democracy: one because it admits variety and two because it permits criticism. (E.M. Forster)

Exercise 23.2

1. d. packed up and headed for Rome
2. a. strong
3. c. ugly
4. b. intelligently
5. b. by boat
6. d. trusted by the media
7. c. watching less television
8. a. increase appetite
9. d. yacht in drydock
10. c. that fair-minded police are visible

Exercise 23.3

1. not parallel
2. not parallel
3. parallel
4. not parallel
5. not parallel
6. parallel
7. parallel
8. not parallel
9. parallel
10. not parallel

Exercise 23.4

1. His basement apartment was small, damp, cold, and dirty.
2. To be a good marriage counsellor, a person must have insight, patience, compassion, and experience.
3. correct
4. Too much coffee can give you nervous days, sleepless nights, and heart palpitations.
5. We require our employees to be honest, reliable, disciplined, and knowledgeable.
6. correct

7. correct
8. Inflation is down, interest rates are up, and unemployment is still high.
9. correct
10. Writing acceptable college-level prose involves applying the principles of organization, sentence structure, spelling, and punctuation.

Exercise 23.5
1. Do you know the difference between polygamy, bigamy, and monogamy?
2. Ahmad has given up not only on the Liberals but also on the Conservatives and on the New Reform Party.
3. Rudolf decided he'd rather be a plumber than a teacher.
4. A good coach must train, discipline, and motivate the team.
5. Two features of the semester system are flexibility and economy.
6. Going to college is good for broadening one's social as well as for learning career skills.
7. Compared to those of ten years ago, today's cars are smaller, more efficient, and more expensive.
8. We find it's more interesting to explore the tide pools at the seashore than to lie in the sun all day.
9. Children who grow up in the city have a different outlook on life than those who grow up in the country.
10. Do Canadians really care if the United States dominates our economy, politics, and culture?

Exercise 23.6
1. The four kinds of prose writing are narration, description, exposition, and persuasion.
2. College fraternities and sororities have become less popular in the past twenty years because they are expensive, they are time-consuming, and they discriminate against some students.
3. Medical scientists are studying the link between weather and such diseases as colds, arthritis, and cancer.
4. If I could have three wishes, I would wish to be gorgeous, brilliant, and rich.
5. Roots products have won international favour because of their reasonable cost, fashionable designs, and high quality.
6. Intramural sports offer three important things to college students: a way to get involved in the school, an opportunity to meet friends, and a chance to stay fit.
7. Freud's psychoanalytic theories, developed in the early years of this century, not only have affected the course of psychology but also have had profound implications for education, art, and literature.
8. Many English words have similar meanings, but they come from very different root languages: for example, *spectre* comes from the Latin *spectrum* (appearance); *phantom* comes from the Greek *phantasm* (image); and *ghost* comes from the Anglo-Saxon *gast* (spirit).
9. Geologists are exploring several phenomena that may lead to an early-warning system for earthquakes: the variation of electrical resistance of rocks under pressure, the release of gas trapped in the crystal lattice of a rock, and the appearance of eerie lights, or luminous flares, in the sky before a quake.
10. It was the best of times; it was the worst of times; it was the age of wisdom; it was the age of foolishness; it was the epoch of belief; it was the age of incredulity; it was the season of Light; it was the season of Darkness; it was the spring of hope; it was the winter of despair.

Exercise 23.7
6. A politician should be well-liked by constituents, respected by colleagues, esteemed by the party, and trusted by the media. (Chronological order)
7. We have all been thinking of fitness, watching our diet, learning to exercise, and watching less television. (Logical order)
8. Excessive use of marijuana can increase appetite, induce lethargy, diminish ambition, and cause psychological dependence. (Climactic order)
10. To lower the crime rate, we must ensure that jobs and adequate housing are available, enough fair-minded police are visible, citizens are involved in their communities, and the courts work justly and speedily. (Random order)

Answers to Chapter 24: Writing the Outline (Pages 248 to 252)

Exercise 24.1
I. Antagonize your teacher
  A. Aim an occasional snort or snicker in the teacher's direction
  B. Wear your Walkman to class and turn up the volume when the teacher speaks
II. Disdain your studies
  A. Don't buy the text for the course
  B. Never take notes in class
  C. Stop going to class
III. Cheat on your work
  A. Copy research assignments out of an appropriate library book
  B. Sit at the back during exams and try to read your classmate's paper
  C. Tattoo your answers on your forearms

Exercise 24.3
"Flunking with Style"
Introduction
  Attention-getter: sentences 1–4
  Thesis statement: To fail your year in the grand style, antagonize your teachers, disdain your studies, and cheat on your work.
I. Antagonizing your teachers
  A. Teachers like enthusiastic students
  B. Show you're bored
    1. slouch in the back
    2. wear your Walkman
    3. talk with classmates
    4. snicker at teacher
  C. Never answer questions in class
II. Disdaining your studies
  A. Buy your books late or not at all
  B. Never take notes
  C. Stop going to class
III. Cheating
  A. Copy out of a library book
  B. Adopt "appropriate" exam behaviour
    1. sit at back, read over classmate's shoulder
    2. write answers on your forearms
    3. stash cheat sheets in washroom
    4. send in a substitute to take test

Conclusion
    Summary: first sentence in paragraph 5
    Memorable statement: The challenge is yours! Become a legend—pick up the torch and fall with it!

Answers to Chapter 25: Writing the Paragraphs (Pages 253 to 267)

Exercise 25.1

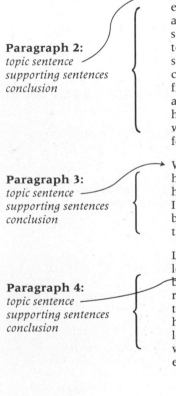

Paragraph 2:
topic sentence
supporting sentences
conclusion

I have sought love, first, because it brings ecstasy—ecstasy so great that I would often have sacrificed all the rest of life for a few hours of this joy. I have sought it, next, because it relieves loneliness—that terrible loneliness in which one shivering consciousness looks over the rim of the world into the cold unfathomable lifeless abyss. I have sought it, finally, because in the union of love I have seen, in a mystic miniature, the prefiguring vision of the heaven that saints and poets have imagined. This is what I sought, and though it might seem too good for human life, this is what—at last—I have found.

Paragraph 3:
topic sentence
supporting sentences
conclusion

With equal passion I have sought knowledge. I have wished to understand the hearts of men. I have wished to know why the stars shine. And I have tried to apprehend the Pythagorean power by which number holds sway above the flux. A little of this, but not much, I have achieved.

Paragraph 4:
topic sentence
supporting sentences
conclusion

Love and knowledge, so far as they were possible, led upward toward the heavens. But always pity brought me back to earth. Echoes of cries of pain reverberate in my heart. Children in famine, victims tortured by oppressors, helpless old people a hated burden to their sons, and the whole world of loneliness, poverty, and pain make a mockery of what human life should be. I long to alleviate the evil, but I cannot, and I too suffer.

Exercise 25.7
1. definition
2. specific details
3. process (series of steps)
4. examples
5. descriptive detail
6. examples
7. descriptive detail (numeric facts)
8. specific details and examples
9. quotations
10. quotation and contrast

Exercise 25.10
    Though I'm new to college, I've discovered three ways of achieving the academic success that most of us desire. First, although going to class is not mandatory, regular attendance enables the student to master course content more readily. Second, the student must take personal responsibility for notes and assignments rather than relying on prodding by instructors. Third, the workload

increases significantly by the middle of each term. Unless the student has made consistent efforts to stay on top of the material, he or she is in real danger of failing. Hence, the keys to academic success are self-discipline and responsibility for one's studies as a college student.

Answers to Chapter 26: Revising Your Paper (Pages 268 to 275)

Exercise 26.1 (suggested answers)

If the Florida Marlins are ever to win a World Series, they must accomplish three things. First, they must develop a first-class scouting department to advise them on the best prospects in the minor leagues. Second, they must establish a quality minor league or "farm" system that will train and develop young players. Third, the new team must make carefully considered trades for emerging young stars. A world championship is a long-term goal, so it is better to build a solid foundation for the future by concentrating on young players and minor league training rather than trying to sign a few established stars at huge salaries.

Chapter 28: Cutting Out Clichés, Jargon, and Slang (Pages 282 to 288)

Exercise 28.5 (suggested answers)
1. When the police officer asked him to, the drunk man got out of his car and raised his hands.
2. You can't judge a book by its cover.
3. Experience is the best teacher.
4. Raccoons live alone, but when they come out at night to look for something to eat, they gather in groups around food put out for them.
5. The dean told the faculty that the college had run out of money and that teachers would therefore be required to begin delivering their courses in ways not involving classroom instruction.

Answers to Chapter 29: Eliminating Wordiness (Pages 289 to 292)

Exercise 29.1
1. I prefer the genuine article to an imitation.
2. There was nothing they could do except repeat the facts.
3. I doubt that this innovation will survive.
4. I think she is pretending to be sick so she won't have to go to work.
5. The results weren't known until he was free to announce himself elected.
6. I will repeat, for those of you who disappeared, that we are lost.
7. Although his ideas seem unique, we must be positive that we don't repeat our mistake.
8. There comes a point when you must reach a conclusion.
9. They circled behind the enemy and, at 4:00 A.M. on July 12, surrounded them, thus eliminating the threat of an invasion.
10. Small, yellow, and ugly, his new car was identical to his old one.

Exercise 29.2

One of the Christmas customs that I enjoy each year is cutting my own tree. I don't do this to save money; I do it because I can cut a tree that is better than a store-bought one, and I can have a good time, too. Friends who share my idea of fun are welcome to come along and help me make the event a memorable experience. Activities that are both inexpensive and enjoyable are rare these days, and tramping off across the fields to a Christmas tree farm to cut one's own tree is a pleasant way to spend an afternoon. I usually select a large, dark-green pine tree. Nothing conveys the spirit of the season like the clean, pungent smell of fresh pine. Bringing home the Yuletide tree is only part of the joy, however. Just as important is the memory of close friends taking part in the ceremony of selecting and cutting the holiday tree.

Answers to Chapter 30: Avoiding Abusages (Pages 293 to 296)

Exercise 30.1
1. I could have done many things, but I chose to become rich and powerful very quickly.
2. Regardless of what you say, I think the media are generally reliable.
3. The reason Marisa came home was that she couldn't do anything to help at the hospital.
4. They teach us many irrelevant things at this school.
5. correct
6. Marco was supposed to be in the race, but he fell off his bike during practice.
7. I should have stayed home, but I went anyway.
8. The reason you are failing is that you don't do any homework.
9. The police department was accused of prejudice against minority groups.
10. Rudolf did nothing to keep Krystal from doing what she wasn't supposed to do. *Or:* Rudolf didn't do anything . . .

Index

READER REPLY CARD

We are interested in your reaction to *The Bare Essentials, Form A*, Fourth Edition, by Sarah Norton and Brian Green. You can help us to improve this book in future editions by completing this questionnaire.

1. What was your reason for using this book?
    - university course
    - college course
    - continuing-education course
    - personal development
    - professional
    - other interests _____

2. If you are a student, please identify your school and the course in which you used this book.

3. Which chapters or parts of this book did you use? Which did you omit?

4. What did you like best about this book? What did you like least?

5. Please identify any topics you think should be added to future editions.

6. Please add any comments or suggestions.

7. May we contact you for further information?

Name: _____

Address: _____

_____

Phone: _____

(fold here and tape shut)

0116870399-M8Z4X6-BR01

Heather McWhinney
Publisher, College Division
HARCOURT BRACE & COMPANY, CANADA
55 HORNER AVENUE
TORONTO, ONTARIO
M8Z 9Z9

THE BARE ESSENTIALS

Form A covers the essential elements of effective communication: organization, syntax, grammar, spelling, punctuation, and diction. Lively, accessible explanations are reinforced by abundant examples and exercises. Now in its fourth edition, this bestselling text contains a new section on using the dictionary, two new readings, and new exercises throughout. Its concise explanations, humorous exercises, and easy-to-use answer key make *The Bare Essentials, Form A* more effective than ever in self-paced learning programs as well as in traditional composition courses. This is a handbook students *enjoy* using!

Also available in Harcourt Brace's *Essentials* series:

- *The Bare Essentials, Form B* covers most of the same elements of composition as *Form A*, but with different exercises throughout.
- *Paragraph Essentials* offers instruction in inventing, developing, and refining well-constructed paragraphs, together with more than a hundred model examples for students to analyze.
- *Essay Essentials* focusses on the skills involved in planning, drafting, and revising essays and research papers. Twenty-one readings by well-known writers provide students with models to analyze and emulate.

ISBN 0-7747-3361-6

HARCOURT
BRACE
CANADA

The Bare

FORM A

ESSENTIALS

FOURTH EDITION

To an employer, any employee is more valuable if he or she is able to write correctly and clearly. No one can advance very far in a career without the ability to construct understandable sentences. Fairly or unfairly, employers and others will judge your intelligence and ability on the basis of your use of English. If you want to communicate effectively and earn respect, both on and off the job, you need to be able to write well. That's the bad news. The good news is that anyone who wants to can achieve the standards of written English that are acceptable anywhere. If you care enough about what others think of you and about career advancement, then you'll put out the effort.

Sarah Norton ∎ Brian Green

Quick Revision Guide